WHAT MAKES SPIRO RUN

THE LIFE AND TIMES OF SPIRO AGNEW

WHAT MAKES SPIRO RUN

THE LIFE AND TIMES OF SPIRO AGNEW

By Joseph Albright

DODD, MEAD & COMPANY, NEW YORK

ISBN: 0-396-06551-1

Library of Congress Catalog Card Number: 75-38525
Printed in the United States of America
by The Cornwall Press, Inc., Cornwall, N.Y.

To Anne, Alice and Kate

Preface

The Vice Presidency is a unique organ in our body politic—
an appendix waiting to replace the heart.

Throughout the last 185 years we have built an unshakable
tradition of pitying the Vice President for being under-
worked. "The chief embarrassment in discussing his office,"
wrote young Woodrow Wilson in his doctoral dissertation, "is
that in explaining how little there is to be said about it one
has evidently said all there is to say." Or as Vice President
Alben Barkley liked to put it, "Once upon a time there was
a farmer who had two sons. One of them ran off to sea. The
other was elected Vice President of the United States. Nothing
was ever heard of either of them again."

When the framers of the Constitution gathered in Philadelphia in 1787, they debated long and effectively on how to
create the Presidency. With their time for deliberation running out, they also established a Vice President, but almost
as an afterthought. Even in the time of George Washington,
the second highest office was widely recognized as an empty

job. One Virginia Senator is said to have referred to the first Vice President, John Adams, as "his superfluous excellency." But the system devised in Philadelphia at least had the advantage of insuring that first-rate men would occupy the Vice Presidency. The Constitution provided that the candidate with the second highest number of electoral votes for President automatically was elected Vice President.

The reason that Hubert Humphrey is not Vice President under Richard Nixon is that in 1804 a Constitutional amendment was passed requiring the Electoral College to vote separately for President and Vice President. During the debate in Congress over the amendment, some warned that the caliber of Vice Presidents would inevitably fall. "The office will be carried into the market to be exchanged for the votes of some large state for President," predicted Congressman Roger Griswold of Connecticut. "The momentary views of party may perhaps be promoted by such arrangements, but the permanent interests of the country are sacrificed." One House member suggested that the Vice Presidency be abolished altogether, but the idea was defeated 85-27.

Despite the warnings of mediocrity, the Twelfth Amendment was swiftly ratified. For the election of 1800 persuaded almost everyone that the method of choosing the Vice President would have to be altered to prevent another constitutional crisis. When the founding fathers wrote the Constitution, they had not foreseen the rise of political parties and the growth of party tickets for President and Vice President. A crisis arose in 1800 because Republican Party discipline was so effective that both Thomas Jefferson and his running mate, Aaron Burr, received 73 electoral votes for President. The tie vote threw the election into the House of Representatives. With Burr angling to make himself President, it took 36 ballots in the House before Jefferson was finally elected President.

The Twelfth Amendment has prevented a repetition of that kind of paralysis, but it has had the unfortunate side effect of electing a good many second-rate men. Before 1804, the Vice Presidency was considered the steppingstone to the Presidency, with two of the first three Vice Presidents going on to get elected Chief Executive. After the Twelfth Amendment, however, only two of the next thirty-five Vice Presidents—Richard Nixon and Martin Van Buren—managed to get elected President in their own right. At least in the nineteenth century, the Vice Presidency was usually a sinecure for the superannuated, the defeated, and the mediocre. Only a few Vice Presidents, like George M. Dallas and Garrett A. Hobart, remained on intimate terms with their Presidents. During the 1900s, four Vice Presidents were propelled into the Presidency when the incumbent died. But John Tyler, Millard Fillmore, Andrew Johnson, and Chester Alan Arthur are not remembered as great Presidents.

Vice Presidents have made a comeback in the last seventy years. Three of the four accidental Presidents in the twentieth century—Theodore Roosevelt, Harry S. Truman, and Lyndon Johnson—turned out to rank among our most important leaders. The fourth, Calvin Coolidge, did not. But he had the distinction of becoming the first Vice President to sit regularly with the cabinet, a tradition which has generally persisted ever since. From the time of Franklin D. Roosevelt, there has been a gradual trend toward transforming the Vice Presidency into an administrative job. Roosevelt sent John N. Garner, his first Vice President, on several overseas missions, thus making "Cactus Jack" the first Vice President to travel officially outside the country. And during World War II Roosevelt gave Henry A. Wallace, his second Vice President, a number of important executive responsibilities, including the chairmanship of the Economic Defense Board. As President, Harry Truman again added to the stature of the Vice President by arranging that he would be a statutory member of the National Security Council. Under President Eisenhower, Richard Nixon was not always satisfied, but he was at least occupied—as a political in-fighter, a foreign traveler, and as chairman of a variety of second-level committees. When Lyndon Johnson and Hubert Humphrey became America's second fiddles, their duties also kept increasing, in number, if not in importance.

Then along came Spiro Agnew. For better or worse, he has emerged as the most important Vice President since Henry Wallace, and possibly since the passage of the Twelfth Amendment. Thanks to his slashing language, and to the media's powers of magnification, Agnew has made himself one of the most beloved—and disliked—figures in our society.

I decided to write a study of Agnew on October 30, 1970, while I was covering the last days of his remarkable campaign aimed at driving the "radical liberals" out of Congress. As the press bus hurried through the slums of East St. Louis, Illinois, we Agnew-watchers were clicking our tape recorders from "reverse" to "play," hoping to reconstruct what Agnew had said at his rally in Belleville, Illinois. Phrase by phrase, I tapped the transcript out on a portable typewriter: "When a President of . . . the United States . . . who is the elected representative . . . of a majority of . . . the people in this . . . country . . . is subjected to rock . . . and other missile throwing . . . it's time to sweep that kind of garbage out of our society . . . Yes, I say . . . separate them . . . from the . . . society in the same . . . humane way that . . . we separate . . . the other misfits . . . who interfere . . . with social progress . . . and interfere . . . with the conduct of business . . . of one of the greatest nations . . . in the world . . . Get them out of our hair . . . where they do not . . . disrupt . . . progress. . . ."

As the motorcade crossed the Mississippi River and the work on the transcript was finished, the images of the last fifty-one days seemed to mash together in my mind. Much of what had happened was obvious to anyone who owned a television set. Who could miss Agnew's alliterative somersaults, his "vicars of vacillation," his "solons of sellout," his "pusillanimous pussyfooters"? Who could remain unmoved by his assaults on the man he called a Christine Jorgenson of politics, his fellow Republican Charles Goodell of New York? Who could fail to be impressed—or turned off—by his pugnacious eloquence when he confronted a panel of college students on "The David Frost Show"?

Interspersed among these highlights were the little glimpses that come only in covering the candidate. As I leafed through my notebooks, I came upon one official's explanation for why in a single short paragraph Agnew had spoken the phrases "nattering nabobs of negativism" and "hopeless hysterical hypochondriacs of history." (Reason: William Safire, the White House speechwriter and pop linguist, coined both phrases, expecting that Agnew would cross out one or the other. But when Safire went to Agnew to get a choice, he replied, "Aw, come on, let's use them both.")

Then I found my notes for the rally in Greenville, South Carolina, where Senator Strom Thurmond introduced Agnew as "the greatest man this country has produced since John C. Calhoun and Robert E. Lee."

On another page were some scrawled statistics suggesting the size of the Agnew caravan: for one eight-hour stopover in the Midwest, the telephone company had to install twenty-eight private telephone lines plus four teletype machines for Agnew's staff, not counting the press facilities.

Finally, there were my notes on what "informed sources" were describing on a background basis as the *real* reason Agnew was attacking Charlie Goodell. (The strategy, which seemed much too cute until it worked, was to hit Goodell hard enough to win him sympathy votes from Democrat Richard Ottinger, thus splitting the liberal vote down the middle, and allowing James L. Buckley of the Conservative Party to win.)

As I mulled over the campaign, what occurred to me was that we were all thinking too much about what Agnew said and where he went. But we were not thinking enough about who he really was. Not that the words were unimportant. When a public figure talks about sweeping "that kind of garbage out of our society," someone has to get the quotes straight. But it was equally important to find out a lot more about the man who spoke the celebrated words. Had he been a promising student? Did his leadership qualities emerge when he served in World War II? Was he a good lawyer? Was he a man driven by ambition? If not, how else could he rise from a county zoning board to the Vice Presidency in eight years? As County Executive and Governor of Maryland, how did he cope with garbage and pollution, race and civil liberties, traffic and taxes? How did he perform under the pressure of a crisis? How pure were his ethics? Then, how did

Richard Nixon happen to pick him out of nowhere as his running mate? And once he became Vice President, what did he do in the Administration besides giving speeches? Finally, the summation of all these question marks: how would he perform as President?

My approach to writing a book on Spiro Agnew has been simply to treat it as a job of investigative reporting: read all the clippings, interview everyone who will talk, find the official documents, put it all together. Although I saw Vice President Agnew twice for personal interviews, I don't claim that I got to know him. Nor did I have access to Agnew's personal papers and letters. However, I was pleasantly surprised at his willingness to let me probe around in his past without trying to shut off my access to his associates. As a result I obtained interviews with nearly all the men and women I wanted to see—except Richard Nixon.

Washington, D. C.
September 1971

Contents

Contents

WHAT MAKES SPIRO RUN

THE LIFE AND TIMES OF SPIRO AGNEW

1

"He pulled up in his Rolls-Royce and the whole
County Office Building seemed to shake."

A Little Help from a Friend

Albert A. Shuger was the biggest gusher the Republican
Party had in the whole state of Maryland when Spiro Agnew
called on him in 1962.

At sixty-four years old, Al Shuger had put together enough
business deals to qualify as an elder statesman. He was president of the Baltimore Paint and Color Works Corporation,
which grossed $20,000,000 a year and was the biggest paint
maker in the South. If you ran a credit check on him, you
would find that he was also part of a group of stockholders
which controlled the BSF Corporation (a holding company
with interests in a Nevada mining operation), a Central
American railroad, an ammunition plant, a hardware company, and three other concerns. He was also a special partner
in a brokerage house in New York and director of a fire
insurance company and of a Chicago bank. What you might
not have learned from Dun & Bradstreet was that Al Shuger
was very quietly speculating in Baltimore County real estate.

All this made for a plush existence. He lived in a new

apartment building that was the closest thing Baltimore County had to Miami Beach, complete with gold-plated bathroom fixtures. A man of culture, he wrapped his life with fine paintings and books. Every day his chauffeur drove him to work in a Rolls-Royce, rented for him courtesy of Baltimore Paint.

The pigment entrepreneur was also a philanthropist, raising money for the old-line Jewish charities and later heading Baltimore City's United Negro College Fund. His tax bracket was high enough that he could give away $55,000 to the University of Maryland at a net cost of $19,000.

Though it was not tax-deductible, his favorite charity was politics. Back in 1943 Al Shuger's brother-in-law got him to make a minor gift to Republican Theodore McKeldin's campaign for Mayor of Baltimore. McKeldin won and later went on to be Governor during the Eisenhower years. All the while, Shuger provided McKeldin with a dependable flow of currency. From time to time he would favor assorted other office seekers, from Democratic perennial George Mahoney to young Republican Charles M. Mathias, now a United States Senator.

Not only could Al Shuger give big money but he could also raise it. The technique was to assemble twenty-five moneyed Baltimoreans and provide them with his own lists of whom to call. When he made a call himself, his motto was "Never be afraid to ask for something really big."

Except that he can now say things like "Charlie Mathias used to run errands for me," Al Shuger never derived much obvious return from politics. McKeldin put him on the state's Welfare Board and Racing Commission, but his public service sometimes seemed more trouble than it was worth.

People kept suspecting that he was in it to get painting contracts. The truth was that Al Shuger enjoyed elections. Winning, he once explained, gave him the same thrill as putting together a major business deal.

Al Shuger should be remembered for one gift for which he has gotten almost no acclaim: he gave us Spiro T. Agnew.

None of the thirty-eight Vice Presidents before him has risen faster or burned a brighter path across the national retina. None since Henry Wallace has been simultaneously so popular and so hated. Take your choice, Spiro Agnew is either the face on your dartboard or else the only politician with enough guts to say exactly what he thinks. To some he is the country's prize boob—a "loudmouth fathead," as one letter writer called him. But he is also the Gallup Poll's sixth most admired man in the world—"Spiro Our Hero," in political poster language.

When Shuger first met him ten years ago, it would be overstating Agnew's prominence to say he was the sixth most admired lawyer in Towson, Maryland. At the age of forty-three, Agnew made his living by defending automobile accident cases for insurance companies and by handling some marginal jobs for the Amalgamated Meat Cutters and Butcher Workers. With a $28,000 mortgage and four kids. Agnew had to scrimp just to pay the bills, without having anything left over for billboards and bumper stickers.

And yet, in 1962 Spiro Agnew had managed through a combination of innate political ability, weak competition, and luck to become the Republican candidate for County Executive of Baltimore County. It was definitely an honor. It might even help his law practice. But nobody thought he could ever win in November. In Baltimore County the

Democrats had such a lock on patronage jobs and such a registration advantage that the Republican Party structure had nearly withered out of existence. There had not been a Republican administering the county since the last days of the nineteenth century.

Al Shuger had just moved out of the city to his fancy new apartment in Baltimore County when he got a telephone call from McKeldin in the spring of 1962. Had he ever met someone called Ted Agnew, McKeldin wanted to know. No, said Shuger, he hadn't, but the name sounded familiar. Shuger pointed out to McKeldin that it would be hard for him to do much for Agnew since the Democratic candidate for County Executive, Mike Birmingham, was an old, old friend.

McKeldin kept talking. And finally Shuger said sure, he would see Agnew. "I didn't think he had a ghost of a chance," says Shuger, who now lives the life of a retired millionaire in a Florida condominium bedecked with art and memorabilia.

Actually, Spiro Agnew happened to possess one qualification that intrigued Al Shuger: he was a former member of the county's Board of Appeals, which handles zoning. At that moment Al Shuger stood to make a six-figure profit if he could get that board to grant him one little rezoning.

Inside of two weeks Spiro Agnew had Al Shuger as an angel and Al Shuger had Spiro Agnew as a zoning lawyer. The growth of their hand-washing relationship is a part of Agnew's life that he has never wanted to publicize. And yet it is worth pursuing for the clues it holds on how Agnew rose, what drove him, and where he pegged his ethical standards.

After getting McKeldin's call, Shuger agreed to see Agnew one Saturday morning in Shuger's apartment, the one with gold-plated faucets. Agnew brought along his campaign manager, a paper-box salesman named Arthur Sohmer, who would later come to Washington and become Vice President Agnew's top assistant. For two hours they talked local politics and then stayed for lunch.

Agnew did not impress the sophisticated Al Shuger as a big leaguer, not at first. "I was surprised," says Shuger. "Ted Agnew was a neophyte. He had no organization. He had not two nickels to rub together. He was living in a little house that he had just bought, and he had hardly any furniture. Looking at him, I thought he needed some clothes. And Art Sohmer, the boy he brought with him, knew about as much about politics as my chauffeur."

Still, Al Shuger decided to help. First he sent Agnew to a wholesale tailor in Baltimore, where Agnew outfitted himself to look like a candidate. ("If you need a couple of good suits, I'll dress you up like I did Agnew," volunteers Nat Molofsky, the tailor.) Then, to launch the campaign, Shuger extended a $4,000 loan, borrowed space for a headquarters, found an advertising agency, and began tapping his associates for contributions.

By his recollection, the campaign eventually cost about $50,000, and he raised more than half of it, including cash contributions of about $6,000 from his wife and himself. Others who were close to Agnew acknowledge that Shuger was the main money man in 1962. Agnew himself now says, "He was a very important fund raiser and he had the experience that I didn't on how to put the thing together." In a letter to Shuger in 1964, Agnew said, "Without your help I couldn't even have gotten off the ground."

As the campaign gained speed, Shuger came in for a surprise. "I've been in politics since 1943," he says, "but never have I seen a man who learned as quickly as Ted did. It was fantastic. At first he made a lot of mistakes. But he gained polish so quickly. Little by little he began to take over the campaign and to use his own judgments, until by the end he was doing it all himself. He kept getting better and better, from a fellow who was in the campaign merely to get his name across to a really serious candidate."

A poll was commissioned by Shuger near the beginning. "I was amazed," he says, "to find out that Ted might have a slight chance to win." Another poll taken for Shuger in mid-campaign showed Agnew steadily improving. But the signal that he was ahead was a private approach by Mike Birmingham, the Democratic candidate and boss of the county, late in the campaign. "We've been friends all these years—what are you trying to do to me?" is the way Shuger recalls Birmingham's message. By then it was probably too late for any single backer to torpedo Agnew, but Shuger believes that is what Birmingham wanted. Shuger made clear to Birmingham that he would not deal.

On the morning after the election, Ted and Judy Agnew had breakfast alone with Al and Nettie Shuger. Richard Nixon had been humiliated by Pat Brown in the gubernatorial race in California. Elsewhere in the country and across most of Maryland it was a dismal year for Republicans, with President Kennedy's success in the Cuban missile crisis in the front of everyone's memory. But in Baltimore County the newspapers told of a "stunning upset" and a "tremendous personal victory" by one Spiro T. Agnew, the first Republican to be elected chief executive of the county since 1895.

Now that he was elected, Agnew was in the middle of his first ethical dilemma. Early in the campaign, perhaps before he had any notion of winning, he had taken on the Seven Slade zoning case for Shuger, who was now his major campaign contributor. Having called during the campaign for tighter conflict-of-interest standards, Agnew now had to draw a line himself. Where did his obligations to Al Shuger cease? Where did his duty to Baltimore County begin?

Shuger was a land speculator only in his spare time, but he knew how the game worked. One of the classic devices for multiplying money was to buy a piece of land zoned for individual houses and then persuade the local government to downzone it to permit a shopping center, an industrial park, or an apartment building.

One of the landmark demonstrations of the efficacy of that technique was Shuger's own apartment building, the one where he and Agnew held their first meetings to plan the 1962 campaign for County Executive. The building, known as Eleven Slade Avenue, was the first high-rise apartment allowed by the Baltimore County government. Shuger's lesson in entrepreneurship on Slade Avenue was not as a mere tenant. Soon after the rezoning was obtained in 1957, he bought into the owners' syndicate as a one-third partner.[1]

Along with his partners, Shuger bought an eleven-acre neighboring parcel in 1960 in hopes of doubling the windfall. Their application for a rezoning to allow a high-rise apartment on this second parcel, known as Seven Slade Avenue, was filed in March 1962—about the time Shuger first met Agnew.

Shuger and his partners had big money riding on the Seven Slade rezoning. Land records in Baltimore County show that they paid $250,000 to buy the land for Seven Slade—$50,000 in cash plus a $200,000 mortgage that fell due within fifteen months. Shuger told me that at the time he met Agnew he had an offer in his pocket to sell the land for $750,000—provided the rezoning was granted. If everything went right with the rezoning, Shuger and his two partners would show a $500,000 profit on a cash investment of $50,000 in a period of two years. But if the rezoning fell through, there was a chance the mortgage could be foreclosed and they would be out $50,000.

One of the prerequisites for putting over a rezoning deal like Seven Slade was a sophisticated local lawyer to handle the inevitable homeowners who didn't want a high-rise for a neighbor. The Seven Slade case promised to be particularly touchy because there were two synagogues down the street whose affluent congregations were signing mass petitions of protest.

Shuger and his partners, who had incorporated as Seven Slade, Inc., already had the best-connected zoning lawyer in Towson on the case, a man named Kenneth Proctor. But one week after meeting Agnew, Shuger decided to hire him as Proctor's co-counsel.

Having served on the Board of Appeals from 1957 to 1961, Agnew knew the tricks of the zoning trade as well as most lawyers. But this was the biggest zoning case he had ever handled as a private lawyer. For Shuger, the rates were cheap. "He only charged me a couple hundred dollars—it was very nominal," Shuger recalls.

The Seven Slade case was moving routinely through the channels of the Baltimore County government at the same time Agnew's campaign for County Executive was progressing. The Zoning Commissioner, John Rose, denied the petition for a rezoning in May 1962, observing that "there are many fine homes on Slade Avenue still occupied by their owners." Seven Slade, Inc., then took the case for a full hearing to the county's Board of Appeals.

The hearing opened in the County Office Building on October 16 and 18, less than three weeks before election day. C. Leonard Perkins, the court reporter, duly noted in his transcript that Seven Slade, Inc., was represented by Kenneth C. Proctor and Spiro T. Agnew. If anyone thought it was strange for a candidate for County Executive to be seeking rezonings, he didn't object.

The transcript indicates Proctor handled most of the questioning and Agnew opened his mouth only on two brief technical points. Aside from setting up a meeting between Shuger and the protesting neighbors to seek a compromise, that is apparently all Agnew did on behalf of Seven Slade, Inc., before the election.

There was nothing in the American Bar Association's code of ethics or in Baltimore County's charter that forbade Agnew from collecting both campaign contributions and legal fees from Al Shuger. Purists might argue that he should have avoided the Seven Slade case anyway, since he would be seeking a lucrative ruling from a county government that he might soon be administering. If elected County Executive, he could scarcely avoid decisions on local sewer routes and road widenings that would help or hurt the owners of Seven Slade. In any event, he took the case openly, and not even the opposing lawyers complained.

It was his services rendered *after* the election that raise real questions of propriety.

That part of the story would never have floated to the surface except that three years later one member of the

Board of Appeals got sore enough at Agnew to disclose what he felt had been an improper effort to apply pressure.

The whistle was blown, ironically, by the only Republican on the Board of Appeals during the Seven Slade proceedings—Charles Steinbock, Jr., a certified public accountant from Catonsville, Maryland, who would later become president of the Maryland Association of Certified Public Accountants. When one interviews Charlie Steinbock now, one finds a nervous and unhappy man who wishes everyone would just forget about the whole thing and go away. He is still a devoted Republican and he has no stomach for renewing a squabble with someone as powerful as the Vice President. In fact, during the 1968 campaign he composed an effusive tribute to Agnew, calling him the best Board of Appeals chairman he ever knew.

But Charlie Steinbock sticks to the story he blurted out in 1965 in the form of a letter to his Congressman:

"Shortly after he was elected, Mr. Agnew telephoned me and asked me to grant the petition [for the Seven Slade rezoning]. I told him I decided cases solely on the evidence presented at the hearings, and that the evidence did not warrant reclassification. He then had [his associate] call me and ask me to grant the rezoning for the good of the Republican party. I told him I was not on the board for the good of any party and promptly denied the petition. . . .

"In my five years on the board, he was the only county official or employee to attempt to influence my decisions."

Grudgingly elaborating, Steinbock now says he got the telephone call from Agnew one night at home, about 11 P.M. They talked about the case for about fifteen minutes, going over matters of substance and not just minor procedural questions.

Steinbock's letter was promptly released by Democratic Congressman Clarence D. Long of Baltimore County, and it led to a one-column headline on page 24 of the third section of the *Baltimore Sun:* "Agnew Named As Pushing Zoning Change." From this piece and a follow-up article in the *Evening Sun* came Agnew's side of the story, which amounted to quite an admission:

"After my election, I obviously had to give up my law practice. But my client was pressing me, so I called Steinbock and asked him if he could accelerate a decision. . . . I at no time suggested how he should decide it."

Such a call, said Agnew, was "common practice among lawyers who for various reasons would like to get a speedy decision on a zoning case."

The County Executive, by then an unannounced candidate for the governorship, was also quoted to the effect that Steinbock's "false allegations are terribly damaging" and might be "actionable" and "entirely misrepresented the incident." Furthermore, "My family's very upset, and I'm pretty sick about the whole thing."

Happily for Agnew, no one thought to point out that the "client" who was "pressing him" was Albert Shuger, who also happened to be his original moneybag. Nor was this connection discovered by the various newspaper and Democratic Party investigators who camped in Towson during the 1968 campaign, although *The New York Times* did publish a few well-submerged paragraphs on Agnew's phone call to Steinbock.

In judging whether Agnew did anything unethical by

calling up Charlie Steinbock at 11 P.M., one begins by asking what standards prevailed among the zoning lawyers in Towson. As luck would have it, the Executive Committee of the Baltimore County Bar Association authorized a policy statement as a result of another zoning dispute a few days before the Steinbock letter surfaced.

"It is fundamentally wrong for any political office holder to attempt to interfere with or influence in any way the actions or decisions of any administrative body," read the statement, which was issued to the press in the name of Bar Association President W. Lee Harrison.

One can telephone Harrison at his law office in Towson today and ask him whether the Bar Association did anything to investigate Steinbock's charges against Agnew. The answer is no. "You have to remember that the Bar Association is a conservative group, and we are not going to act on something as nebulous as an alleged telephone call which was not disclosed until two years later," Harrison says.

There are a few things Harrison is not likely to volunteer. First, the Agnews and the Harrisons are intimate friends and part of a social group that has regularly gotten together on Saturday nights ever since World War II. Second, when the Steinbock letter became public, the Seven Slade case was still dragging on, and Seven Slade, Inc.'s attorney was now none other than W. Lee Harrison.

When asked whether Agnew's telephone call to Steinbock was ethical, Harrison says Agnew had a right to support his client's interests vigorously up until the time he became a county official. After he was sworn in, says Harrison, he could not ethically represent a client before a county agency because of the conflict-of-interest section of the Baltimore County charter.

A cloud of uncertainty could be puffed away if there was some proof of exactly when Agnew made his telephone call to Steinbock. But the evidence is in conflict.

Agnew, in two interviews in 1971, told me he was sure he telephoned Steinbock during the four-week interval between his election on November 6, 1962, and his inauguration on December 3. "I had no contact with Charles Steinbock about this matter after I became County Executive—I'm wholly positive about that," said Agnew. "I was County Executive-elect, I think, when we had this conversation. I was in the process of closing out my law practice."

Albert Shuger—the anonymous client Agnew said was pressuring him—also has a sharp recollection, but it does not match Agnew's. The time he raised the Seven Slade question with Agnew, he says, was at a meeting in the County Office Building right *after* Agnew took office. "I asked him why in hell it was taking so long [to get a decision on the rezoning petition]. He said, 'I'll see what I can do about getting you a hearing.' " Shuger says he is certain that Agnew never put any pressure on Steinbock to decide the case in his favor.

Agnew's confidential secretary from 1962 to 1967, Ormsby S. "Dutch" Moore, provides independent confirmation that Shuger's visit came shortly *after* Agnew was sworn in. "He pulled up in his Rolls-Royce and the whole County Office Building seemed to shake," remembers Moore. He does not know all they talked about.

In 1965 Steinbock said that Agnew's attempt to pressure him occurred "in 1963," which would have been after Agnew was in office. He now says he doesn't know the exact date because he never wrote anything down about it. All he knows is that it was after Agnew's election on November 6 and before the final Seven Slade hearings, which turn out to have been on December 18 and 20, 1962. He has no independent recollection of whether Agnew was already sworn in or not; the last thing he wants to do is contradict the Vice President.

Up to now, there has never been any hint that Agnew talked to any other officials about the Seven Slade case beside Charlie Steinbock. However, it develops that Agnew also brought the case up with G. Mitchell Austin, the other Board of Appeals member who heard the case. Austin, a Democrat who likes Agnew and thinks Steinbock was wrong to make a big stink about the phone call, told me he happened to pass Agnew in the hall of the County Office Building shortly *after* Agnew had become County Executive. Austin says Agnew asked him when the Seven Slade decision was coming out. He replied it would not be long.

A previously overlooked official document provides backing for one of two conclusions that are unflattering to Agnew: either he still was Shuger's zoning lawyer two weeks after becoming County Executive, or else he neglected to make clear that he was out of the case.

This dusty document is the transcript of the hearings which Agnew told Shuger he would try to arrange. On the first page, under the heading "Appearances," court reporter Perkins typed the names of two lawyers representing the Seven Slade syndicate on December 18 and 20, 1962. One was Kenneth C. Proctor. The other was Spiro T. Agnew.

Did Agnew really interrupt his new duties as County Executive to represent a client at a zoning hearing? The transcript does not show him asking any questions. His co-

counsel, Proctor, now says Agnew was already out of the case. The court reporter can't remember. Of the witnesses who testified that day, one is a surgeon and another a retired hat manufacturer. The surgeon says he is positive Agnew was not there; the hat manufacturer says he is sure he was. On balance, it appears he probably was not.

Yet if Agnew had withdrawn from the case, somehow the court reporter was not told to remove his name from the list of appearances.

Obviously Agnew's ethics cannot be calibrated by one isolated episode ten years ago. Yet when all the facts on Seven Slade are in, it is difficult to avoid a harsh judgment: Spiro Agnew didn't come into his first elected office with an infallible sense of public morality. For a man who had just been elected County Executive to make a private appeal to a Zoning Board member at 11 P.M. on behalf of his largest campaign contributor was obtuse, to say the least. If the contact did occur after Agnew was sworn in, it was flatly unethical and illegal under the conflict-of-interest section of the Baltimore County charter.

Nor was this Agnew's last part in the story of Seven Slade. Despite Agnew's phone call, the rezoning was blocked by a 1-1 split vote of the Board of Appeals early in 1963, with Charlie Steinbock supplying the no vote and Austin voting yes. Steinbock's position was later upheld by the Maryland Court of Appeals. But the neighborhood's worries about a high-rise were not over. In October 1964 the owners of Seven Slade made a new application to get the land rezoned. They got it in five months.

The second time around Shuger and his partners had a stronger case, thanks to a seemingly insignificant provision in Agnew's budget. The crucial item was $490,000 in construction money to widen and extend Slade Avenue. As a perhaps inadvertent consequence of that provision, Agnew eliminated one of the County Planning Board's main objections to the Seven Slade rezoning.

Traffic congestion on Slade Avenue had been one of several grounds cited by Deputy Planning Director George E. Gavrelis when he formally opposed the rezoning in April 1962. "Widening and improvement at those points will come about only as a result of as yet unbudgeted expenditures by the county," Gavrelis warned. Although the improvement of Slade Avenue had been on the county's back burner for four years, the project was being held in abeyance for lack of construction money. However, in the spring of 1964 Agnew's Department of Public Works decided to move ahead with widening Slade Avenue, and Agnew included it in his 1965-66 budget plans. The files of the County Bureau of Engineering suggest that the pressure to go ahead came not from Seven Slade Inc. but from the neighboring Baltimore Hebrew Congregation. Still, for Shuger it was great news. When the Seven Slade rezoning petition went back to the Planning Board, Gavrelis wrote a formal memo reversing his earlier position. "From a planning viewpoint, the nature of this petition is substantially different from the previous petition," he wrote. "With the extension of apartment zoning elsewhere and with scheduled improvements on Slade Avenue, the Planning staff would concur with apartment zoning here." Gavrelis also noted that Seven Slade Inc. was now planning a somewhat smaller apartment building with more off-street parking, and that these refinements had satisfied some of the protesting neighbors.

Another plus for Al Shuger the second time around was that the Board of Appeals no longer included Charlie Steinbock, the man who blocked the original rezoning. When his term expired in March 1964, Agnew intervened with the Democrats on the County Council to get him dumped in favor of another Republican. Charlie Steinbock would later contend he lost his job because Agnew was "infuriated" when the Court of Appeals sustained his position in the Seven Slade case.

It was a bittersweet victory for Al Shuger and his partners. By cutting the planned size of their building to mollify the neighbors, they also cut into their profit potential. Although they could have sold out for $750,000 if they got the rezoning in 1962, they had to settle for $428,000 six years later. Still, for a cash investment of $50,000, it wasn't a bad deal.

Agnew assured me in 1971 that his relationship with Al Shuger had nothing to do with his decision to have Steinbock dropped from the Board of Appeals. "It was just that he didn't do anything," explained the Vice President. "When I say he didn't do anything, he didn't participate in the nuts and bolts of the elective process or get heavily involved in the campaigns or anything else."

No dishonesty, in other words. Just patronage politics.

2

The Orphan and the Immigrant

Vice President Spiro Theodore Agnew inherited his genes from a man and a woman with enough gumption to quit their ancestral surroundings to seek a new and faster life in the city. Even now, he knows only vaguely about the life his parents left behind.

The girl who would become his mother, Margaret M. Akers, was born in the Allegheny Mountains of the southwestern tip of Virginia, where the state protrudes into Tennessee, North Carolina, and Kentucky. Her home was Bristol, which straddled the Tennessee border and thus employed two full sets of local officials for a population of less than ten thousand.

Akers was an old if not aristocratic name in Virginia. There is documentary evidence that two of Agnew's grandparents and four of his great-grandparents were Virginia-born. John Akers, who was born in Virginia in 1758 and later fought as a private in the Revolutionary War, could well have been a relative. As an old man John Akers lived not far from

Lynchburg, where Agnew's grandfather William L. Akers lived as a young man.

Vice President Agnew has up to now been unaware of one bit of genealogy that might help him in certain precincts: his grandfather William Akers was a Confederate soldier in the Civil War. To trace this previously unknown bit of Agnewiana one starts at the National Archives in Washington, a repository for federal census records from the nineteenth century. Checking through the 1860 census lists, one finds a twenty-one-year-old clerk named W. L. Akers living in Lynchburg, Virginia. He was the city's only W. L. Akers in 1860.

The next piece of proof must be found in Lynchburg. There, in the City Clerk's office, is an aging Register of Marriages which establishes that on January 23, 1861, a William L. Akers, age twenty-two, married one Eugenia B. Porter, age eighteen.

Back at the National Archives are microfilms of all the personnel records maintained by the Confederate Army. One file belonged to William L. Akers, a twenty-two-year-old clerk who was recruited in Lynchburg in the spring of 1861 as a private in the 11th Regiment, Virginia Volunteers. Originally, Private Akers was assigned to a rifle company, the Lynchburg Rifle Grays. But within a year his commander, apparently impressed by his talents as a clerk, reassigned him as commissary sergeant for the whole regiment.

The assignment of handling the unit's provisions lasted through the rest of the war, as the 11th Virginia Volunteers fought their way through the battles of Sharpsburg, Fredericksburg, and Gettysburg. Although Akers filled a sergeant's billet, he was never promoted beyond his rank of private, which earned him $11 a month. But the job had other compensations. According to his personnel records, he came through the war unscathed except for a minor wound he suffered while at home on furlough.

When the census taker came around to see William L. and Eugenia B. Akers in 1870, they had moved to Nelson County, Virginia, near a private academy known as the Norwood School. William was listed as a bookkeeper. Their household included five children, ranging from infancy to eight years, and a boarder, Walter Holliday, who counted as a "professor in mathematics."

In 1880 the census taker found the Akers family living at the Norwood School, with William now identified as "clerk for school." There was no boarder but the family had nearly doubled. By now there were seven sons and a daughter— Wade, Cora, James, William, Wallace, Porter, Joseph, and Jno. Although Agnew's Virginia grandparents evidently spent much of their adult lives around educated people, they were not a wealthy family. No servants lived with them. And the census takers left blanks in the columns where they were supposed to record the family's real estate and personal property, except in 1860 when W. L. Akers was shown as having property worth $800. Still, he was one of the relatively few men in that part of Virginia who didn't work with his hands.

Vice President Agnew's mother, Margaret, was born to William and Eugenia Akers within a year after the 1880 census. Subsequently a tenth child, Lilly, arrived to round out the family. Although the evidence is sketchy, the Akers family apparently moved from Nelson County, Virginia, to Bristol before the last two children were born.

When Margaret was a young girl, both of her parents died. What killed them is a minor mystery. Until recently the Akers family assumed they simply died of old age. But the census schedules at the National Archives indicate that in the year Margaret was born, her mother was forty and her father forty-five.

"It is my understanding that my Aunt Margaret spent most of her childhood in an orphanage," says Miss Lucille Akers of Roanoke, who is the Vice President's first cousin. That, at least, is the story told to Lucille Akers by her father, William Eugene Akers, who was Margaret's older brother. After Margaret and her sister Lilly had lived in the orphanage for a time, they came to stay with another older brother, James Akers, in Bristol. Jim, who was sixteen years older than Margaret, was a trainmaster for the Norfolk and Western Railway, which ran south through Bristol into Tennessee.

By 1901 Margaret was a dark-haired belle of twenty, sometimes known to her friends as "Maggie." Unlike most of her contemporaries, she had no mind to sit at home and tend house. A Bristol city directory published in 1901 discloses that Margaret M. Akers held a job as a stenographer for Bailey and Byars, a two-man law partnership at 18½ Lee Street. She was living with her Uncle Jim.

Something of the spirit of Bristol, population 9,850, still pervades the crinkling pages of that old city directory. "Fine mountain scenery—bracing climate," boasted one advertiser. "Above malaria," said another. The index of Bristol businesses included two architects, twenty-nine lawyers, three funeral parlors, two coal-mining companies, one baking powder manufacturer, seven butchers, and thirteen bakers. The introduction to the volume listed some of the reasons

Bristol was a thriving city: "Cheap fuel . . . and progressive people."

All this was not enough for Margaret Akers. If it was unusual for a Virginia lass to enter the world of commerce, it was virtually unheard of for a Victorian lady to venture forth to a distant city to find a job. Nevertheless, at the age of twenty-two or twenty-three, she packed her clothes and moved to Washington, D.C., which was more than three hundred miles away. With her went a friend, Miss Mittie DeArmond, and also Mittie's uncle, Roland L. Davidson, who had landed a 50-cents-an-hour patronage job in the Public Printer's office. At first Maggie and Mittie shared quarters in a house on Capitol Hill; later Maggie moved to Q Street, closer to downtown Washington.

Mittie, who later returned to live in Bristol, told retired Bristol newspaper publisher C. J. Harkrader that she and Maggie had two goals in mind when they left for Washington. "They were looking for work, but principally they were looking for romance," says Harkrader.

Maggie Akers found both.

In the Washington city directories published in 1904 and 1906, Margaret M. Akers was listed as a stenographer. For whom she worked is still unclear, however. Vice President Agnew's own version is embarrassingly muddled. In a letter to Harkrader in 1969, Agnew wrote, "Basically, most of the detailed information is very hazy because my mother never talked a great deal about her early life. However, I can confirm the general information that she lived in Bristol and left there to work in Washington in the office of the Secretary of State, Cordell Hull [sic]."

The flaw in Agnew's account is that Cordell Hull was a

Tennessee judge when Margaret Akers came to Washington. He became a United States Congressman in 1907, the year she moved away. Hull didn't join the State Department until twenty-six years later.

The government's Official Register, listing every federal employee, made no mention of a Margaret Akers in its biennial editions of 1903, 1905, or 1907. It is possible, however, that she did work for a short time for the government between editions. During the 1968 campaign Agnew's mother was sometimes described as a former White House secretary, but Agnew subsequently passed the word to me that he never heard that story from his mother. His latest version is that he thinks his mother worked at the War Department.

Romance entered Margaret's life right on schedule, but not with Spiro Agnew's father. According to the story Mittie brought back to Bristol, Margaret found an attractive young beau from New England shortly after she got to Washington. His name was William S. Pollard, and he was studying to be a veterinarian while holding a patronage job with the Public Printer—the same bureau where Mittie's Uncle Roland worked.

Marriage ensued in 1906. The following year Margaret and William Pollard moved to Baltimore, where he had gotten a new job as a veterinary inspector for the Agriculture Department's Bureau of Animal Industry. Their only child, a son whom they named W. Roy Pollard, was born in November 1907. The elder Pollard's salary while Roy was a child was $150 a month, enough to provide very nicely for the family in the days when $14 a week was a decent living wage. For a onetime orphan girl who had been so bold as to leave her home town in Virginia in search of a new life, William Pollard must have seemed like quite a catch.

One of the curiosities about Vice President Agnew's ancestry is that within a few months of the time his mother was deciding to leave Bristol, Virginia, his father was making his choice to emigrate from Greece.

Theofraste Spiro Anagnostopoulos was born into a prosperous family in the village of Gargalianoi on the southwestern slopes of the Peloponnesus. The town used to be right on the blue Ionian Sea, but after raids by some Algerian pirates about 1850, the townspeople moved a few miles inland. Today Gargalianoi is a village of 7,000 inhabitants who live in whitewashed stucco houses with red tiled roofs, making a living chiefly by tending olive trees, fig orchards, sheep, and cattle. It is eight hours from Athens over a bumpy road.

At the corner of Socrates and Aristotle Streets is an ample two-story house with a small balcony and an inner courtyard where Theofraste grew up. When he was born in 1878, the Anagnostopoulos family owned acres of olive groves and was considered rich by Gargalianoi standards. In addition to being a landowner, his father was a notary public, a position of considerable stature in the village. Thanks to his father's affluence, Theofraste acquired far more than an average education. Many years later he told a friend in Baltimore that he had finished high school and then enrolled in the medical school at the university in Athens.

About the turn of the century hard times befell the family and he left medical school, apparently after one semester. "There was, not a depression, but some sort of disaster in the olive industry and they were pretty well wiped out financially," Vice President Agnew has explained. With the future looking glum in Gargalianoi, the family decided to send Theofraste, the eldest son, to make a new start on the gold-paved sidewalks beyond the Atlantic.

The best authority on the young immigrant's life in America is Daniel St. Albin Greene, a reporter for *The National Observer* who spent weeks researching Agnew's background in 1970 but then published only part of what he learned. What follows about Agnew's origins and childhood depends heavily on Greene's spadework.

An authorized campaign biography of Agnew published in 1968 stated that his father arrived in Boston in 1897. The actual immigration records, which turned up later, demonstrate that Theofraste's entry into the promised land occurred on September 19, 1902, through the port of Hoboken. Quickly the twenty-four-year-old immigrant shortened his name to Theodore Anagnost and made his way to Schenectady, New York, a chilly city of 56,096 people and 2,588 dogs on the Erie Canal. Knowing very little English, young Anagnost had no choice but to take a job as a barber. "The proprietor apparently took pity on him and kept him on and taught him barbering," said his son Spiro much later. Judging from successive entries in the annual Schenectady city directories, the Vice President's father was a barber until 1907, five years after he arrived on these shores.[1]

But restlessness drove him to go into business for himself, as in the case of many of his former countrymen. Another Greek immigrant who happened to meet Agnew in America, Luke Carmen, has given an apt description of what success was like for a typical immigrant: "The Greek is a great individualist. He doesn't want to work for another person. If he can get away and do something for himself, he will do it. He would get a little stove and start selling chestnuts in the street. Then he'd sell hot dogs on the street with a push-cart. The next thing, he had a wagon with a horse, and expanded to pork chop sandwiches, hamburgers, fish sandwiches.

"The next thing he'd open the corner store—it had to be the corner to get traffic from both sides—or the old-time quick lunchroom. Then that fellow who opened the lunchroom, he would need help and he would bring his brother, his cousin, or his nephew over from Greece and put him to work in the kitchen. But that doesn't last for long because the cousin starts thinking, I am going to go do something for myself."

Thus it was that in 1908 Theodore Anagnost became the proprietor of a lunchroom at 436 State Street, Schenectady, in the same building where he had worked as a barber. The following year he moved a few doors down State Street and opened another lunchroom, which he named the Hygienic Lunch. Within the next two years, his brother George and his girl cousin Angeliki arrived from Greece to live with him. Another Greek cousin, who Anglicized his name to Pete Lambert, became his partner at the lunchroom.

Theodore was apparently in no mood to cling to all the symbols of his past. By 1909 he had learned enough English to become a United States citizen. By 1911 he again shortened his name to Theodore S. Agnew. Of the forty-five restaurants in Schenectady, at least three featured Greek cuisine, but the Hygienic Lunch was not one of the three. Its quarter-page advertisement in the 1911 Schenectady directory read as follows:

P. Lambert   Theo. Agnew
Hygienic Lunch
Open Day and Night
Steaks and Chops Cooked to Order—Lunches put up to take out
412 State Street, Near street railway waiting station
In the heart of the city.

For a while the Hygienic Lunch did a good business, good enough so that Theodore Agnew could open another Hygienic Lunch in nearby Troy, New York. But in 1912 something happened that made him sell out and move away. The only available explanation comes from his onetime Schenectady acquaintance, Pandelis Chrissikos, who was interviewed after the 1968 election when he was eighty-five years old and again living in Greece. According to Chrissikos, Theodore Agnew's restaurants simply failed to support him.

Then came three quirks of chance. First, Theodore Agnew and his brother George happened to settle in Baltimore, perhaps simply because they liked the Maryland climate better than that of snowy New York. Theodore opened a restaurant on North Howard Street called the Brighton Lunch Room.

The second coincidence was that Mr. and Mrs. William S. Pollard stopped in at the Brighton from time to time for a meal, and in the process they got to know Theodore Agnew, the proprietor. Occasionally the Pollards would invite him over to dinner at their house on West Fayette Street, knowing that he had almost no friends in Baltimore.

The final quirk was that William Pollard, who was in his late thirties, suddenly died of leukemia in April 1917.

A widow at thirty-six, Mrs. Margaret Akers Pollard probably considered going back to Virginia. Instead, she took her nine-year-old son, Roy, and her maiden sister, Lilly, and moved to a two-bedroom apartment over a florist shop which happened to be several blocks from the Brighton Lunch Room. Like Theodore Agnew, she was also something of an outsider to Baltimore. It was not surprising that they saw more and more of each other, despite their differences in origins and the fact that she was Episcopalian and he was Greek Orthodox. Agnew, who was still unmarried at the age of thirty-nine, was handsome in the way Vice President Agnew is handsome today, although about four inches shorter. The widow Pollard was good-looking and nearly as tall as Theodore.

The wedding of Theodore S. Agnew and Mrs. Margaret Akers Pollard took place less than a year after William Pollard's funeral. "I just recall that one day they were married," says her son Roy Pollard. "They went to some church unknown to me and they were married. All I know, in my childish mind, they suddenly got married, that's all."

A son, who would be their only child together, was born on November 9, 1918. With Solomon's wisdom they agreed to raise him as an Episcopalian—and name him Spiro Theodore Agnew. The melting pot had melted.

3

The Perpetual Lieutenant

The rearing of young Spiro Agnew did not always involve the sort of stern parental guidance that he would ultimately hark back to as part of his appeal to the simpler values of the good old days.

"There wasn't an awful lot of home life," his half-brother Roy Pollard has recalled. "But there was an obvious reason. When Mr. Agnew had the restaurant, he and also my mother were at the restaurant most of the time. You don't have an awful lot of home life under conditions like that."

Much of the child raising and discipline fell to Spiro's maiden aunt, Lilly Akers, who lived with them and was known to all as "Aunt Teddy." As Pollard told interviewer Daniel Greene, "Teddy was a spinster and her entire life was centered around Spiro and me. To her we could do no wrong. No one would ever criticize us around Aunt Teddy because she wouldn't believe it."

Spiro's mother was the dominant member of the family, if Roy Pollard is correct. "I have to be honest," he once said.

"If he [Theodore Agnew] didn't let her do what she pleased, in all probability she'd have raised hell with him and his life would have been miserable. . . . Except every now and then he'd put his foot down and it had to be just as he said. [But] if my mother really set her mind to something, she would argue until she got the doggone thing."

Pollard's recollection is that Spiro got more authoritarian treatment from his mother than from his father. "If Mr. Agnew disagreed with something the boy wanted to do, he would explain why the boy should not do such and such a thing. However, with my mother the answer was, 'You can't do it,' and that's all there was to it."

A similar impression of the family relationships in Spiro's household formed in the mind of Katina Agnew, his first cousin, who was the daughter of Theodore Agnew's brother George. "I think my aunt dominated my uncle," remembers Katina, who is now married to a retired can company salesman in Georgia. "It was not in any ugly way, of course, but he just kind of let her do whatever she wanted. It didn't bother him." Katina, who is one month younger than Spiro, recalls that her father and her Uncle Ted were almost never home for dinner. "When they were in the restaurant business that took all their time, evenings and weekends and everything."

Agnew's mother was a woman who cared greatly about her appearance—which may help explain her son Spiro's sartorial fastidiousness. Her other son, Roy Pollard, once said, "I don't ever remember my mother reading a book. My mother was more interested in buying beautiful clothes and things like that. She was a little on the vain side." Even when she was in her eighties, Mrs. Agnew went to the hairdresser every week.

One of her favorite diversions in her younger days when Spiro was growing up was playing poker. One of her husband's friends, Luke Carmen, remembers that Margaret learned the names of the cards in Greek so she could play with the menfolk. She also liked to go to the racetrack occasionally and bet on the horses, although her husband didn't.

Spiro grew up with what his half-brother, Roy Pollard, remembers as "a tremendous admiration for his dad, almost an idolization, you might say." Today, Agnew knocks down various published suggestions that his father was ever a vegetable peddler. "My father . . . was a very successful businessman," said Agnew after his election as Vice President. "He was wiped out in the Depression and then he had to start over and then work his way back."

Between the time Spiro was two and eight years old, his father ran a confectionery shop in Baltimore, probably selling homemade candies, taffy, pecan rolls, and chocolates. While Spiro was nine, ten, and eleven, his father was back in the restaurant business, this time as proprietor of the Piccadilly Restaurant on North Howard Street in Baltimore. During those years, the elder Agnew was also a mover in local Greek activities and a district officer in AHEPA, the American Hellenic Educational Progressive Association. However, he never was elected to the highest offices in the organization.

The Piccadilly went broke in 1930, long before most Baltimore small businesses felt the impact of the stock market crash. To earn a living Spiro's father, who was in his early fifties, got a job as a salesman for the Koontz Dairy. On the side he ran a small fruit and vegetable business, taking orders from his friends who were still running restaurants. He would buy produce at a wholesale market and then deliver the orders in his truck, usually tipping the dishwasher a nickel so that he wouldn't have to carry the groceries himself.

"He was a very distinguished gentleman," remembers Luke Carmen. "His appearance in public was always immaculate. Even when he was delivering the produce, it was always with a coat and tie and with his hair parted in the middle and combed down on each side."

Theodore Agnew's final fling in the restaurant business in Baltimore began in the 1940s, when he was past sixty. For about ten years he ran the Chesaco Inn out on a highway toward Philadelphia, doing the cooking himself while his wife worked the cash register.

To his friend Luke Carmen, Theodore Agnew would sometimes lament his modest successes as a businessman. "He'd always say, 'I can't get the breaks, I can't get the breaks—either in AHEPA or in business.' He became famous for that saying," recalls Carmen.

Richard Nixon once said, in justifying the nomination of Spiro Agnew as Vice President, "He has experienced poverty and prejudice and risen above them on his merits." For his part Agnew denies that the family ever experienced hardship or poverty—only hard work.

"My admiration for my father is very high," Agnew once told Jim Naughton of *The New York Times*. "I didn't have the admiration for him, to this degree, until he got wiped out in the Depression. I saw he just shrugged it off and went back to work with his hands without complaint and kept the food coming in and the coal coming to keep the house warm. I'd watch him come in, just dead tired, and, having lived a rather affluent life up to that point, now hauling sacks of potatoes around. He'd come home so tired, go in the living room with a newspaper on his lap, pull out a sack of Old Durham and roll the next day's cigarettes. And then right after dinner, right to bed because he had to get up about three.

"With all of that [he was] a very aware person politically. This sort of helped my interest in politics, that he always knew what his Congressman was doing and he had strong opinions about political figures and political issues. After he'd finished his rounds from the produce market to the restaurants he served, he'd sit with a cup of coffee—and I'd be with him sometimes—and talk politics, not football. That was the big thing to talk about in those days."

Despite his father's inspiration, Spiro Agnew was not an especially promising youth.

Glenn Owens, the principal of Forest Park High School in Baltimore, had a motto: "All for sports and sports for all." That meant nothing but frustration for the future Vice President. From the time he was thirteen he was over six feet tall, but he was skinny as a pole. "Thank God I put on weight later," he once said. The varsity athletic coach at the high school in the thirties, Andy Anderson, still remembers young Agnew trying out for basketball but failing because he couldn't match his peers in natural ability. As for football, says Coach Anderson, "He couldn't possibly have made my football team—you had to be tough to make my team in those days, and I'd have broken him in half."

He did, however, get fairly proficient at playing the piano, shooting pool, and playing tennis. On Saturdays he often played street hockey on roller skates, using a hard rubber ball and a hockey stick. He now remembers swinging a warped and rusty golf club when he was thirteen years old, mainly to impress a neighborhood girl "with the power and coordination of my swing." There was also softball, soccer, and basketball after school in a vacant lot known as "The Field."

When he graduated from Forest Park High School, his yearbook listed no school activities at all beside his name, only the cryptic motto "An ounce of wit is worth a pound of sorrow." In a sense he was overshadowed by his cousin Katina, who was in his class. Katina was president of the Girls Leaders Club and the Opportunity Club and was active in the glee club, dramatics, and sports. "He was an avid reader," remembers Katina. "He was much quieter than I was."

Jim Ringold, who was the school's star football player, got to know both Agnews. "He was a very quiet, very gracious fellow. He was the least likely person to be where he is today." On the other hand, Ringold remembers Katina as "a spark of life."

Although quiet and shy, Agnew "was no sissy by a long shot," according to his school friend I. H. "Bud" Hammerman, who later became a major campaign contributor. Hammerman likes to tell the story of how Agnew one day whipped several other boys with his fists after they grabbed his lunch bag.

Agnew's grades were only average, even though at some point his IQ was tested at 135. His chemistry teacher, Joseph L. Krieger, recalls him as a quiet, industrious student who did not make any special impression on the class. Krieger gave him an E for excellent. Apparently Agnew did well in

English, but poorly in history and other subjects. He refuses to release his report cards.

Theodore Agnew was sorry that his son Spiro never learned to speak Greek. For one thing, there were occasional rumbles from Schenectady, where Theodore's aging cousin Angeliki used to complain about Spiro being raised as a Protestant. But ethnic consciousness was not much of a factor in Spiro's development, except for occasional cutting remarks he heard in the neighborhood about "that Greek family up the street." [1]

"I was a little surprised," says Roy Pollard, "when, while campaigning, Spiro went so heavily to the fact that he was of Greek ancestry because, very frankly, up till the time he began campaigning, I never thought of him as a Greek at all, I thought of him as an American."

Like many Depression kids, Agnew worked after school as a matter of necessity. "He was always hustling—I think he made more money in junior high than any of the teachers," says Bud Hammerman with a dash of exaggeration. "He had an express wagon at the supermarket, and he had four or five kids working for him, delivering groceries for two bucks and picking up a quarter. He also had a big circular business. He hired me once. Some hardware store was having a sale, and we delivered the circulars door-to-door. After a while, we had about 500 left so we stuffed them down the sewer. Ted caught us and got mad as hell."

Agnew's father, who had great hopes for the boy, tightened his belt and sent him to Johns Hopkins University to study chemistry. "Ability is something, and you have a sufficient amount of that, but application is the key," his father told him. Or sometimes, "It's not how intelligent you are, but how much you apply yourself and discipline your thinking."

Spiro graduated from Forest Park High School in February 1937, and entered Hopkins the same month. When the spring semester ended, he stayed on for summer school, hoping to finish college as soon as possible. At first his grades were pretty good, but they began to drop in the 1937 fall semester and kept dropping. Part of the problem was that he didn't like the messy, smelly chemistry labs. And, he once explained, "I was more interested in having a good time than studying."

After five semesters Agnew dropped out in February 1939. "Hopkins was not an inexpensive school and [my father] was not a man of affluence," he told a campaign biographer. "He was dismayed at how little attention I was paying to my studies. . . . Finally my father said he couldn't keep me in Hopkins any longer and perhaps it would do me a lot of good to get out and get a job to pay for my education."

After telephoning half a dozen fellow students, I found one who does remember Agnew. "He was just a quiet, nice fellow," said W. H. Callahan, a contractor. "He was not the dynamic person he is now, but he sure was a nice guy." It says something about Agnew's college days that during his later career in politics he never depended on a friend he made at Johns Hopkins as an important ally or advisor. In his Vice Presidential years, his main contact with his alma mater was a private letter to Baltimore labor lawyer H. Raymond Cluster, a classmate who has been involved in alumni affairs, complaining about leftwing radical professors now populating the campus. "Nobody that I know ever knew that Agnew was there when we were," says Cluster.

After leaving college, Spiro decided to take a job in the

insurance business following his half-brother's footsteps. He went to work for $11 a week in the file room of the Maryland Casualty Company, and at the same time enrolled in night courses at the University of Baltimore Law School. Agnew, a tall, well-built man with a boyishly handsome face, smoked a pipe at that point in his life. One day in the file room at the Maryland Casualty Company he happened to meet a short, dark-haired fellow employee named Elinor Isabel Judefind. Impressed, he took her to the movies and then to have a chocolate milkshake at a drive-in stand. They found that they had grown up four blocks apart in Forest Park but had never met each other, since she was three years younger. "Judy," as she was nicknamed, was not the flamboyant type. She came from a family that believed that on Sunday it was a sin to play cards or go to a movie. She was the granddaughter of a Methodist minister and the daughter of Dr. W. Lee Judefind, who was vice-president of the Davison Chemical Company in Baltimore.

Ted Agnew and Judy Judefind were engaged in April 1940, five months after they met. About that time, Agnew's insurance career took a great leap forward, or so he thought. "I was taken out of the file room and given a job as assistant underwriter in the Sprinkler Leakage and Water Damage Department," he told his campaign biographer. "I got an office and a secretary and $13 a week." Shortly there was another promotion to $18 a week. The only hitch was that his grades in law school were bad because he was, he says, "cutting a lot of classes."

Along came World War II and with it Spiro T. Agnew's first chance to demonstrate whether he had any extraordinary leadership qualities to contribute to his country.

If he did, his superiors never discovered them. The quick summation of his military career is that he got through Officers Candidate School early in the war and then became a good, average lieutenant, but never was promoted to captain. Agnew was drafted in September 1941, two months before Pearl Harbor, and did his basic training at Camp Croft, South Carolina. "I remember it so well," he said in 1969. "We had all Regular Army NCOs and they were really tough boys. Most of the draftees came from New York and Brooklyn and they were pretty rough boys too, and I'd led a very sheltered life. I became unsheltered very quickly."

After Pearl Harbor, Agnew was picked for Officers Candidate School at Fort Knox, Kentucky. When he emerged as a second lieutenant in May 1942, he got a short furlough, just time enough to marry Judy Judefind. Their first offspring, Pamela, was born on July 5, 1943.

After nearly two more years of shuffling between stateside Army bases, with Judy living just off base most of the time, Lieutenant Agnew was shipped to Europe in 1944. On the day before the Battle of the Bulge, he reported for duty at the 54th Infantry Battalion, 10th Armored Division, which was advancing not far from Bastogne, Belgium.

The best indication of what his initiation into combat must have been like is a passage from the battalion's daily log four days later: "Due to withdrawal of the 501st on our left flank and our right flank was already open, enemy on three sides of us. Team O'Hara was preparing for all around defense when it received orders from Combat Command B to withdraw approximately 1,500 yards and hold commanding ground approximately 2½ kilometers east of Balogne. The withdrawal of our force started at approximately 2200 and is something every member of this command will remember.

"With enemy forces on three sides of you, armored vehicles moving would certainly draw enemy artillery fire. However, we infiltrated vehicles and men back to our new position on the one remaining road in our hands; blew trees and mined the road without receiving one casualty in our force. The 54th Reconnaissance Platoon with the Light Tank Platoon is holding Marvie (they knocked out enemy volkswagen and killed three men there at 1200). Wardin is afire burning like hell."

Company A, in which Agnew was apparently an infantry platoon leader, was spared the worst of the fighting. But nobody could escape the discomfort of the battle, which lasted for thirty-nine days. In 1971, when the Vice President searched for an example of the most unpleasant experience he had ever gone through, he would remember that winter. "During my service time, in the Battle of the Bulge, I slept on the ice for a week," he said. "I was so cold that when I finally got into a warm place, the simple pleasure of having the heat from the stove wash over me was one of the most enjoyable sensations I have ever known."

From the Battle of the Bulge until V-E Day, Agnew bobbed up and down between assignments. On January 12, 1945, he was promoted to commanding officer of the Service Company, the outfit responsible for convoying rations and ammunition up to the 54th Battalion's front-line troops. On March 27 he was relieved as company commander and made the Service Company motor officer, only to bounce back as its company commander on April 12. On May 5, a few days before the

German surrender, he was again relieved as company commander and resassigned as motor officer of Company A.

Judy Agnew believes the Army experience was the most important influence that shaped her husband's "attitude." In a 1970 interview on NBC's "Today Show," Mrs. Agnew said: "It gave him self-confidence because he was a commander." His experience in combat "and having to command troops and having to make decisions, I think this helped him develop, well, very rapidly."

Since Agnew's sudden fame, war stories have been coaxed from the fading memories of several of his army companions. The most bloodcurdling came from John F. Bevilaqua of Chattanooga, Tennessee, who was the first sergeant of Agnew's Service Company. In an interview published in the tabloid *National Enquirer,* Bevilaqua, now a Post Office employee, said:

"We were in a small convoy of ragtag military vehicles near Bastogne, creaking along on a torn-up road. Our trucks were hauling green replacements, weapons, ammunition, and canned rations. All of us were dog-tired. Suddenly there were short swishes and loud roars as German 88-millimeter cannons began to bracket the convoy. Within seconds Lieutenant Agnew had stopped the convoy and had everyone in ditches. As round after round fell on us and all around us, many of the recruits began to panic and wanted to run, but the Lieutenant kept hollering at them and telling them to be calm. He said everything would be all right.

"He used a firm, confident voice and the soldiers believed him. When the shelling stopped, Agnew ordered everyone back on the vehicles. He and I, along with a driver and a radio operator, were up front in a jeep. Then the Lieutenant noticed a young soldier still lying in the ditch. He and I went to check. The boy had been hit in the head by a piece of shrapnel and had been killed instantly. He had been in the ditch right next to our commander. That shrapnel must have missed Agnew only by inches to hit the soldier. The company suffered only eight casualties and I believe the leadership of the man who was later to become our Vice President of the United States had a lot to do with this low casualty rate."

Another brand of leadership—or should one say a higher proof?—was recounted to the Hearst papers by former Second Lieutenant George Van Emburgh, now a dressmaker in Easton, Pennsylvania. "We spotted this building where they made champagne," he said, "but someone posted a couple of guards out front by the time we got there. So Spiro T. decided on a night raid. We slipped in behind and pried the stones out and we filled up a three-quarter-ton truck with champagne. We all got bombed, Spiro T. too. We were drinking champagne instead of water for days. It was a very happy company."

When the war was over, Agnew took home a combat infantryman's badge and a bronze star which was awarded without a citation. But he was still a lowly first lieutenant, having been passed over for promotion each time he was considered for captain. The June 15, 1945 personnel roster of the 54th Infantry Battalion tells something about Agnew's qualities as a leader: of the 41 officers assigned to the battalion, the man who had gone the longest since his last promotion was First Lieutenant Spiro Agnew. Typically, by 1945, first lieutenants were being promoted to captain within fifteen months, according to statistics maintained by the Army's Office of Military History. However, Agnew had gone thirty-three months since his last promotion, a feat that took some doing in the wartime Army.

Part of Agnew's problem, apparently, was an unpromising efficiency rating. Like all officers, Agnew was graded periodically by his superiors, and the composite grade was recorded in his personnel folder. His numerical efficiency rating is a secret, but one can at least deduce that he was not rated either "superior" or "excellent." Any first lieutenant with those efficiency ratings was automatically promoted to captain when he returned to civilian life, provided that he had been a first lieutenant for eighteen months. But Agnew wasn't promoted. This would suggest that Agnew was rated in one of the Army's two lesser categories, either "satisfactory" or "very satisfactory."

Retired Colonel James O'Hara, who was his battalion commander during the Battle of the Bulge, has this explanation for why Agnew was never promoted to captain: "The only thing I can think of is that he came into the battalion later than the other lieutenants." O'Hara, incidentally, was Agnew's liaison to veterans' groups during the 1968 Presidential campaign. When I wrote to Victor Gold, the Vice President's Press Secretary, about Agnew's non-promotion, Gold replied, "The Vice President's service record speaks for itself and requires neither explanation nor apology."

Throughout high school, college, his first job, and the war, Spiro T. Agnew had done a brilliant job of concealing any talents or qualities that would elevate him above the crowd. He was, based on performance, a consistent mediocrity.

4

Postwar Blues

Spiro Agnew may be the world's most stunning proof of the theory that life begins at forty. In his first thirty-nine years he blundered through a series of false starts and failures that might have destroyed another man. If he left any clues of impending stature along the way, they are hard to unearth.

As a gawky first lieutenant of twenty-seven, Agnew came back from Europe in the winter of 1945–46 to resume life with Judy and their daughter, Pamela, now two and a half. "I had an insatiable desire to learn and get on with my education," said Agnew later. Released from the service in February of 1946, he was admitted to the Maryland Bar later that year under a special dispensation for servicemen whose education had been interrupted.

He still lacked many law school credits, however. He made that up by enrolling for night courses at the University of Baltimore Law School, where he had begun his legal training before the war. It was a meat-and-potatoes law school—not much theory but plenty of torts, contracts, accounting, and wills. Its reputation was such that the American Bar Association had not seen fit to accredit it. From the University of Baltimore Law School Agnew emerged in June 1947 with diploma in hand, convinced that he could make it on his own.

That was to be the end of his formal education, except for three later years of night school aimed at completing his undergraduate education. From 1952 through 1955 he would study cost accounting, public administration, elements of business, and public speaking at McCoy College, a night school affiliated with Johns Hopkins. His grades were Bs and As, including an A in public speaking. In the end, however, he quit night school before accumulating enough credits for his undergraduate degree.

While in law school he worked as a law clerk for Smith and Barrett, a politically-connected law firm in downtown Baltimore. The job, which he got through one of his father's contacts at Koontz Dairy, paid $25 a week. In addition he got $25 a week from the federal government under the GI Bill for on-the-job training. With the two paychecks combined, he was able in September of 1946 to get out of a cramped apartment and buy a house in the suburbs for the first time. It was a diminutive ranch-type home in Lutherville, out in Baltimore County, complete with a $9,000 mortgage and its own back yard.

Agnew's financial position turned for the worse the day he got out of law school. Suddenly he was minus the benefits he had collected under the GI Bill as long as he was a student. To complicate matters, their second child was born on September 9, 1946, a boy they named J. Rand Agnew.

One day law clerk Agnew strode into the office of Michael Paul Smith, the imposing senior partner of Smith and Barrett who would later become a judge. Gathering his courage, Agnew suggested that it was only right for him to get a raise. Specifically, he thought he should get an extra $25 to make up for the GI benefits he was losing. Michael Paul Smith did not say no. But he did not say yes either. As Agnew sat there wondering, Smith simply walked out of the office and did not come back. Although hurt and mad, Agnew had no alternative except to stay on as a $25-a-week clerk.

Lester Barrett, Smith's partner, took more of a liking to Agnew. It was Barrett who gave him the most valuable piece of political advice he ever got: change your registration to Republican. Agnew had registered Democratic in January 1940, the first election year when he was old enough to vote. If he stayed a Democrat, Barrett told him, he would have a terribly tough time getting anywhere in politics because the Democratic Party organization was already brimming with ambitious young lawyers. In the Republican Party, to which Barrett himself belonged, he would have a much better chance because there were very few young lawyers to compete against. Taking Barrett's advice, Agnew registered as a Republican on October 4, 1948. The two men shared another bond: when the Baltimore Colts got a football franchise in 1947, they bought season tickets together.

Barrett, now a Circuit Court judge in Towson, maintains he thought a lot of Agnew's legal abilities. But the firm did little to advance him. Bravely, Agnew left Smith and Barrett in late 1947 or 1948 to set up his own law practice. It promptly failed. Meanwhile, a third child was born to the Agnews on October 23, 1947. They christened her Susan.

On New Year's Day, 1948, at the age of thirty, Agnew reverted to the line of work he had tried before the war. He took a job as a claims adjuster for Kemper Insurance. For $60 a week, he examined wrecked cars to see that the body shop was not padding the bill. It was not what he had in mind at law school, but at least it was a steady paycheck.

Early in 1950 a classified ad attracted his attention. Some unidentified employer, with only a box number, was prepared to pay well for a qualified assistant personnel manager. Agnew applied. The prospective employer turned out to be Schreiber Brothers, an overgrown family-owned grocery store in downtown Baltimore that also sold drugs and liquors. Schreiber's, which thrived by buying in huge quantities and selling cheap, had about four hundred employees. Although the job did not seem to point toward the practice of law, Agnew snapped at it. "The salary was $100 a week, and that seemed like all the money in the world," he once explained.

A story got around during the 1968 campaign that Agnew worked at Schreiber Brothers in a white smock with a sign on the front saying "No Tipping Please." Like many a delicious anecdote, it isn't quite true. On especially busy days Agnew, like the other executives, did appear on the floor in a white smock. But it didn't say "No Tipping Please"— smocks with that sign were only for the delivery boys who carried groceries to the customers' cars. As a management man, Agnew was not in the union and could not wait on the customers.

His real duties were only slightly grander. Every morning he would stay in front of a window in the second-floor hallway checking off the employees as they came to work. At lunchtime he would check each one out again. After lunch he would check each one back in. There was a final check when the employees left for the day. Since the shifts were staggered, the human-time-clock function was shared between two assistant personnel managers.

The job had other duties. When a butcher needed a clean uniform, Agnew supplied it. When a store detective caught a shoplifter, Agnew took down a statement to prevent a lawsuit. When a customer claimed to have been injured in the store or poisoned by the food, Agnew handled the insurance forms. He was not responsible for negotiating labor contracts, but sometimes he was allowed to deal with the union on grievances.

Alvin Schreiber, nephew of the boss, was personnel manager when Agnew was hired. As Agnew's direct superior, he came to know and like him. "Agnew was conscientious, bright, hard-working, and he related well with people," says Alvin Schreiber. "Despite all that has been written, he is not just a stupid idiot."

Agnew's career in the grocery business was halted in October 1950 by an order from the United States Army commanding him to report to active duty for the Korean War. Like thousands of World War II veterans, Agnew was jolted into the realization that the slot in the Reserves he accepted in 1946 was more than a piece of paper.

Unlike many of his peers, Agnew managed to get back out of uniform in May 1951, without being shipped to Korea. Of the 40,000 Army captains and lieutenants who had been involuntarily recalled, he was among the first to get out. The precise grounds for his release are locked away inside Agnew's Army personnel records, which were shipped to the Pentagon from the Army Personnel Records Center in St. Louis when he became Vice President. Sam Kimmel, Agnew's longtime friend and law associate, says Agnew once told him that he got out of active duty only after intercession by his Congressman, Representative James P. S. Devereaux, on the grounds that he had three children. According to Kimmel, the plea for Agnew's release was transmitted to Devereaux by Lester Barrett—who was not only Agnew's former boss but also one of Devereaux's main political backers. "Ted is not ashamed of this," said Kimmel. Former Congressman Devereaux, a celebrated Marine general in World War II, has no recollection of seeking Agnew's release.

After seven months of refresher courses and parade drills, Agnew came back to Baltimore and returned to his old job at Schreiber Brothers. He was still full of bitterness at the Army. Carl O. Gleitsmann, who worked beside him in the personnel office, says, "He often remarked that it was a hell of a thing for a married man with children to be called back, and how close he had been to going to Korea." By the time of his recall, Pamela was seven, Randy was four, and the baby, Susan, was two. (The youngest Agnew, daughter Kimberly, was not born until December 9, 1955.) It is Alvin Schreiber's recollection that Agnew told him he had applied for release on hardship grounds.

The Korean War forced on him a change of address that turned out to make a difference, although it seemed inconsequential at the time. When he got his recall notice the Agnews could not afford to keep their little house in Lutherville and they sold it for $11,000, just about what they had paid for it in 1946. A year later, after he was released, they bought an equally modest brick two-story row house at 1830 Aberdeen Road in Loch Raven, again for $11,000. Loch Raven was an amorphous, variegated suburb of twenty thousand residents in Baltimore County, teeming with community activities, from the Optimists Club to the Little League. In Loch Raven, Agnew would ultimately construct his power base—moving from president of the Dumbarton Junior High School Parent-Teachers Association to president of the Loch Raven Intercommunity Council to president of the Loch Raven Kiwanis Club.

Agnew got into the Kiwanis Club on the strength of his musical abilities. "We felt we needed some music and we were looking for a piano player, so he could accompany the happy birthday, the anniversaries, and all the other fellowship things we like to do," says his fellow Kiwanian Clarke Langrall. "Ted Agnew was introduced as a prospective member who could play the piano."

For seven years Agnew maintained a perfect attendance record at the Kiwanis Club, and in 1960 he was elected vice president. If there was any clue about Agnew's future, it was that he liked to use 25-cent words. "This is only the Kiwanis Club, Ted; where do you get words like this?" Sam Kimmel once joshed him. "I like to look them up," Agnew replied. "And I read that 'Increase Your Word Power' section in the *Reader's Digest*."

He advanced to president of the Kiwanis Club in 1961 and distinguished himself, according to Langrall, by straightening out the finances of the Loch Raven community swimming pool. "Had it not been for Ted's ability to take hold of this thing, I'm afraid it could very well have resulted in the complete dissolution of the club because there were some very serious things going on," says Langrall.

But in 1953 he was not yet ready to scale such peaks as presidency of the Kiwanis Club. On a Monday in August Agnew was suddenly informed by Martin Schreiber, the tough, unpredictable boss of Schreiber Brothers, that the company no longer desired his services. The words "You are fired" were never used, but that is what the scene amounted to. By the time of his departure Agnew had been promoted to personnel manager, a step up from assistant. Eugene Schreiber, then controller, thought enough of Agnew to protest his termination to his Uncle Marty, but Uncle Marty would not change his mind. Later that week Agnew telephoned his friend Carl Gleitsmann, who was called back from his vacation to fill in when Agnew abruptly left. "He told me he wasn't going to take that kind of stuff off of Marty," says Gleitsmann.

There are two things Carl Gleitsmann remembers about Agnew at Schreiber's. One, he was a rabid Baltimore Colts fan. Two, he once helped a black fish-handler get out of trouble with a loan company by calling up the company and threatening to take it to the Maryland Commissioner of Small Loans. "I thought he treated the coloreds better than anyone else did around there," says Gleitsmann.

Although the chief executive of Schreiber Brothers got rid of him, a member of its board of directors helped him find another position. It was through the help of Herbert Moser, a Democratic Baltimore City judge who was also a director of Schreiber Brothers, that Agnew was able to land a job in a top-drawer Baltimore law firm.

It must have struck Agnew as a real break. Suddenly at the age of thirty-four he would join the law offices of Karl Steinmann, who had about fifteen lawyers working for him and a client list that ranged from the *Baltimore News* to American Oil. The pay was about $5,000 a year, not bad for someone who had just lost a job.

Eight or nine months later Agnew left the employ of Karl Steinmann for reasons that may never be entirely clear because Steinmann is now dead. Agnew's side of the story, as he told it to his friend Sam Kimmel, is that he quit because his only assignment was handling dry research chores for Steinmann's corporate clients. Corporation law did not fascinate him, he told Kimmel; there wasn't even any courtroom work.

After leaving Steinmann he once again set out as an individual practitioner, using a desk in another downtown lawyer's office as his base. He had only two steady clients throughout the rest of his private practice as a lawyer. The first was his former employer, Kemper Insurance, which used him to defend routine automobile accident suits in Towson. The second was the Amalgamated Meat Cutters and Butcher Workmen of North America.

His connection with the Meat Cutters later gave rise to the belief in some quarters that he was a prominent labor lawyer. The first proponent of this theory was Richard M. Nixon, who wrote in 1968 that Agnew was an "experienced and effective labor relations lawyer." Agnew's admiring biographer Jim G. Lucas expanded on the legend: "His brief tenure as assistant personnel manager at Schreiber Brothers—even though he may also have been a floorwalker—had aroused interest in him at the Meat Cutters' national headquarters. They were eager to obtain his services, and his quick grasp of labor law, for themselves.

"Agnew found their offer attractive. He was also deeply interested in the meat cutters—many of whom ran butcher counters in the big chain markets—and felt their cause was a good one. He became legal counsel to Local 117 in Baltimore, and conducted its contract negotiations. He seemed always to bring the two sides together. There were no strikes. . . ."

The union officers who hired Agnew do not remember it that way.

Their story is that shortly after Agnew left Schreiber Brothers he was retained by the Meat Cutters Local 162 in Baltimore, a 1,200-member union that represented Schreiber's as well as some other meat markets. John Tennyson, the secretary-treasurer, had dealt with Agnew at Schreiber Brothers and thought he might be useful in keeping him posted on changes in the labor laws as well as representing the union in arbitrations. However, he told Agnew when he retained him that negotiating contracts was not part of the job. The pay was a $100-a-month retainer, plus a per diem for extra work.

At the time Tennyson judged that Agnew did an adequate job. However, Roy C. Manns, Jr., who was number-two man in the local (even though his formal title was president), formed a much less flattering judgment. "We got into a jurisdictional dispute with a supermarket chain in Baltimore," says Manns. "We were trying to prove that they were a chain and not just individual stores. It resulted in a National Labor Relations Board hearing that lasted eighteen days. That's where I got my strong impression that he [Agnew] didn't know what he was doing. It was just he and I at the hearing, and I had to tell him the questions to ask. . . . The thing that gets me is the articles about Agnew that say he was a good labor lawyer. What he did as a labor lawyer was nothing."

In one instance Manns got the impression that Agnew was too militant for the union's good. The incident arose when one store owner in the same supermarket chain wanted to get out of a unionization agreement he had just signed. As Manns recalls it, "We had one of the store owners down on his knees, so to speak. If he went to the union, the rest of the stores in the chain were going to ban him from any connection with the parent corporation, which he needed for financing. I couldn't see crucifying the guy, and I was going to release him from his agreement. Agnew got quite upset about it—he said we should put him out of business just to show the rest of the employers. I told him I was the boss, and that I was going to release him from his agreement. But he didn't like it."

Local 162 was the smaller and less militant of two Meat Cutters' locals in Baltimore. During the mid-1950s the larger Baltimore local lodged a complaint with the union's district headquarters in Washington that Local 162 was settling its labor negotiations too cheaply, and thereby establishing city-wide wage patterns that were holding down the pay scales of the larger local. The solution doped out by the international headquarters was to merge the two locals into one tough, united union.

Within Local 162, the leadership was split on the advisability of merging, with Tennyson against it and Manns in favor. The issue was fought to a conclusion in 1959 when Manns beat Tennyson in an election for the top job in the local. One of Manns's first official acts was to telephone Agnew at his office in Towson and inform him that his $100-a-month retainer was finished and he was no longer the local's lawyer. A few days later Manns and Agnew almost came to blows when Manns drove out to Towson to reclaim some papers from Agnew's office. "He was real unhappy about it," says Manns. "It was to the extent that I was working myself around to where I was ready to knock him down the stairs." Manns claims Agnew told him he needed the money from the union but he told him no.

Another officer of the local goes so far as to say, without allowing his name to be used, that "Agnew turned out to be a heel. He was for what he could get and to hell with everyone else."

Undaunted, Agnew took his problems to Leon B. Schachter, the union's district director who was in charge of merging the two locals. As Schachter remembers it, he knew Agnew was hard up for income and could not afford to lose the union business. "How am I guilty?" he remembers Agnew asking him. Schachter agreed that it was not Agnew's fault that the two locals had to be merged.

To make up for the Local 162 business Agnew had lost, Schachter decided to seek approval for putting him on the payroll of the union's district headquarters in Washington. "It was kind of an interim thing," explains Schachter. "It was an extra kind of thing to tide him over." Schachter persuaded Patrick E. Gorman, the International Secretary-Treasurer of the Meat Cutters, to approve a temporary position for Agnew. "Okay, let's give him a chance to find other clients" is the way Schachter remembers Gorman's directive.

At the age of forty, Spiro Agnew had achieved a state of absolute averageness in almost every respect. He had been fired by his last two employers, although some of his fellow employees thought he was a nice, quiet guy. He bowled in a bowling league, played softball, and struggled to pay the bills on an income not far above the $7,000 median income of Baltimore County. If anything made him unusual, it was that he held a part-time political job in Towson on the county Board of Appeals.

In the remaining years of his legal practice, from 1959 to 1962, he began to make some headway, but not enough to qualify him as an outstanding advocate, either in brilliance or financial success. The Martindell-Hubbell law directory, which assigns ratings to lawyers based on confidential questionnaires to their colleagues, rated seventy-four lawyers who practiced in Towson for its 1962 edition. Agnew wasn't one of the eleven Towson lawyers accorded Martindell-Hubbell's top "av" rating. Nor was he among the twenty-five unlucky ones with a "cv" rating, which is the lowest. Agnew belonged, along with thirty-seven others, to the middle category known as "bv"—which meant his legal ability was "high" but not "very high." Agnew's partner, Owen Hennegan, was a "cv"—meaning his legal ability was "fair." Martindell-Hubbell estimated Agnew's net worth in 1962 at $10,000 to $20,000—a range that Owen Hennegan says was about right. Along with his private practice, Agnew taught a few courses, including labor relations, at his alma mater, the University of Baltimore Law School.

Agnew's assignment with the Meat Cutters' district office consisted largely of helping Melvin Tyler, a staff organizer, in an attempt to unionize a fleet of commercial fishing boats that ranged off the Atlantic coast from North Carolina to New Jersey. The crew members, nearly all of them blacks, were hired on a seasonal basis to net menhaden, a "trash fish" that is processed into fish flour and chicken feed.

All the boats and processing plants were owned by a single family named Smith from New York. However, each boat and factory was separately incorporated to impede unionization. This meant long drives for Agnew and Tyler to meet the widely scattered union committees and boat captains from southern Virginia to New Jersey. In the end, the fishing fleet and the factories were organized for the first time, and without a strike. In 1960 the Menhaden Fish Workers Union Local 315 of Lancaster, Virginia, had grown big enough to collect $14,063 in dues. Of this, $1,456.19 went to Spiro T. Agnew for salary and expenses. Schachter believes that Agnew was making about $5,000 a year in all from the Meat Cutters, including payments from district headquarters.

Schachter thought Agnew performed his assignment with the Menhaden fishermen pretty well, in part because he could get along with the Smith family's lawyer better than a labor organizer like Melvin Tyler could. However, Schachter was never convinced that Agnew was a top labor lawyer. "He might have developed into one," says Schachter. "But he was not a seasoned labor lawyer like the others I dealt with. He was too limited—after all, he came to us from a small local union."

The Smith family's lawyer, Thomas Kerrigan, was evidently more impressed, even though his clients were constitutionally opposed to the union. "He was very able—he had his feet on the ground," says Kerrigan. So impressed was he that at one point he hinted to Agnew that he could get a job for $25,000 a year at his firm in New York if he wanted to move. This was apparently about the time of Agnew's campaign for County Executive and he said no.

The contract which Tyler and Agnew negotiated for the menhaden fishermen was not the most favorable one the Meat Cutters' district headquarters had ever seen. It guaranteed men only two days of shore leave every two weeks and allowed the boat captains to withhold part of each crewman's pay to insure that he would work through the season. The wages were not paid by the hour. Instead, each man got about 10 cents for every thousand pounds of fish the boat caught.

"It was," says management lawyer Kerrigan, "a pretty loose contract. It had to be because of the nature of the business." Schachter says he won't praise the Menhaden agreement or criticize it. "I thought it was good because we had nothing before," he explains.

Defending the rights of poor black fishermen makes fine fodder for campaign biographies, but Agnew earned the bulk of his income by defending insurance companies, mainly those in the Kemper group, against automobile liability claims. The typical case was an out-of-court settlement with someone who claimed a back injury—"I've never seen one that was very glamorous," says his partner Hennegan. In the early 1960s, a change in Maryland state law brought Agnew a spurt in personal injury business. The law required insurance companies to split up a pool of claims filed against uninsured motorists; Kemper assigned Agnew all those in the Towson area. Edgar Fulton, Kemper's claims manager at the time and a friend of Agnew, offers this judgment on Agnew's legal ability: "Recognizing that he had not had a great deal of trial work, he was substantially above average as a lawyer."

A minor client during 1959 and 1960 was the Eastern Conference of the Teamsters Union, with headquarters in Washington. Thomas E. Flynn, then the international director of the Eastern Conference and Agnew's boss, ducked half a dozen phone calls seeking information on Agnew's work for the Teamsters. Finally Flynn's secretary telephoned to say that Agnew had worked part-time from his office in Towson "and he was extremely competent." She also said Flynn considered Agnew "a good friend." One of Agnew's jobs for the Teamsters, ironically, was helping a Baltimore local organize the Koontz Dairy, for which his father had long worked as a salesman before retiring.

Throughout his legal career Agnew, like most lawyers, had little to do with criminal law. The one murder case he defended before a jury brought some minor headlines—not because he won it, but because he lost and then his client formally charged that he had been incompetent. In the end Agnew was exonerated.

Late in 1961 Agnew was appointed by the Circuit Court in Towson to defend Lester L. Grogg, a thirty-eight-year-old chicken farmer with a record of mental illness, a subnormal IQ, and a past criminal conviction. Grogg was charged, along with an eighteen-year-old friend, with murdering a ninety-one-year-old woman in the course of robbing her of $28. Before Agnew was appointed, Grogg had given the police a full confession.

At the trial Agnew attempted to prove that Grogg was innocent by reason of insanity. However, one of his own witnesses, a psychiatrist, cut the ground out from under that defense by testifying that Grogg was legally responsible for his acts. The jury found Grogg guilty of first-degree murder and he was sentenced to life in prison.

Another lawyer, Roger C. Duncan, was appointed to handle the appeal. Duncan took the case to the Maryland Court of Appeals, citing the refusal of the trial judge to allow Agnew to ask the potential jurors a question on whether they believed there had been "great progress, some progress, or no progress" in treating mental illness.

The Court of Appeals slapped down the appeal in a decision that implied that any harm in the question had been caused by the inexperience of the unnamed defense attorney, who was Spiro Agnew. "In the form used it was a vague, blunderbuss-type question," said the Court of Appeals in June 1963. "Since the ruling of the trial court merely held that the question was objectionable in form and there was no hint that the court intended to preclude more suitable questions, no error is apparent."

From the Maryland State Penitentiary, Grogg then filed a semicoherent post-conviction petition alleging, among other things, that Agnew and Duncan had both been incompetent. As a result Agnew, who was by now County Executive, had to be cross-examined for nearly two hours in November 1964 in the county courthouse in Towson. He was pressed on why he had not tried during the trial to prevent the prosecutor from introducing his client's confession and why he had put on as a defense witness a psychiatrist who testified that Grogg was sane.

The presiding judge, W. Albert Menchine, issued an opinion two months later that defended Agnew's trial tactics and rejected Grogg's petition. "Hindsight will forever be better than foresight, but it has not yet been decreed to require two trials for every offender," he wrote.

The question of Agnew's competence at the trial was routinely appealed to the Maryland Court of Appeals, to the Federal District Court in Baltimore, and to the United States Circuit Court of Appeals in Richmond. At every level Grogg lost. The issue was quietly put to rest during the height of the 1968 campaign when the United States Supreme Court declined to review a lower federal court ruling which held that Grogg had been represented by a "competent attorney experienced in criminal matters." The newspapers missed a story they could have headlined "Supreme Court Won't Review Agnew's Competence."

5

"He called me day and night to line up votes."

Politics on a Shoestring

Spiro Agnew paints a romanticized picture of the way he got into politics, showing himself as a young campaign worker toiling to help elect James P. S. Devereaux, the World War II Marine general known as the "Hero of Wake Island," to the United States Congress.

"I worked like a Trojan in those campaigns," Agnew told me. "I wish that we had people who were willing to work as hard in campaigns as I worked in that campaign. I can still remember the tremendous amount of work I did."

The way Agnew likes to remember it, he was responsible for inventing one of Brigadier General Devereaux's most successful campaign gimmicks.

"I got the idea that these Burma Shave commercials were very effective," Agnew told me. "We didn't have a lot of money to spend, so we made up these little jingles. Then I recruited these girls from Goucher College, who were very attractive young ladies. I'd pick them up and we'd have cars take them twice a day at the rush hours onto the principal

61

arteries coming out from the city to the suburbs and station these girls with these signs.

"It's a wonder we didn't cause a few accidents," he chuckled. "But it was tremendously effective."

Every spectacular career must have a curtain raiser. The only trouble with this one is that a few small details do not check out.

E. Scott Moore, then a politically aggressive young Republican lawyer from Towson and later an aide to Agnew, isn't reassuring. "As far as I know, all he ever did for Devereaux was work in a precinct in Lutherville and hand out ballots on election day," says Moore. "I was deeply involved in every one of Devereaux's campaigns and I never remember Ted Agnew being involved."

One then turns up the paid campaign organizer and publicity man who ran all the Devereaux campaigns, Edward Hanrahan. "Actually," says Hanrahan, "the idea for our so-called 'Pickets for Peace and Progress' was mine. The only job I remember Ted taking was to get people to put up Republican Party banners in their houses. The premise was that it would look as though the Republicans had an organization even though they really didn't."

Finally one interviews the Hero of Wake Island himself, now almost seventy and living on top of a hill in the horsy part of Baltimore County. "As far as thinking up the idea for the girl pickets," says General Devereaux, "that was Hanrahan."

The General does remember Agnew as a "very intelligent and forthright sort of person" who did help out in several of his campaigns as a volunteer. (Later, recalls Devereaux, he and Agnew once discussed how they felt inside during combat. Agnew told him about how scared he had been the first time his unit was strafed by German planes. Was Devereaux ever scared in battle too, Agnew wanted to know. The general told the former first lieutenant yes, sometimes he was scared too.)

The fact is Agnew got into county government by badgering the local Republican patronage wielders until they gave him a job. His main supporter was not Devereaux but Mrs. Christine Nathan, a longtime Republican worker from Agnew's area who thought he might be a comer.

Agnew told me he "got sort of interested in the periphery of politics" in the late 1940s and "became involved really more out of admiration for Lester Barrett and Devereaux than out of any ideological discernment of issue variances." As he recalled that era, "Those were the years of overpowering United States strength. We were the only people with atomic energy and we were feeling very benign toward the world, and it wasn't a period of great trauma." (Apparently the Berlin Airlift and the other great events of the Cold War were not indelibly burned in his memory.) The first manifestation of his political hankerings came in 1948, when he served as an election judge in a precinct on election day.

Agnew had his sights set on becoming Governor of Maryland not long after he was terminated by Schreiber Brothers in 1953. At Goucher College in Towson there is a professor of political science, Dr. Brownlee Corrin, who happens to be a Republican as well as the director of the college's Field Politics Center. Corrin recalls that in 1954 Agnew came to him and tried to solicit his active support for a political career he wanted to start. Agnew's only power base was the Loch Raven Improvement Association, a local pressure group that worried about everything from potholes to green space. But his horizons were out of sight. Corrin clearly recalls Agnew talking about how he could first get into local government and then work his way up to governor. Corrin said no, but wonders where he'd be today if he said yes.

Agnew made a pass at getting the Republican nomination for the Maryland House of Delegates in 1954, but was turned down cold by the local party organization. He tried again for a seat on the County Council in the 1957 special election, but again the Republicans were unmoved. "None of the people in the party knew Agnew, really," says Moore, who worked in every one of Devereaux's campaigns.

His chance finally came early in 1957 because of a flukish result in the 1957 County Council election. The fluke was that the Republicans won. Baltimore County is historically a Democratic duchy, with nearly four registered Democrats for every registered Republican. But in 1957 the county held a special election with no primary to narrow down the slates. Because of Democratic factionalism, twenty-four Democrats got their names on the ballot for the seven County Council seats. The Republicans, weaker but more cohesive, put up a single ticket of seven names. On election day the Democrats as usual got a majority of the votes. But their votes were fractionalized among the long list of competing Democratic candidates, and to everyone's astonishment the Republicans captured a 4-3 majority on the County Council.

When the balance of patronage automatically shifted toward the GOP, Agnew was up near the head of the line for goodies. What he wanted was one of the three $3,600-a-year jobs on the Baltimore County Board of Appeals, which dealt almost entirely with zoning cases.

Agnew wasn't coy about it. "He wanted this thing, he wanted it badly," remembers Scott Moore. "He called me day and night to try to line up votes."

With Moore and Christine Nathan on his side, Agnew went after the newly elected chairman of the County Council, a Republican lawyer named Gordon G. Power. "He kept pushing me," Power says. "He must have called a dozen times. He said he wanted it so that he could move his law office out to Towson. He said he didn't have enough business to justify a Towson office otherwise, and he needed the income from this appointment to justify the move."

Since the Board of Appeals was a quasi-judicial body, Agnew's legal diploma seemed a helpful qualification, although it wasn't necessary. His willingness to get people to put Republican precinct signs in their windows during the 1956 Devereaux campaign was probably a better litmus of his ability to serve on the Board of Appeals. "Besides," explains Power, "we didn't have hardly anyone else."

Since they held the majority on the County Council, the Republicans had two out of the three seats on the Board of Appeals to fill. They gave the first to a Chevrolet dealer named Charlie Irish, who had periodically demonstrated his Republican credentials with his checkbook. When the *Baltimore Sun* printed its first story on the new Board of Appeals, it noted that Charlie Irish had been named chairman. In a beautifully prescient typographical slip, the *Sun* reported that the other new Republican member was "Spiro T. Anger."

There is a temptation to view all of Agnew's later progression as an inevitable escalator ride beginning when he made the Board of Appeals. However, at the time there was no way of telling whether the escalator was going down or up. The new job meant making yes-or-no decisions that could alienate whole neighborhoods of voters. True, there were also opportunities for racking up headlines in the local papers, but there was no guarantee that the stories would be helpful.

With these caveats, the fact remained that for the first time in his life Agnew had power. He could not escape it. The authority to change zoning is the power to multiply or divide the value of other people's land, to make some men rich and others miserable. His power increased in 1958 when Charlie Irish went back to selling Chevrolets and he became chairman of the Board of Appeals.

Agnew acquired this power in the middle of a decade in which his county's population was surging from 270,000 to 492,400. The flight of the middle class from Baltimore City to the independent suburban ring called Baltimore County created a lusty demand for split-levels, apartment complexes, row house developments, shopping centers, convalescent homes, power plants, TV towers, animal hospitals, and gas stations. As tract after tract of estates and farmland were being suburbanized, a canny crowd of land speculators kept a step ahead of the bulldozers, buying up undeveloped property farther and farther from downtown Baltimore. To turn a profit, they needed rezonings.

Although Agnew and his colleagues had authority to change zoning, it was narrowly restricted by law. The zoning of every piece of land in the county was specified on a series of large multicolor zoning maps that hung on racks in the County Zoning Office. The maps were revised periodically by the County Council, with the members signing each map in pen and ink to signify their approval.

Between these County Council revisions, the law provided two circumstances under which a rezoning could be authorized by the Board of Appeals: first, if there was an error in the original map; and second, if there had been a change in the condition of the surrounding land that was not foreseen when the map was drawn. The flexibility of the Board of Appeals was especially limited when Agnew joined it because at that point most of the maps were only a few years old.

The Board of Appeals was the second stage of a four-stage process of hearings and appeals. The first step was the presentation of arguments for and against the rezoning to Baltimore County's full-time paid Zoning Commissioner. If the losing side was dissatisfied with the commissioner's ruling and could afford the appeal fees, it then took the case to the part-time Board of Appeals. Automatically the Board heard a new round of testimony and cross-examination at a public hearing which was something like a courtroom with a Greek chorus. While the rezoning applicants and the protesting neighbors glowered at each other in the audience, the three Board members sat behind a long table in the front of the hearing room, insisting on order and decorum. Some weeks after the hearing, the Board delivered its decision in written form. If the losing side was still dissatisfied, the Board's decision could be appealed to a Circuit Court judge in the County Courthouse across the street. After that, there was still a final appeal to the Maryland Court of Appeals in Annapolis.

If one looks through the dockets preserved by the Board of Appeals, it is hard to see any statistical evidence that Agnew was biased either for or against those seeking rezonings. During his tenure the Board decided 133 cases, almost all of them unanimously. Of these Agnew voted to grant 69 rezonings and to deny 64. In 81 of the 133 cases, Agnew simply agreed that the Zoning Commissioner was correct in his original ruling—40 to grant the rezoning and 41 to deny. In the remaining 52 cases where he disagreed with the Zoning Commissioner, he favored previously denied rezoning 29 times and was against previously granted rezoning 23 times.

If anything, the Circuit Court judges across the street felt the Board of Appeals was too restrictive on rezonings rather than too lenient. Of 47 Board of Appeals decisions appealed to the Circuit Court, 40 were affirmed. All seven reversals had the effect of granting rezonings that the Board of Appeals had previously denied.

In those days, nobody thought to keep score.

Whatever faint imprint Agnew's name was tracing on the public consciousness was made through scattered newspaper articles. One day he was cracking down on a junk dealer who was violating an ordinance. Another time he was cutting short a trailer park hearing with a pronouncement that "This Board will not permit this hearing to degenerate into a political football." A third clipping quoted Agnew on the intolerable burdens imposed on small-property owners "smeared M-R (manufacturing-restricted zone) by the broad brush of the mappers."

What mattered most was that the newspapers said nothing bad about him. During Agnew's service, Baltimore County had its share of zoning scandals of the everyday variety that made zoning offices suspect throughout the country. In a single month in 1959, a Democratic member of the Board of Appeals was indicted for malfeasance and the wife of the Zoning Commissioner was found to have made a $20,500 questionable profit in a land deal. The following year, the Zoning Commissioner himself was fired after he admitted receiving $20,000 in "consultant fees" from a supermarket chain interested in developing a shopping center.

For many, the whole zoning process in Baltimore County in the fifties and sixties seemed to be a matter of who had the most clout. Richard Kilroy, president of the Wayside-Timonium Heights Community Association, summed up the prevailing cynicism in a letter to the editor: "This erection [of apartment buildings in an area zoned for one-family residences] by unscrupulous exploiters of our quiet communities is usually preceded by a familiar pattern of petitioning, minimum publicity, and favorable action [for the builder] by the Zoning Commissioner. The whole process is carried out so cleverly and quietly that the neighborhood affected does not realize what is taking place until construction is commenced. Then it is too late.

"Schools are overcrowded, water and sewer facilities are inadequate, recreational areas are reduced, and property values are depressed. . . .

"Unless the residents retain a lawyer and make a strong show of political force, their protests will fall on deaf ears. If a large enough segment of the community's residents contribute their time and money to the protest efforts, the petition may be denied. But this is not the end of the matter. Eighteen months later it starts all over again [if the owners submit a new rezoning application]. More money for lawyers, more time off from work. . . ."

Throughout, Agnew managed to keep his nose cleaner than Baltimore County cynics had come to expect of their zoning officials. "He was holier-than-thou on that board," said one admiring Republican lawyer.

Agnew did all he could to reinforce the image of untouch-ability. Typical was his remark when the county Planning Board told the Board of Appeals about a new road plan which affected a current zoning case. The Planning Board's action, said Agnew, "easily could be construed to be an improper attempt to influence the Board on a matter now under advisement." He said he would refuse to accept "any new evidence by way of corridor correspondence."

From Clarke Langrall, an intimate friend of Agnew's since Kiwanis days, comes the word that Agnew believed he could have made $500,000 a year in bribes if he had only wanted to. Searching to give me an example of Agnew's moral fiber, Langrall thought back to a long trip in a car with Agnew about 1960.

"He was telling me about the monetary opportunities in-volved in his job," said Langrall. "He said there was never a case before the Zoning Appeals Board that doesn't mean a lot of money to someone. He said he hadn't been approached directly, but he happened to know that there was never a case which came before him worth less than $50,000 to somebody. He said, 'I know I could make $10,000 a week with no problem at all.' "

Langrall says when he facetiously asked Agnew why he didn't take the money, Agnew replied, "No money is worth that much to me; the important thing is the service I per-form. And secondly, I wouldn't allow $10,000 or $100,000 or $1,000,000 to get in the way of the heights I aspire to, which are much greater than being just a county zoning commissioner."

Actually two of the heights to which Agnew aspired would have been dead ends if he had reached them.

Early in 1958 Agnew got word of a $14,000-a-year job opening on the State of Maryland's Workmen's Compensation Commission. Would he like to be considered for it, he was asked by County Council Chairman Gordon Power. Yes, replied Agnew, he certainly was interested. Power recalls Agnew saying that he owed it to his family to provide for their security.

The duty of a workmen's compensation commissioner was to sit through scores of injury cases and decide from the evidence whether the victim was entitled to "10 percent of a back," "90 percent of a leg," or sometimes nothing. It was a long-term, full-time job. If Agnew had gotten it, he could never have moved back onto the political track in time to position himself for Vice President in 1968. As things turned out, the appointment went not to Agnew but to a former Baltimore City judge named Helen Elizabeth Brown. Miss Brown kept the job until sixteen months after Agnew was nominated as Vice President.

The other dead end he pursued was his ambition to become a judge—an ambition which his friends believe he harbors today.

In a vault in the Baltimore County Courthouse there is a dusty brown folder that would make a nice trophy for an autograph collector. Leafing through dozens of documents about campaign spending for the 1960 Maryland primary elections, one first comes across a letter signed by the late John F. Kennedy appointing a local representative for the Maryland Presidential primary. If one keeps on looking, there is also a letter signed by Spiro T. Agnew announcing that he was a candidate for Judge of the Baltimore County Circuit Court.

Established Republicans like Scott Moore had told Agnew he didn't have a prayer. As they all knew, the tradition around Baltimore was that the incumbents always won in judgeship elections. Although this was only a matter of practice, the Bar Association and the local newspapers regularly served as enforcers of the so-called "sitting judges principle."

Nothing would dissuade Agnew from what seemed to everyone to be a foolish gesture. His first campaign opened on April 16, 1960, with the erection of three billboards paid for by one of his father's Greek-American friends. His slogan was a wordplay on his name: "Agnew A New Judge."

Agnew, who filed as both a Republican and a Democrat, was swamped in the Democratic primary by the sitting judges. On the Republican side he got 3,594 votes, which put him in second place in a field of seven. It was enough to get him on the ballot in November. That month cost $2,975 plus the three donated billboards, according to his campaign expenditure report. Of that, Agnew put up $1,955 of his own, and he raised the rest.

As November approached, Agnew highlighted his campaigning with a slam in the newspapers against both the Bar Association and the sitting judges principle. "Under our judicial system, judges must be elected by the people," he told the *Baltimore Evening Sun*. "If the intent of the law was to have judges appointed by the Bar Association, the law would so read. . . . The sitting judge principle is a cloak which can be donned or discarded, depending on the severity of the weather, or more bluntly, whose ox is being gored."

The Bar Association was not provoked into direct combat.

But just before the election, Bar Association President John F. Whitney made a simple announcement. "The lawyers of our county are almost unanimously in favor of the election of these three [sitting] judges, and intend to let the voters know it through personal contact at the polls."

When the votes were in, the ox gored was Agnew. Each of the sitting judges polled more than 100,000 votes. The other Republican on the ticket, Agnew's 1957 benefactor Gordon G. Power, came in fourth. Number five out of five was Spiro T. Agnew with 49,764.

The conventional wisdom is that Agnew blundered when he ran for judge because it was clear he would lose. But Agnew figured it differently. Not long after the election he unburdened himself to his friend and client Edgar Fulton from Kemper Insurance. Although he lost, Agnew said, the whole campaign had cost only $5,000. And where else could he get $50,000 worth of publicity at a cost of $5,000?

After four years on the Appeals Board, Agnew was beginning to make an indentation on the minds of the diligent readers of weekly newspapers. And there was evidence at the beginning of 1961 that he was beginning to find success in the law business. One sign of his confidence in the prospects was his decision, along with several partners, to expand their practice by renting a larger suite of offices for $803 a month in a new building in Towson. Edward Hardesty, a Democrat and then an Assistant County Solicitor, remembers he was watching the inauguration of President Kennedy on January 20, 1961, when he got a telephone call from Spiro Agnew.

"He said he was very impressed with my legal ability, and he was looking for a young lawyer from the western end of the county," says Hardesty. "He said, 'Maybe you can cut some red tape, because you are close to the County Executive.' " A few weeks later, Hardesty joined the Agnew firm as an associate, and he has been an Agnew fan ever since.

Despite the first glimmerings of prosperity in his law business, his prognosis as a politician was not good. He was tiring of the Appeals Board, having served longer than he ever expected or wanted to. For the last year, the Democrats held a 2-1 majority on the board, and that meant he had been obliged to step down as chairman. Although he had ambitions to move on to some other niche in government, there was no obvious escape route. The only thing he had going for him was that the Republicans on the County Council who gave him his job originally had been swept out of office by the Democrats, leaving him as the highest-ranking Republican in the county government.

The problem was right upon him. His term on the Board of Appeals was due to expire in February, and he was getting rumbles that the Democrats, who held every seat on the County Council, were thinking about giving his job to some other Republican.

The Council president was Dale Anderson, a shrewd real estate man from the eastern prong of the county. On January 19, 1961, Spiro Agnew signed a zoning decision that allowed a large development of row houses in Anderson's own district. Anderson started getting calls and letters asking for Agnew's scalp. What made the neighbors maddest was that the Board of Appeals had overruled the Zoning Commissioner's judgment that the rezoning should be denied.

As soon as the first Dump Agnew talk began, a Keep Agnew campaign materialized. On January 31 the *Evening Sun* carried a squib that the members of the Loch Raven Village

Association had endorsed their home-town boy for retention on the Board. Within the next two weeks, seventy-one local lawyers, many of whom had tried zoning cases before him, signed a petition urging the County Council to keep Agnew. Then the respected Citizens Planning and Housing Association declared that his past record "entitles him to reappointment."

Whether or not he wanted to stay on the Appeals Board, Agnew was sharp enough to see the ingredients of a newspaper splash.

"I think it is about time for me to publicly state that it is an open secret who the people are who are opposing my appointment," Agnew announced. "They are the same group who were so successful in ramming the unfortunate Hubers appointment down the throats of the County Council . . . the Pine-Boone faction." Linguistically, it may have fallen short of more recent Agnew. But as a gut-fighting lunge it showed native talent. In one paragraph he had accused the county's two most powerful Democratic state legislators, James Pine and A. Gordon Boone, with trying to get his job. And he had linked both of them with Daniel Hubers, a man who had recently been indicted for malfeasance.[1]

Agnew couldn't have gotten a better headline in the *Baltimore Sun* if he had written it himself: "Agnew Calls Foes Afraid—'They Can't Control Me.' "

The County Council met the following evening, still stinging from Agnew's denunciation. For a variety of reasons, the consensus was to slap down this pesky gnat. Some of the Democrats were saying privately that it was a good chance to stop Agnew before he became a threat in some future election. But the decisive voice was that of Dale Anderson, who says now he was mainly swayed to vote against Agnew by his constituents, who were in an uproar over the row house rezoning.

"It was politics," acknowledges Anderson, who followed Agnew as County Executive of Baltimore County. "It was damned stupid politics. It made Agnew a martyr and that helped him tremendously."

The smallish County Council meeting room was packed with several dozen vocal Agnew partisans when Anderson started speaking. There was, he said, "an extreme amount of political pressure on this appointment . . . the vast preponderance of that political pressure on behalf of the incumbent." But there had also been pressure against Agnew, he said, and in the circumstances he thought the fairest thing to do was to see that neither faction got the man it wanted.

Under the county charter, both parties had to be represented on the Board of Appeals, and this seat had to go to a Republican. An Agnew backer stood up in the audience and proclaimed that the county Republican organization was behind Agnew all the way.

Someone else cried out, "Castro was right!" and "Cuba had it bad but Baltimore County has it worse!"

Before going into the meeting, Agnew had worked out a scheme in which every other qualified Republican would decline the job and the Democrats would have to reappoint him. To his surprise Dale Anderson had unearthed a substitute Republican candidate. He was Charles Steinbock, the same man Agnew was to telephone twenty-one months later on the Seven Slade case. Friends of Agnew say he has always believed Charlie Steinbock let him down by agreeing to take his job on the Appeals Board. It was a grudge that would hurt both men.

The vote in the County Council against Agnew was 5-2. It might have gone differently if Agnew had fought in private to keep his seat. As Councilman Robert R. Gill explained, he had planned to vote for Agnew but switched because he "chastised us all in the press and burned his bridges." Councilman J. Cavendish Darrell, who sided with Steinbock in the end, said he too admired Agnew, but "I'm not going to vote for a man I'm not sure is going to win."

Agnew said nothing about the treachery of Charlie Steinbock, but he did keep up his tirade via the press against the Democrats. "The reasons for my removal given by some of the Councilmen would make a new edition of *Grimm's Fairy Tales*," he said. "They are fantastic insults to the public intelligence. Such weak, small-caliber excuses hide the real reason about as effectively as a coat of cellophane. The job was being done honestly and with reasonable efficiency. Perhaps in the minds of some, those traits require immediate extermination."

After Agnew went to Washington to be Vice President, Sam Kimmel would lean back in his chair and reflect: "I've never seen him so mad as he was over getting dumped from that post. If the Democrats had left him alone, he might well be still sitting there handling zoning cases."

6

"Ted, you are asking me to do a hell of a thing."

The Sinking of Iron Mike

"It is apparent to even the most casual observer of the local political scene that the leadership of Baltimore County must be pried from the tired but still greedy hands of the feuding majority party factions." So saying, Spiro T. Agnew announced in October 1961 that he was a candidate for County Executive of a suburban county as populous as the cities of Denver or Atlanta. If the voters wanted a reformer, a man with a flair for the cutting phrase, here was their man. The Republican organization in the county, known somewhat confusingly as the Republican State Central Committee, waited less than forty-eight hours before unanimously endorsing Agnew as the party's official candidate. The *Sun* editorial writer called him "a good choice" and "well-known and well-liked throughout the county."

The swiftness of his selection masked an outbreak of factional turmoil within the county's minuscule Republican organization. One main source of the turmoil was Agnew's longing to advance himself. What Agnew really wanted in

1961 was to run for the United States Congress, not for County Executive. A leap from the zoning board to the House of Representatives took gall to contemplate, but then it also had taken gall to buck the Bar Association and the *Sun* papers when he ran for judge. The problem was not that he lacked the background, although that was skimpy; rather, there was the fatal defect that he lacked the financial backing. When Agnew went around to ask the members of the Republican State Central Committee to support him for Congress, he got enough turndowns to realize it was hopeless.

His main putative rival was J. Fife Symington, a handsome forty-nine-year-old gentleman farmer from Lutherville, Maryland, who did not hurt for money. Symington's wife, Marsie, was granddaughter of Henry C. Frick, who helped found United States Steel. They lived on a five-hundred-acre estate in the upper-class stretch of Baltimore County known as the Valley, where there were no factories or subdivisions. An accomplished horseman, Symington had been master of the Green Spring Valley Hunt Club. Recently, he had retired from his building supplies business to run his estate and experiment in politics.

Symington, who would later be a Barry Goldwater loyalist, began as a conservative Democrat. In 1956, the year Agnew was handling minor chores in the Devereaux campaign, Fife Symington had the more glamorous assignment of heading a committee known as "Democrats for Devereaux." Through his friendship with Devereaux, Symington was later able to make a quick switch to the Republican Party and walk off with the 1958 Republican nomination for Congress when Devereaux retired. Symington was snowed under in the 1958 congressional election, and again in 1960 when the Republicans let him run a second time. But in 1962 the incumbent Democrat was due to depart, and Symington thought he could finally win.

When Symington, the patrician, heard that this fellow Agnew from Loch Raven also wanted to run for Congress, he contacted Scott Moore and told him, "I want to run for Congress, and I want you to get Agnew out of this. He is a lawyer and he has a growing family—it doesn't make sense for him to go to Congress." Then he left on a jaunt to Spain.

Agnew had no choice but to step aside, even though a few scattered factions such as the 237-member Dundalk Consolidated Republican Club did endorse him for Congress. Agnew had never had much affection for Fife Symington, ever since the late forties when he lived near the railroad tracks in Lutherville and Symington lived a few miles away, at his estate on the hill. Now he loved Symington even less.

When Agnew saw that he could not get the congressional nomination for himself, he signaled his availability to run for County Executive through his friends Sam Kimmel and Scott Moore. On the strength of his newspaper clippings during his ouster from the zoning board, Agnew was given the endorsement. "We didn't have a half a dozen of us in the county that anyone had ever heard of—we were glad to give it to him," recalls John K. Davis, who was a Republican Councilman.

Although he couldn't run for Congress himself, Agnew resolved to knock Symington off the ticket if he could. His vehicle for opposing Symington was a slow-talking cattle farmer named George H. C. Arrowsmith, who announced that he too wanted the Republican Congressional nomination.

George Arrowsmith sounded like another upper-class farmer out of the Symington mold. The son of a clergyman, he was an heir to part of the Dow Jones & Company fortune. After prep school he had been sent to Princeton and Johns Hopkins, but judging from his campaign literature he did not graduate. After finding the business world stifling, he settled down to become a gentleman cattle breeder in the northern reaches of Baltimore County. In announcing his qualifications for Congress, Arrowsmith noted that he was a former president of the Maryland Shorthorn Breeders Association.

As long as anyone could remember, there had never been a real contested primary among the Baltimore County Republicans. The party was so weak and the odds against winning so enormous that there were usually not enough candidates willing to fill all the places on the ticket. In fact, throughout the state of Maryland there had not been a hard-fought Republican primary in more than a decade. Thus once Agnew was endorsed by the Republican State Central Committee of Baltimore County in October 1961, it was a foregone conclusion that he would win the primary in May 1962, provided he stayed out of trouble.

But that wasn't Agnew's idea of how to get ahead. Although he was not impressed with Arrowsmith's brilliance, he was impressed enough with his money to become his most vocal booster. Sam Kimmel, who was Agnew's associate in both the law office and Republican politics, tells what he thinks went through Agnew's mind: "This may not be too complimentary to Ted, but Arrowsmith was a rather affluent person. And it appeared to Ted that if the Republicans were going to have any success against the Democrats in the fall, that they were going to have to spend some money. Arrowsmith indicated that he would spend more money to support the whole ticket, if he was nominated, than Symington would. It is my opinion that this is what influenced Ted to go along with Arrowsmith."

Arrowsmith, now just a farmer but still an admirer of Agnew, says: "They did not hold me up or anything, but Ted simply said he wanted somebody on the ticket who would pull for the whole ticket." Arrowsmith said he did agree to put up some money for the whole local ticket, which was headed by Agnew, but no exact dollar figures were negotiated.

Dollars were not Agnew's only motive. Arrowsmith, like Agnew, tended toward the liberal side of the Republican spectrum, whereas Symington was an unreconstructed conservative. What mattered more, Symington had blocked Agnew's own ambition to run for Congress, and there was even some talk that Symington wanted to keep Agnew off the Republican ticket entirely. "It could be described as a political battle for the sake of power," Agnew explained to me, "because power was a very important ingredient—who was going to have the power in the county as far as setting the Republican Party in the direction we felt it should go."

With a shove from Agnew, Arrowsmith won the endorsement of the State Central Committee by a vote of 4-3. Predictably, Symington went ahead to create his own slate as though Arrowsmith didn't exist. Agnew then led a charge against Symington, using the kind of truculence that would become his trademark eight years later.

"I wish to make clear," he said in a press release, "that any so-called 'rift' in the Baltimore County Republican Party is no more than an illusion solely attributable to the efforts of one man [Fife Symington] who places his pride and personal ambitions before the welfare of the Republican Party and our excellent chances for a county-wide Republican victory in November.

"Symington's efforts to divide this unity have fizzled, even backfired, because of his devious methods, obvious inconsistencies and his penchant for hiding behind and using, for personal gain, the good name of well-meaning citizens who are not now active or in touch with Republican affairs in Baltimore County."

The Symington-Arrowsmith campaign cracked the tiny party in two, and soon Agnew found himself fighting most of the established figures in the Baltimore County Republican firmament. Gordon Power, who helped put Agnew on the Board of Appeals in 1957, joined forces with Symington even after accepting the endorsement of the State Central Committee as the official candidate for the State Senate. Former Representative Devereaux also made a public statement for Symington, and so did the Chairman of the Republican State Central Committee, Osborne P. Beall.

Any obligation Agnew may have felt to Gordon Power was now buried. Just before the filing deadline for the May primary, Agnew went before the State Central Committee and got it to withdraw its endorsement of Power for the State Senate on grounds that he was not behind the official Arrowsmith ticket.

Devereaux, the war hero, presented another sort of problem. Agnew's response was to portray him as a kindly, honorable old general who had been used by Symington "in his fast-sinking campaign to rule or ruin." Agnew charged that

Symington had agreed to be chairman of Democrats for Devereaux in 1956 only after extracting a promise from the general that he would support Symington for Congress after his retirement. "In our opinion," said Agnew, "Fife now proves his insensitivity to the feelings of others by forcing Devereaux, who regards his word as his most important obligation, to take a public position on this matter."

A week before the primary Agnew wrote another blast at Symington for trying to use the party "as a part-time plaything rather than a solemn responsibility." He asserted that he was acting to restore leadership to the State Central Committee at the request of "a large group of greatly concerned Republican workers" who asked him about a year earlier to "spearhead" such a movement.

Symington replied by accusing Agnew of exerting influence on the State Central Committee "to impose his personal whims upon party candidates and the voters." And two days before the primary the chairman of the Republican State Central Committee, Osborne Beall, announced that he was disavowing Agnew's pink sample ballot, which represented Beall as backing the Arrowsmith slate. Actually, said Beall, he was behind Symington.

Although Agnew was unopposed in the 1962 primary, that election became a test of whether he was the maximum leader of the county party or just another candidate. Agnew flunked the test, as both Symington and Power smashed the candidates Agnew was promoting. Hard as this was on his ego, he suffered even greater damage in the balloting for the seven seats on the county Republican State Central Committee. Five of the six names on Agnew's slate were defeated, mostly by conservatives and friends of Symington and

Power. The only winner he endorsed was Beall, and Beall was endorsed by the other side too. What it meant was that for the next four years Agnew could expect no warmth from the official structure of his own party.

To make things worse, people close to Arrowsmith felt that in the final days Agnew could have worked harder to pull in votes around Towson that he was supposed to control. There was even a suspicion among some Arrowsmith backers that in the end Agnew deliberately let Symington win. Considering Agnew's hopes of latching onto some Arrowsmith cash for the general election, the suspicion that he dumped Arrowsmith seems preposterous. Whatever happened, Agnew was left without a money man when Arrowsmith went down— that is, until he found the aforementioned Al Shuger.

After the primary Agnew had a tense talk with his old benefactor, Gordon Power. "Ted, I don't understand—I made your political career and you just tried to destroy mine," Power recalls telling Agnew. Nonetheless they agreed, using the cliché for such occasions, "to try and mend fences." The symbol of the mended fence was a party thrown by Symington at his estate with Agnew and Power serving as official co-hosts.

Fife Symington is now the United States Ambassador to Trinidad and Tobago, a fitting reward for his generosity over the years to the national Republican Party treasury. If it had been up to Spiro Agnew, Symington would be back in Lutherville tending the livestock.

Despite the velocity of his verbiage, the Baltimore newspapers printed almost nothing about Agnew's role in the Symington-Arrowsmith primary. The big news in Baltimore County was the clash among the Democrats, since it was assumed that the Republicans would lose in November anyway. Of the Republican contest the *Baltimore Sun*'s political editor wrote, "By comparison with the massive divisions among the Democrats, this is hardly a ripple. When the primary smoke clears away, the Democrats will have 40 defeated, disgruntled and possibly disaffected candidates to be placated. The Republicans will have no more than four."

Primary elections are designed to pick each party's most electable candidates, but sometimes primaries backfire. In 1962 the Baltimore County Democrats settled on their worst and least electable candidate to run against Spiro Agnew. Then they compounded their mistake by failing to reunite their factions after the election. This combination of blunders was sufficient to make Agnew the next County Executive.

The man chosen by the Democratic primary was Michael J. Birmingham, widely known as "Iron Mike" because of the way he had ruled the county Democratic Party for ten years. Already over seventy, he was a character out of *The Last Hurrah* except that few found him lovable. Bald, potbellied, and nearly inarticulate on a podium, he belonged to an old school of politics that depended on a permanent organization to deliver the votes.

Like a minor league boss, Michael Birmingham based his power on patronage. Your garbage collector was likely to be your Democratic precinct captain, and it seemed only natural to let him drive you to the polling place on election day. If you wanted to get that old refrigerator carted away, or a sidewalk paved by the county, it was probably better to register Democratic. The game wardens, the constables, the dogcatchers, the court clerks, the police magistrates—all were part of the anthill of Democratic patronage. Even the police were in the system. Once when a reporter checked the registration of every county policeman and found not a single Republican, Birmingham conceded it was no coincidence. "To me, a Republican is a guy who wasn't brought up right," he said.

Baltimore County looked on the map like a horse collar nearly encircling the city of Baltimore, and Birmingham's power was concentrated in the lower right corner of the collar. His strongholds were Dundalk and Essex, where lower-middle-class factory workers lived in packed proximity. Many worked at Bethlehem Steel's huge Sparrow's Point steel mill in the southeast tip of the county. Often, the Democratic Party was more than just a matter of belief. Instead of belonging to the Elks, it was common to join the 15th District Democratic Club just for the social life.

There was another regular Democrat, Christian H. Kahl, who had a personal organization of his own, concentrated in the northern and western parts of the horse collar. Both Kahl and Birmingham had been powers in local politics since 1938, alternately squabbling and reuniting. As 1962 approached, the two men locked into a petty combat that turned out to be irreconcilable.

Birmingham had been the first County Executive, serving for two years, when the county went to the County Executive form of government in 1957. Facing a hard election in 1958, Birmingham agreed to step aside and let Kahl take over. After Kahl was elected the two men wrestled continually over the next three years, largely over dividing the pork. Then Birmingham announced that he would come out of retirement and take on Kahl, then the incumbent County Executive, in the 1962 Democratic primary.

If Kahl had beaten Birmingham, he would have made a far tougher candidate against Agnew. More articulate than Birmingham and less tainted by grafting associates, Kahl demonstrated a modern outlook as County Executive. Ironically, Kahl could have won the primary if he had been a more adroit politician. As it turned out, Kahl lost to Birmingham by only 4,500 votes, while another anti-Birmingham candidate siphoned off 18,000 votes. If the third candidate, maverick liberal W. Brooks Bradley, had been offered the proper inducements by Kahl, he might well have stepped aside, since he was basically running to beat Birmingham.

Even after Birmingham won the primary, the Democrats could still have beaten Agnew in November if they had arranged to solidify for a few months. But "Iron Mike" Birmingham would not bend a millimeter.

The test case, as far as Kahl's troops were concerned, was an opportunity to nominate candidates to fill seven more seats in Maryland's House of Delegates which were assigned to Baltimore County in a reapportionment. Kahl demanded three out of the seven for his faction, but Birmingham took all seven. If that was the way Birmingham would treat the Kahl faithful, what hope did they have for keeping their jobs once Birmingham was County Executive? There was no gesture from "Iron Mike" to lure them back to the fold.

All this gave Spiro Agnew no more than an outside possibility to pull an upset. He still faced multiple problems— not much money, a nonexistent precinct organization, factional problems of his own, and a ratio of nearly four registered Democrats for every registered Republican.

The arithmetic of the problem was obvious to him: if he was to win, he would have to win with Democratic votes.

"There is no point spending much time talking to Republican clubs because they are going to vote for me anyway," he explained to one Republican worker.

It happened that one of the part-time associates in Agnew's law firm, Edward Hardesty, was also a part-time Assistant County Solicitor in Kahl's administration. After the primary, Hardesty remembers Agnew coming to him and offering to put him on the payroll of Agnew and Hennegan full-time if he lost his county job. Hardesty says in midsummer Agnew approached him again. "First they [the Birmingham faction] knocked you down and kicked you in the teeth," said Agnew. "Now I would like to talk to you about supporting me."

"Ted, you are asking me to do a hell of a thing," Hardesty replied.

Hardesty had his own mini-machine of several hundred Democratic workers, many with patronage jobs he had arranged for them, down in the southwestern corner of the county. Naturally, he was raised to believe it was fatal to cross party lines. At first he put Agnew off, but Agnew kept after him several times a week. After about a month, he agreed to a half step—he would put an Agnew bumper sticker on his car. Finding it torn off the next morning annoyed him so much that he told Agnew he would back him 100 percent.

"Can you get your organization to go along?" Agnew shot back.

"Yes," replied Hardesty, "provided they get a promise that their jobs would be protected."

"He gave me his word," says Hardesty. "And I did deliver my district for him."

Hardesty was the first Kahl lieutenant to come out publicly for Spiro Agnew, but by the end of September he was joined by such pro-Kahl luminaries as the county Registrar of Wills and the Clerk of the Circuit Court, along with the whole Middle River Democratic Club. Another convert was independent Democrat Brooks Bradley, the third man in the Kahl-Birmingham primary. At a testimonial dinner for Agnew on September 24, Democrats almost outnumbered Republicans. The former president of the local AFL-CIO Executive Council was seated at the head table, along with Baltimore Colts Captain Gino Marchetti.

Kahl, who could have prevented the defections, chose to stay publicly uncommitted. Privately he told his troops they would have to make their own calculation of the risks, but he would never take reprisals against them if they went for Agnew. Kahl believes that if he had told them to stay with Birmingham, Agnew's chance to win would have vanished. Later, when Agnew was Governor, he gave Chris Kahl a state job.

With no Republican organization and limited money, Agnew had difficulties in getting the unorganized voters to recognize his name, let alone grasp what he stood for. For one thing, many people believed that Ted Agnew and Spiro Agnew were two different people. Repeatedly he tried to taunt Birmingham into a televised debate, but the Democratic candidate would not be hooked. "Why should I set up an audience for him?" he sneered. Sick during the campaign, Birmingham appeared at almost no public functions, and even declined to respond to a routine questionnaire from the League of Women Voters. Finally Agnew sneered back, "Why doesn't somebody wind up Mr. Birmingham so he can talk?"

Agnew and his advertising agency cooked up a slogan they used throughout the campaign: "The Man with a Plan." That slogan, along with his picture, was imprinted on several hundred thousand cards for commuters. On the other side of the card was a map of the newly opened Baltimore Beltway which circled the city. "We had to do something so that people wouldn't immediately throw his cards away," says his advertising man, Louis Cahn. If pressed about the details of his "plan," Agnew talked glibly about a coordinated blueprint for long-range county expansion. The main thing he wanted to get across was that he was a reformer trying to oust "Boss Birmingham."

Agnew's positions during the campaign were eminently progressive. He was for a county ordinance guaranteeing equal public accommodations to all races, patterned on the law just adopted by Baltimore City. He was for more women in government, for local laws against air pollution, for mandatory anti-smog devices in automobile exhaust systems, and for more money for local libraries.

The *Sun* papers, tired of the Birmingham machine and pleased to see a refreshing newcomer, fell into place behind Agnew on November 1. The *Sun*'s editorial endorsement said, "In his vigorous and thoughtful campaign he has shown that he knows where the sore spots in county affairs lie—in the need for making common cause with the city on matters of mutual interest, in speeding the adoption of land use maps, and in eliminating conflicts of interest."

Once the candidate looked as if he might win, campaign money was much easier to raise. Scott Moore remembers copying down lists of Democratic contributors and asking each donor whether he didn't want to give something to the

Republicans too. A good many, particularly those with county contracts, agreed to hedge their bets. But money was a constant problem on Agnew's mind throughout 1962 even with the help of Al Shuger. He had just moved into a new $36,000 house, which carried a $28,000 mortgage. The rent on his new law office was $803 a month. And he'd had to co-sign two notes for political expenses. During the Cuban missile crisis in October 1962, Agnew began to despair about his debts and chances of winning. "Why did Kennedy have to come up with this Cuba shit?" he complained to his law associate Joe Pokorny.

The results showed Agnew needn't have worried:

Spiro T. Agnew (Republican)	78,738
Michael J. Birmingham (Democrat)	61,313
Earl R. Van Gorder (Independent)	2,246

Whether he knew it or not, Agnew was on his way to the Governorship. Within a month the *Baltimore Sun* called it "Maryland's most remarkable political upset" of the year and ventured prophetically: "The momentum could, if all goes smoothly, carry him even farther four years from now."

What must have made victory sweeter was that both Symington and Power lost.

7

"I'm under tremendous pressures from the kindergarten people
and the vocational schools people."

Running Baltimore County

For all his self-confidence during the campaign, the "Man
with a Plan" was awash with qualms about his ability to
perform as County Executive. He worried about his talents
for getting a message over to the public and even about his
capacity for making the right decisions. "The biggest fright
I ever had in government was the first office I went into," he
confessed in December 1968.

Considering his inexperience, he turned out to be a good
County Executive. In the process he got his on-the-job training in the big three domestic issues of 1968—law and order,
inflation, and race.

The current County Executive, Democrat Dale Anderson,
was a close and somewhat admiring observer of Agnew's
performance from his own vantage point of chairman of the
County Council. "He came in here under a severe handi-
cap," declares Anderson. "He had never been in public office
as an elected official. But he is a smart man and he learns
fast, so he did a fairly good job. I couldn't rate him as excel-

lent, and I certainly couldn't rate him as poor. I think he was a good County Executive. Probably if he had been re-elected, in 1966, he would have been outstanding." Naturally there were others who found him brilliant and some who rated him a disaster. But on balance Anderson's judgment isn't far wrong. The only necessary codicil is that Agnew should get credit for advancing a series of fresh and sometimes highly unpopular ideas, even though not many got adopted.

Perhaps it was a harbinger of Agnew's future that he began his term with a law-and-order problem: the magistrate's court in Halethorpe (population 349). Less than a week in office, Agnew dispatched his first executive recommendation to the County Council on December 10, 1962, calling for a new courtroom to replace the "woefully inadequate" facilities in the present Halethorpe magistrate's court. By a unanimous vote, the six Democrats and one Republican on the Council approved a new lease immediately. As legislative triumphs go, it wasn't much. But over the next four years he would not have many big ones. On any issue more controversial than restoring law and order to Halethorpe, the Democrats on the Council were not exactly receptive to change.

His first burst of reformist energy was aimed at eliminating patronage in the county police department, which naturally meant Democratic patronage. One of his first acts was to summon Patrolman Herman W. Diesel to his office. Agnew had noted down Diesel's name as the policeman he met one day while campaigning in a tavern. Diesel, who was off duty and out of uniform, had snubbed him, saying, "I'm not going to shake hands with a Republican." His message to Diesel now was blunt: stay out of politics. The meeting was arranged in such a way that the local press could publish Diesel's name and the rest of the police department could draw the proper inferences.

Agnew immediately replaced the old police chief with Robert J. Lally, who was just then leaving his job as Assistant Special Agent in charge of the Baltimore Federal Bureau of Investigation office. The job of Director of Public Safety he gave to retired General James P. Devereaux, the former Congressman for whom he had once labored in the precincts.

Despite impressive new talent at the top of the police department, Agnew made little lasting progress toward eradicating politics in the Baltimore County Police Department. The bill he sent to the County Council early in 1963 to accomplish that objective was, in his word, "emasculated." Lally went to Annapolis with Agnew in 1967 as his Superintendent of the Maryland State Police.

Another early proving ground for Agnew's law-and-order credentials was gambling. "We feel," he said less than a month after taking office, "that pinball machines especially are gambling in its worst form when played by juveniles. The machines bring together a group of youngsters in a situation that has nothing to recommend it."

Two months later he widened his focus to include the "slot machine counties" on Maryland's Eastern Shore, far from his jurisdiction but close to the hearts of *Baltimore Sun* editorial writers. "A great deal of potentially assessable wealth in these counties flows undetected, uncounted and untaxed into the hands of the nation's gambling cartels," Agnew thundered. "I believe there is sentiment for driving the racketeers entirely out of the state."

Attacking pinball machines and one-armed bandits made sense politically. The tavern owners who kept them were a dependable source of political contributions to whatever political organization was entrenched. Both in Baltimore County and on the Eastern Shore, the dominant party was the Democratic Party. "We knew this was where the Democrats were getting an awful lot of money, and we decided to break it up," explains Scott Moore, who was Agnew's County Solicitor. Breaking it up didn't turn out to be so simple. When a bill to outlaw payoff pinball machines came to a vote, the County Council said no.

If deploring pinball was painless, calling for gun control measures took political courage. In October 1964 Agnew proposed a bill to the County Council that would have required anyone wanting to buy a handgun, rifle, or shotgun in Baltimore County to get a license from the police department. The pastor of the Universal Christian Church was the only one of twenty-five speakers at a public hearing who liked the bill. The other twenty-four, representing the gun collectors, the hunters, the gun dealers, and even the Timonium Optimists Club, were hotly opposed. With 300 in the audience, it was the largest turnout for a public hearing in more than two years. Realizing he could not win, Agnew agreed to amend the bill to omit rifles and shotguns. Then he named a commission to study the whole subject of gun control, headed by Lieutenant General Milton A. Reckord, state adjutant of the National Guard and a member of the National Rifle Association executive board.

A revived gun control bill was submitted to the County Council in February 1965, this time with Reckord's stamp of approval. Although it covered only handguns, it included a licensing procedure for gun dealers and a prohibition against selling guns to convicted felons or mental defectives. This time five witnesses, including Reckord and Lally, spoke in favor and twenty-three testified against. In June it was defeated 4-3 by the County Council on the grounds that gun control should be handled by the state legislature. Once again Agnew resubmitted the bill in January 1966, and once again the County Council promptly tabled it.

Baltimore County was no sylvan sanctuary. Chief Lally outlined the dimensions of the county's crime problem for Agnew early in 1964. On the one hand, the county's crime rate (2,080 serious crimes a year per 100,000 population) was double the national average. On the other hand, Baltimore County had only about 130 policemen for every 100,000 residents, compared to 210 in an average city. To bite into the county's crime problem Lally proposed to add 122 policemen in the forthcoming budget and another 112 every year after that.

For Baltimore County politicians, the statistic that applied the stimulation to the cranial nerve was not the crime rate but the tax rate. In preparing his next budget Agnew sliced 47 policemen out of Lally's request, leaving an increase of 75 slots. Even that was too much for the City Council, which cut out still another 50 policemen. In the next two years Baltimore County's crime rate increased 32 percent, almost double the increase in the national rate.

The issue of inflation, or at least inflating costs of municipal services, was a constant ulcer for Agnew during his four years in the County Office Building. It was typified by the great kindergartens-vs.-football controversy. When he came into office, the county schools had neither high school football nor kindergartens. Pressure groups lined up to push one or the other. Then new groups turned up advocating vocational schools. Asked by one sports fan why he did not introduce football, Agnew let out his frustration: "I'm under these tremendous pressures from the kindergarten people and the vocational schools people. Can you imagine the reaction from them if I went ahead and okayed something they consider an amenity?"

Agnew sent his first budget to the County Council in November 1963. In it there were salary increases for policemen and firemen and more money for schools and libraries. But there was not enough revenue left for either football or kindergartens. Even without them, Agnew had to ask for a 9 percent increase in the real estate tax, despite his windfall of a $63,000,000 increase in assessments.

The following year the county Board of Education leaned on Agnew for funds to cut the pupil-teacher ratio and to start football, a kindergarten program, and a vocational high school. In order to hold down taxes, Agnew chopped all of these proposals out of the 1964-65 budget. Under continual pounding from parents and school officials, Agnew changed course a few months later, saying, "I have tried to adjust my thinking" about kindergartens. In the spring of 1965 he announced that his upcoming budget would contain money for vocational education as well as a summer pre-school for the "disadvantaged." The county would get a full-time kindergarten, he promised, but not until the following year. Nor was football left out. When the Board of Education refused to set priorities, Agnew simply cut the pie in thirds.

Even after all his economizing, the last budget Agnew submitted was 67 percent higher than the first. Over his three and a half budget years, the cost of running the county swelled an average of 19 percent annually. Much of the bulge was caused by a rising population and the need to increase wages of county employees, rather than by any blossoming of new services.

One costly service which Agnew did feel compelled to expand was sewer construction. His 1965-66 budget contained $3,000,000 for sewers, which he proudly proclaimed as two-and-a-half times as much as any previous County Executive had provided. Unlike his predecessors, Agnew set out to install sewers even in some communities which opposed them out of fear that the homeowners' share of the costs would run too high. When Agnew's accomplishments are totaled up someday, one of his measurable legacies will be 150 miles of Baltimore County sewer pipes.

Had he not been thwarted by the County Council, he would also have bequeathed the county three much-needed incinerators to burn garbage. Agnew told the Council in December 1964 that the county was running out of room to dump garbage in landfills. His answer was three huge incinerator plants to dispose of ten million pounds of garbage a week. He promised they would be "smokeless and odorless."

When prospective neighbors began circulating petitions against them, Agnew offered to charter a bus to Hempstead, Long Island, so that doubters could see that a modern incinerator was not a smelly, smoky monster. The program might have gone through except that the John Deere Company, which owned land across from one of the incinerator sites, announced it would cancel its planned sales center in Baltimore County unless the incinerator was relocated. Agnew flew to Moline, Illinois, hoping to persuade the company to relent, but the trip was futile. After that, the incinerator proposal could not be revived. Today Baltimore County still has no incinerators and no answer to its hills of garbage.

Like all municipal executives, Agnew felt constant pressure to come up with new sources of revenue so that the full weight of government would not fall on the real estate tax. But the Democratic-controlled County Council found most of his money-raising proposals unpalatable. The Council rejected his requests for a one percent sales tax in 1963; for higher "nuisance taxes" on fuels and telephones in 1964; for increases in pinball and house-trailer taxes in 1965; and for a one percent tax on salaries and investment income as well as corporate profits in 1966. Even his County Solicitor, Scott Moore, balked at the idea of a tax on unearned income. To this Agnew replied, "Sometimes you are too damn much of a Republican."

With no new broad-based taxes, Baltimore County had to increase its real estate tax rate an average of 9 percent a year during Agnew's tenure. And when it came to building roads and schools, the county had to borrow money either by selling bonds on Wall Street or by getting advances from the state. By using these time-honored devices Baltimore County borrowed about $100,000,000 under the Agnew administration. Only about $40,000,000 of past debts were retired in that period, a fact that considerably upset an old-line citizen watchdog group known as the Economy and Efficiency Commission. To escape the county's debt limit, Agnew and the County Council set up a separate Revenue Authority to build a new office building and then lease it to the county.

Dealing with county debt wasn't always so painful. Twice a year or so, the County Executive and a small delegation of officials and friends would hustle off to New York, primarily to keep up contacts with the bankers and underwriters who helped float the county's bond issues. A bond trip was also a fine opportunity to hit some good restaurants and take in the best shows on Broadway. "We ran up some pretty big bills, and the banks paid the bills," recalls Scott Moore, who accompanied Agnew on at least one bond trip.

The first stress test of Agnew on the civil rights issue came in the summer of 1963.

The focal point was the Gwynn Oak Amusement Park, a sixty-eight-acre emporium of kewpie dolls and thrill rides that had a policy against admitting blacks. Gwynn Oak was in Baltimore County, which was 97 percent white, but it was just a few blocks beyond the limits of Baltimore City, then 50 percent black. Since 1955 civil rights protesters had been sporadically demonstrating for an end to segregation at Gwynn Oak.

James Price, one of the two brothers who owned the park, always insisted that he would be driven out of business if he integrated. "The white man in this area does not accept the Negro on a social or recreational basis," he said. Price was not far wrong about the race prejudices of many white Marylanders. It was only under President Kennedy that the federal government got around to asking the restaurateurs along Route 40 in Maryland to stop discriminating against black diplomats en route from Washington to the United Nations. By mid-1963 most of Baltimore County's restaurants were integrated, but some public swimming pools and roller rinks were still white-only.

When the Price brothers again refused to integrate Gwynn

Oak for the summer of 1963, an interfaith trespass-in was planned for the long July 4th weekend. From all over the East came busloads of students, clergymen, and housewives. Leaders included Reverend William Sloane Coffin of Yale, Monsignor Austin Healy of the Archdiocese of Baltimore, and the Reverend Dr. Eugene Carson Blake, executive officer of the United Presbyterian Church. Most of the faces were white.

James Price met the demonstrators near the ticket booth and read aloud the trespass law. Chief Lally warned that the invaders could either leave or get arrested. When they refused to move, the police locked up 283 persons, including the chief executive officer of the United Presbyterian Church, an Episcopal bishop, a Roman Catholic monsignor and a rabbi.

A knot of white toughs jeered from the sidelines and someone threw a cherry bomb at the demonstrators, injuring a young woman from the Bronx. What looked like an ugly situation got even uglier on Sunday, July 7, when the demonstrators returned for another bout. Alerted by news film on TV, the white hecklers now numbered about 1,500. One demonstrator, a young white girl, caught a flying brick above her right eye as she was trying to sneak into the park. Later, about ten hecklers caught a glimpse of two black women entering a bathroom inside the park. It turned out they were Gwynn Oak cleaning women, but the hecklers did not discover that until they had burst into the bathroom and pummeled one of the cleaning women. Lally deployed a line of leashed police dogs to keep the two sides separated.

Agnew was of two minds. "Morally, I feel the park should be integrated," he declared. But he also felt that he had to enforce the trespass law since the state's new public accommodations law specifically exempted amusement parks. While sympathizing with the moral objectives of the demonstrators, he also felt obligated to lash out at them for "hasty and immature" actions which had cost the taxpayers money.

Confronted with his very first executive crisis, Agnew sought to apply his talents as a mediator. To get the picketing temporarily called off, he agreed with the integration leaders to press the County Council to establish a powerful Human Relations Commission. Its first role would be to find a solution to the Gwynn Oak controversy, but later it would turn to "employment, housing, education, public accommodations, and any other field where intergroup relations may be in question." A law establishing a Human Relations Commission and assigning it broad responsibilities passed the County Council less than a week after the protesters stepped from their buses at Gwynn Oak. To some protesters, the creation of a Human Relations Commission sounded like a breakthrough. To Agnew, it was a means to an end.

Over the next two weeks Agnew and the Human Relations Commission tried independently to work out a compromise with CORE, which was making the loudest sounds about renewed picketing. Meanwhile, on the Senate floor Senator Hubert H. Humphrey reacted to the arrests at Gwynn Oak by charging that the leaders of Baltimore County were "not privileged to be despots" under an "anachronistic" trespassing law.

The Price brothers, fearful of more picketing, reluctantly agreed to integrate the park, but an impasse was reached over the timing. CORE demanded integration by mid-August. However, the Prices refused to accept blacks until the following summer. On July 19 the Human Relations Commission met until 3 A.M. trying to end the deadlock but could not get the Prices to bend. At that point Agnew moved back into the negotiation and worked out the final compromise—integration on August 28. Years later, when he was called upon to cite his accomplishments during his term as County Executive, Agnew would proudly point to the Gwynn Oak settlement.

The upstaged members of the Human Relations Commission have sometimes wondered what Agnew told the Price brothers to win that final compromise. The answer comes from County Solicitor Scott Moore. According to Moore, the way Agnew pulled it off was by telling the Price brothers that if they were driven out of business by integration, he would do what he could to get the land at Gwynn Oak rezoned for industry.

Agnew was equivocal on this point during an interview in 1971: "I made no promise about any zoning—I wasn't in any position to," he told me. "But I did say to the Price brothers that I thought if they were driven out of business as they feared, they weren't exactly sitting on a piece of land that didn't have any other use. I pointed out to them that they were not on the brink of disaster if they had to close the amusement park, because you can't take that kind of acreage so close to a big city and lose money on it."

With Gwynn Oak resolved, Agnew still had to contend with the two-week-old Human Relations Commission, with its sweeping charter covering employment, housing, education, public accommodations, and all other race-related issues. The breadth of the charter hadn't been Agnew's idea. But CORE had demanded it as its price for a truce, and he had agreed. To make the matter even pricklier for Agnew, a young idealist named Michael G. Holofcener had been elected chairman of the commission, despite the efforts of certain unshakable allies Agnew had put on the commission, including his former law partner Owen Hennegan. They had tried to throw the chairmanship to someone safer, like Gordon Power. But Holofcener, a thirty-three-year-old white insurance agent, won.

Holofcener and Agnew got into their first public hassle almost immediately, when Agnew put out a statement urging the Gwynn Oak demonstrators to settle for integration the following year. Holofcener responded with a statement of his own: "Considering the delicate nature of the discussions and the high feelings on both sides, we fail to see any useful purpose in such pronouncements."

Holofcener, naively assuming that the Human Relations Commission's charter was meant to read literally, began after Gwynn Oak to pursue forbidden subjects, such as racial housing patterns in Baltimore County. He went so far as to invite federal housing officials to the county to discuss publicizing a list of homes in white neighborhoods which were legally available to blacks. Then, in the fall of 1963, Holofcener brought Agnew to a boil. Holofcener was trying to get the County Executive to allocate $20,000 to the Human Relations Commission for a staff man. When Agnew wouldn't do it, Holofcener told a meeting that Agnew had acted out of "political expediency." To Agnew, those words were a grave insult. The upshot was that Agnew told the Human Relations Commission that he wanted Holofcener out. What was required, he said, was a "diminution of the aggressive posture favoring racial integration reflected by the chairman of this commission." To borrow a latter-day Agnewism, he was a querulous complainer.

At first the Commission stood behind Holofcener, but his position weakened as Agnew kept up the attack. A showdown came on December 18, 1963, when Agnew again went before the Commission to lay out his case for ousting Holofcener. Stepping out of the meeting, Agnew told a reporter that Holofcener's behavior amounted to "complete and utter boorishness." The plea from the County Executive was persuasive enough to get two of the more agressive commission members to call for Holofcener's resignation as chairman, supposedly for the good of the commission. One said Holofcener's "political expediency" remark was evidence of insubordination.

Holofcener turned in his resignation as chairman the next day, but Agnew's troubles with the Human Relations Commission were not over. In March 1964 Agnew charged that Commission member Eugene L. King, Sr. had acted improperly by urging demonstrators at a roller rink to go limp when they were arrested. King called this a "bold lie." Agnew struck back with a charge that King had been wrong to contribute $25 to CORE.

Before that dissonance died down, one of the three blacks on the eleven-member Commission, Hural Thompson, resigned in disgust. "I didn't like his holdback on the [civil rights] program," said Thompson. "He told me the county was not ready for a full-blown civil rights program." According to Thompson, Agnew had told the Commission it should spend its time worrying about jobs and schools instead of public accommodations and open housing.

In June, when Holofcener's term came up for renewal,

Agnew arranged to have him dropped from the Commission entirely. Looking back after eight years, Holofcener is now convinced that Agnew really never wanted a strong Human Relations Commission despite his commitment to CORE for a body to investigate housing, employment, education, and public accommodations. "I don't think he was completely truthful from the beginning," says Holofcener. "He just wanted the Commission to calm the situation, not attack these basic problems."

Agnew's feud with Holofcener is worth recalling if only for the clues it yields on the shape of Agnew's philosophy of race relations at a time three months after Martin Luther King Jr., delivered his "I have a dream" oration in Washington. The best evidence of Agnew's thinking is a long dissertation on the race problem which he gave to the Human Relations Commission in December 1963 to buttress his case against Holofcener. The document is worth quoting at length to show how Agnew's mind approached a moral crisis:

Not since the early and bloody days of the labor movement has there been more fertile soil for the malcontent opportunists than the hatreds of segregationist dogma on the one hand and the unreasonable ultimatums of some power-crazed integrationist leaders on the other.

Caught up in the searing heat of deprivation by the decade, the Negro is eager to have civil equality legislated and enforced. This he is entitled to as a moral right if our system of government and our way of life is to have meaning. I repeat, so that I may never again be misunderstood, the Negro is entitled as a matter of moral right to have his civil equality legislated and enforced....

The fact that the Negro lacks confidence in those who select the surer but the less sensational path is not surprising. He looks at a history of unfulfilled promises while he is concurrently being goaded by those same self-seeking opportunists who constantly demand the sensational. When the rash conduct of others makes his position untenable, those same fair-weather friends depart for distant geographical points and leave the local Negro holding the bag.

The heart of his position was that discrimination in public accommodations was wrong but discrimination in private housing was permissible. "I take a strong position," he said, "that it is wrong to tell the owner of a private dwelling place, be it single-family or multiple unit, that he must offer it for rent or sale to anyone with whom he does not want to do business. This applies whether or not he is biased and applies regardless of what his bias may embrace. If he dislikes Greeks, he should not have to deal with Greeks, and the government that infringes upon his discretion in this respect abrogates his freedom of selection and disregards the intent of the Constitution of the United States."

His stance on restaurants and other public facilities, like the ones his father used to operate, was more liberal: ". . . when an individual openly or impliedly seeks the good will and business of the general public, I believe he thereby waives his rights to personal preference. He then becomes obligated to sell his product or render his services to all persons who present themselves as prospective customers, so long as they do not by their conduct or demeanor offend his other clientele."

Although it sounds like a stack of timid legalisms in retrospect, it was a fairly bold statement for a Baltimore County politician to make in 1963.

Agnew again risked provoking a white backlash against

himself when he decided to throw his weight behind a county urban renewal project in mid-1963. Agnew liked the plan because it would add $80,000,000 to the county's tax base, and most of the cost would come from federal and private investments. He gave the project a go-ahead even after Vladimir Wahbe, his urban renewal director, cautioned him that similar plans in other communities around the country were getting defeated because of an open housing requirement included by the U. S. Department of Housing and Urban Development.

It was minuscule as urban renewal projects go. The idea was to renovate two suburban business centers, Towson and Catonsville, which were losing out to the big shopping centers. To meet federal standards, the plan had to include a small low-cost housing project for the few hundred blacks who would be pushed out of their homes in East Towson. Because it required a $3,800,000 county bond issue, the urban renewal plan had to be submitted to the voters in the November 1964 election.

Almost overnight, urban renewal turned into a fierce local issue in the spring of 1964. A militant conservative faction set out to defeat the bond issue by exploiting fears that low-cost housing would cause an influx of blacks from Baltimore City. The campaign mushroomed just at the time George Wallace was running strong in Maryland's Democratic Presidential primary. One fair barometer of Baltimore County's racial tolerance that spring was that Wallace carried 49.2 percent of the Baltimore County Democratic vote.

Having endorsed urban renewal before the controversy broke out, Agnew now went way out on a limb to get it passed. The anti-urban renewal faction was led by Joshua

Cockey, member of an old Baltimore County family and owner of a segregated public swimming pool. At one packed rally at the Towson American Legion Hall, Cockey attacked Wahbe, Agnew's urban renewal director, for not being an American citizen in the course of calling urban renewal a "malicious, socialistic cancer."

His words dipped in sarcasm, Agnew congratulated Cockey for reaching "a new pinnacle of bigotry" when he called attention to Wahbe's Lebanese ancestry. Then he insisted that the low-cost housing project in Towson would be too small to attract anyone except the local residents who would be displaced.

As the hot weather arrived, the county was again threatened with CORE demonstrations aimed at desegregating the remaining all-white swimming pools and roller rinks. Squeezed between hostile whites and militant blacks, Agnew maneuvered toward another deal. Meeting with CORE representatives, Agnew promised to deliver a county public accommodations law to the County Council in August if CORE would refrain from picketing. CORE privately agreed to call off demonstrations in exchange for a public accommodations bill.

Cold-eyed pragmatism rather than morality was driving Agnew, or so it appeared to his close advisors. One political confidant, who was more liberal than Agnew, tells of hearing Agnew remark that he decided to support the local public accommodations bill only after he was convinced that the Democrats on the County Council would kill it.

Another Agnew ally, County Solicitor Moore, says, "The real purpose of our civil rights bill was to get the jurisdiction out of the federal court and into the local courts, but Mr. Agnew couldn't say that."

The churches, the Baltimore AFL-CIO, and the League of Women Voters mobilized in support of Bill No. 90, Agnew's public accommodations bill. Joshua Cockey and the other segregated-swimming-pool operators tried to fight back, but their position was undercut by the fact that the federal government and the city of Baltimore had just passed their own public accommodations bills, which contained nearly identical prohibitions. On October 5, 1964, the County Council passed Bill No. 90 by a vote of 4-3, thus handing Agnew perhaps his principal achievement in Baltimore County.

A month later the voters got their chance to express themselves on the urban renewal plan, for which Agnew had campaigned with all his might. With Judy at his side patting his arm for reassurance, he spent election night watching the votes being tabulated. It wasn't even close. Urban renewal was crushed 94,466 to 58,988. "Agnew seemed really shattered," said one friend who was with him. "He told me he thought his term was over." [1]

When the reporters asked him how the County Executive felt about the defeat of urban renewal, he replied sadly, "I feel worse about this than I did when I lost the judicial election in 1960."

8

"Mainly, we were selling sex."

The Itch to Be Governor

The surface explanation for Spiro Agnew's incredible acceleration in the last ten years is that he rode a streak of blind luck. There is a lot of truth in the "Spiro the Blessed" theory, as Garry Wills has named it. But there is more to the story than luck. Inside his soul, Agnew had an itch for power that would not let him rest.

The driven quality of the inner Agnew was not part of the image he presented to the public. But it was manifested with chilling clarity in a previously unpublished letter he wrote in 1964 to his benefactor Al Shuger. It must have been a difficult letter for Agnew to compose. Shuger, who had just assembled a $35,000 testimonial dinner for Agnew and who had been his main money man in 1962, informed him that he would like to be a delegate or an alternate at the 1964 Republican National Convention. But at the state Republican convention, Agnew voted for another man, Joseph Dukert, instead of Shuger. Now Agnew had to explain why:

112

Baltimore County, Maryland
County Office Building
Towson, Maryland 21204

June 23, 1964

Mr. Albert A. Shuger
11 Slade Apartments
11 Slade Avenue
Baltimore 8, Maryland

Dear Al:

This will acknowledge receipt of your letter of June 19th concerning Joe Dukert's position at the Convention.

Your reaction to the failure of the nominating committee to place your name before the Convention as a delegate was very distressing to me. Although you said nothing definitive, I was forced to interpret your general comments as a reflection of your feeling that I had let you down. If there had been any indication that the delegates were available to elect you I would have seen that you were nominated from the floor or would have pressed for your nomination in committee.

Al, the delegates just weren't there. McKeldin's personal squeak through should indicate to you that they weren't there.

Because of our long friendship and my very sincere appreciation for what you have personally contributed to my political success thus far, I would hate to see a misunderstanding develop between us. It would seem to me that it is much more important to you and to me that I amass the utmost in political strength so that I can continue to be successful. To take a controversial position which would weaken me personally, when nothing but a delegate's seat at the Convention is at stake, does not make much sense to me. By this I do not mean that my career should be the most important thing in every decision. But in politics there have to be people who go before the electorate and people who work behind the scenes. You have elected to be behind the scenes. Consequently, you are nowhere near as vulnerable as I to public opinion. Of all people I would have thought that you would have been the first to subscribe to this view.

In short, I think it is more important to both of us that I make a show of strength in the Republican Party rather than be weakened by a needless intra-Party dispute.

In office, with your guidance and the help of other unselfish people, I can implement the type government you wish to see in effect in Baltimore County. Out of office, I am completely ineffectual.

In closing, I sincerely trust that we can reestablish our close personal relationship. I shall never forget that you were among the very first to give my candidacy support and that without your help I could not even have gotten off the ground.

Sincerely,
(signed) TED
Spiro T. Agnew
County Executive

STA/adf

A turning point in Agnew's political flight path came a few months after his letter baring his ambitions to Al Shuger. Although he would say nothing publicly for more than a year, he reached a decision late in 1964 that the way to "amass the utmost in political strength" was to run for governor.

One man whose political judgment he sought was his former law associate, Ed Hardesty, whom he had appointed Deputy Zoning Commissioner of Baltimore County over the violent objections of the Birmingham Democrats on the County Council. A few days before the 1964 election Agnew invited Hardesty and his wife, Barbara, to join him and Judy on a weekend bond junket in New York.

Hardesty, an Irishman with a wide face and a sharp memory, remembers that on a Saturday morning Agnew led the two couples on a shopping expedition down Park Avenue. Soon they found themselves in what was for Hardesty an expensive dress shop. First Judy saw a dress she liked and immediately the County Executive insisted that she buy it. Then Barbara Hardesty took a fancy to a two-piece tweed suit with a fur collar. Ed Hardesty was stunned by the $125 price tag, but Agnew shamed him into saying yes. "You goddam Greek, what do you think I am, made of money?" sputtered Hardesty.

That same day, Agnew asked Hardesty to join him for a drink at the old Astor Bar to talk over something big on his mind. "You are the first person I've talked to about my ambition," Hardesty recalls Agnew telling him. "I want to run for governor. I don't want to wage a hopeless campaign— what do you think my chances are?"

From what Hardesty had heard, George Mahoney and three or four others were angling for the Democratic nomination. Hardesty recalls telling Agnew that he was intelligent and good-looking enough to be a candidate, and if the Democrats got into their usual bloodbath, he might just win. Agnew then put out his hand and said, "I'm asking for your support." Hardesty, the first Democratic politician to defect from Birmingham in 1962, promptly gave Agnew his pledge.

The next morning the two men met in the hallway of their hotel. Before Hardesty knew what was happening, Agnew pressed $50 into his hand. "I embarrassed you by putting you on the spot about Barbara's suit," Hardesty recalls Agnew saying. "I know you can't afford that kind of money." The Deputy Zoning Commissioner, figuring that he really couldn't afford it, stuffed the bills into his pocket and they headed back to Towson.

The decision to go for the governorship had been banging around in Agnew's mind for a long time. As early as 1954, when his only launching pad was the Loch Raven Inter-community Council, he had talked soberly with Professor Brownlee Corrin of Goucher College about his ambition to be Governor. After his freakish victory in 1962, the newspapers routinely elevated him to the status of a potential statewide candidate. What finally convinced him to make a run for Governor was his realization that he would be beaten if he ran for reelection as County Executive in 1966.

To his mind, the clinching evidence was the overwhelming sentiment in the county against his urban renewal plan, soon to be confirmed in a referendum landslide. Dale Anderson, then the County Council chairman and a Democrat, says Agnew told him over lunch in late 1964 that he knew he could not get reelected because of the urban renewal issue. Anderson said Agnew told him he was thinking about running for Governor as an alternative. (Although Agnew did not tell Anderson, he had one other alternative in mind: a judgeship appointment. That proved impossible to engineer, however.)

Maryland's state Republican Party was so anemic that there were only three men who had a stronger claim on the gubernatorial nomination than Spiro Agnew. One was Rogers Morton, the gargantuan Congressman from the Eastern Shore who would one day replace Walter Hickel in President Nixon's Cabinet. The second was Charles M. Mathias, the young liberal Congressman from the Washington suburbs. The third was garrulous backslapper Theodore McKeldin, who had been Mayor of Baltimore in the 1940s, and Governor of Maryland and even a Vice Presidential possibility in the

1950s. Now in the 1960s he was Mayor of Baltimore for the second time.

One by one, the others eliminated themselves. Mathias never wanted the nomination. His wife, who was the daughter of former Massachusetts Governor Robert Bradford, was staunchly against it. And Mathias was aiming for the Senate anyway. For Morton, the gubernatorial nomination had some strong attractions. In the end, however, he examined the odds against winning and decided to run again for his relatively safe seat in the House of Representatives. Then in August 1965 Mayor McKeldin also stepped out of the picture after examining a private poll.

There being no one else of any prominence who wanted to run, the party turned to a very eager Spiro Agnew. In September he had a private meeting with the leading Republicans from around the state and secured pledges of support for his unannounced campaign. From then on, his selection in the September 1966 Republican primary was virtually a sure thing.

If anyone wanted to fight him for the nomination, there was plenty of ammunition to be found right in Towson, where icy hostility existed between County Executive Agnew and his own county Republican organization.

After his candidates for the Republican State Central Committee were erased by Fife Symington backers in the 1962 primary, Agnew had made a point of ignoring the Committee whenever possible. Once elected as County Executive, he judged that it was more important to take care of the Democrats, both those who helped elect him and those who controlled the County Council, than it was to please his own party. "We thought the plums were ripe and naturally we were disappointed," says Republican Gordon Power.

Some of the plums in Baltimore County came in tiny packages, but that did not reduce their succulence. There was a continuing struggle over dogcatchers, which according to Agnew's confidential secretary Dutch Moore, "caused us no end of headaches." The attraction of a dogcatcher's job was not chasing stray animals. It was the chance to sell dog licenses for $2 and keep 50 cents on every license. At one time Agnew's patronage empire consisted of 18 dogcatchers, 55 garbage collectors, 37 court clerks and bailiffs, 4 sidewalk inspectors, 2 zoning officers, 15 lawyers in the County Solicitor's office, and 5 personal aides.

The Republican State Central Committee took the position that Agnew should clear all his appointments with the Committee, but Agnew simply refused. Instead, he allowed the Democrats who had supported his candidacy over Birmingham to control many of the jobs. Other appointments went to Republicans whom he considered personally loyal. The Republican county organization often pushed deserving Republicans for specific jobs, but Agnew would generally ignore the suggestions. "He didn't care whether he got along with the State Central Committee or not," says Dutch Moore. "He didn't have any respect for the Committee."

In his apostasy Agnew went so far as to promote a maverick Democrat, Brooks Bradley, for the Republican nomination for Congress. "Spiro originated the idea that I run," said Bradley, and Agnew did not deny it. That did not delight state party treasurer Fife Symington, who once again was maneuvering for the congressional seat. Nor did it please the Symington allies who controlled Baltimore County's Republican State Central Committee. In the end Agnew pulled back his tentative endorsement when it was clear that Bradley could not attract enough other support to make a race.

Even so, Baltimore County Republicans were treated to the strange sight of State Central Committee Chairman Elliot P. Hurd resigning his chairmanship in May 1964 with a public attack on Agnew—the first Republican elected to run the Baltimore County government in sixty-seven years. "Keep faith with the taxpayers!" he challenged, pointing out that Dutch Moore was performing political tasks on the county payroll. Hurd went on to complain about Agnew's refusal to heed party recommendations about jobs, as well as his fund-raising activities outside the party. Agnew was a fine County Executive, concluded Hurd, but he had "failed the party."

Happily for Agnew, the state party had no other candidate of any stature who thought the 1966 Republican gubernatorial nomination was worth taking, in the wake of the Lyndon Johnson landslide in 1964. In one important respect Maryland resembled a Deep South state: usually the real contest for the governorship was not in the November election but in the Democratic primary. There was little reason for anyone to think that the Republican candidate had any chance of winning the governorship in a state with seven registered Democratic voters for every two registered Republicans.

The common assumption was that the Democrats would nominate either State Attorney General Thomas J. Finan or Congressman-at-Large Carleton Sickles. The smart money was on Finan, a cautious middle-of-the-roader of comely visage who carried the flag of the regular Democratic Party organization. With the organization behind him, Finan figured to overcome not only his essential colorlessness but also the accumulation of eight years of gripes against the incumbent administration of Governor Millard J. Tawes. The man Finan had to beat, Carleton Sickles, was expected to run strong in the bedroom suburbs around Washington, D.C., and in the black precincts of Baltimore City. But the real pros knew Sickles was too liberal and too tightly tied with labor unions to beat Finan.

Then there was George Mahoney, the sixty-four-year-old paving contractor who liked to call himself "the boy from the other side of the tracks who made good." In a way he had made good. The eleventh child of a Baltimore policeman, he had started as a laborer and ended up with custom-made suits, a pretty blond wife, and a multimillion-dollar net worth. The only thing he couldn't do was win elections. He had run six times for Senator, Governor, and a variety of lesser offices. Invariably he had lost. In one of his more recent also-ran performances, he had told the voters: "If you don't want me, I won't come back and bother you anymore. I won't impose on you again." When he turned up again as a candidate in 1966, people guffawed.

After six campaigns, Mahoney had a hard time thinking up a new slogan for 1966. But one day a few of his pals were kicking around ideas when one of them got an inspiration: "Your Home Is Your Castle—Protect It." Mahoney had never angled for the segregationist vote before, and in fact he had been quoted in 1965 as favoring an open housing law. However, the implications of George Wallace carrying 43 percent of the 1964 Maryland Democratic Presidential primary changed his mind. Both Sickles and Finan hedged on open housing, but Mahoney left no doubts: if elected, he would veto any open housing legislation that passed the legislature. When someone accused him of being a racist, he replied, "I am not biased—85 percent of my employees are colored."

By midnight of primary election night, it was obvious that Agnew had easily won the Republican primary against his token opponents. But the Democratic primary looked like an upset: Carleton Sickles was running ahead and the favored Finan was third. If Sickles had gone on to win, the public's perception of Spiro Agnew would have turned out quite differently. His only chance to win in November would have been to induce enough pro-Mahoney or pro-Finan Democrats to cross over and vote for him. With Sickles for an opponent, Agnew would have been viewed as the more conservative candidate.

In the primary Sickles figured to sweep the black ghettos of Baltimore, but he failed to live up to his potential. Of the two important black Democratic officeholders, Sickles got the endorsement of only one, House of Delegates member Clarence M. Mitchell. The other, State Senator Verda F. Welcome, was loyal enough to the Tawes organization to stick with Finan. Thus the black vote split.

When the last precincts came in from Baltimore County early on the morning of September 14, George Mahoney finally won an election, even though he got only 31 percent of the votes. The official canvass later showed that 148,446 people voted for Mahoney, compared to 146,507 for Sickles and 134,216 for Finan. Four unknowns trailed far behind.

Until the Democratic primary, the sole aim of Agnew's campaign was to increase his name recognition factor, which was close to zero except in his home county. The instrument he chose was a song written by the head of his advertising agency, Robert Goodman, to the tune of "My kind of place, Chicago is. . . ." In Goodman's hands it came out: "My kind of guy, Ted Agnew is . . . my kind of guy, Ted Agnew is. . . ." It was the voice-over for every TV spot and the slogan for his billboards, radio commercials, and even his newspaper ads.

When asked many months later by a reporter from *Baltimore* magazine to name his predominant theme in the Agnew campaign, Goodman gave an answer that he claims was no put-on. "Mainly," says Goodman, "we were selling sex."

The reporter, Nancy B. Gabler, sounded dubious: "You mean you promoted Ted Agnew as a sex symbol?"

"That's right," insisted Goodman. "His record was kind of undistinguished because he had a County Council made up of six Democrats and one Republican. Most of the good things Agnew fought for were denied him. . . . So we didn't have a good record to run on, but we did have what we thought was a really beautiful guy and we ran a sex campaign. The song was a sex appeal type of song and we almost screwed it up by having a male singer in one of the versions. Maybe that wasn't so bad after all. Maybe we got the homosexual vote, who knows?"

While pounding away at Agnew's name recognition problem, Goodman and the rest of the campaign staff tried to stay loose on the issues. As Goodman told me, "I didn't know how we were going to play him after the primary, liberal or conservative."

Ever since the middle of his term as County Executive, Agnew and his friends had been pinning down campaign contributions which could be used in 1966. Dutch Moore, who handled Agnew's initial fund raising, explains how the

early money was actually raised: "You just went around to
the architects, builders, developers, and people who do business with the county. These are the guys who will give
heavily. . . . I was sitting where I could make recommendations on who should get architectural or engineering contracts. I knew every one of them—I could pick up the phone
and call any one of them and ask for a contribution. . . .
Don't think a contractor contributes to a political campaign
unless he knows that whoever he is dealing with is in a position to make a favorable recommendation. . . ."

With the official opening of the campaign in April 1966,
a ten-man finance committee was formed, featuring Clarke
Langrall as chairman and land developers Bud Hammerman
and J. Walter Jones, Jr., as the big hitters.

Before the primary, the biggest splash of the Agnew campaign was his disclosure that he had turned down a six-figure
bribe in the form of campaign contributions if he promised
not to veto any legislation to extend the life of slot machines
in Maryland. As he told the story, he was first offered $20,000,
then $75,000, and finally $200,000 for a no-veto pledge. The
District Attorney of Baltimore County, naturally a Democrat,
demanded that Agnew reveal who offered him the money.
Lamely, Agnew refused on grounds that the solicitation had
been transmitted by an innocent third party. That incident,
among others, led *Baltimore Evening Sun* columnist Brad
Jacobs to describe one quality of Agnew's before anyone
else saw it: "his curious weakness for blurting out the wrong
thing at the wrong time."

The election of George Mahoney, who had obviously hit a
vein of gold with his opposition to open housing, caused
much agonizing in the Agnew camp. Agnew's problem was

that his real feeling about open housing legislation was not far removed from what Mahoney had been saying. Although Agnew believed that discrimination ought to be illegal in the sale of future developments and apartments, he was on record as thinking that a homeowner in an existing neighborhood had every right to be "selective, discriminatory, even arbitrary," in choosing a buyer for his house.

When I asked Vice President Agnew in 1971 to recall his philosophy on open housing during the 1966 campaign, he gave it in the form of a revealing analogy: "A man has some responsibility to his neighbors. And if someone—whether white or black—comes to buy his house, he has a right to say no, I'm not going to sell my house to that person if he thinks he is going to be a disaster for neighborhood relations. It is the same as if a man has a litter of puppies for sale. He is not going to sell one of his puppies to someone who comes to the door if he doesn't like his looks."

Mahoney had used an oddly similar analogy in 1966: "I don't care if you're a white man or a Chinaman or a Negro. Suppose someone wants to rent your house and he has fifteen children and ten dogs. You turn him down. You could be fined or go to jail if you say no. I'll fight a law like that to my last breath."

The strategy Agnew finally picked was to gather all the black and liberal support he could by picturing Mahoney as a racist who would turn Maryland into another "Maddoxville." That was not his first impulse, however. As late as three weeks after the primary, Agnew actually narrowed his differences with Mahoney on open housing by promising to veto any open housing bill "affecting the right of the individual homeowner to sell to whomever he wished." It was mid-October before he switched his position back and said he would accept an open housing bill for existing homes if it was passed by a big majority of the state legislature and if it was backed by strong public sentiment. "The word 'veto' . . . may have been somewhat strong," he now asserted. "I would be inclined to leave the question of constitutionality to the courts."

Seeing from the start that open housing was Mahoney's issue, Agnew tried to focus the campaign elsewhere—on mass transit, water pollution, education, and the like. A *Washington Post* reporter wrote, "In public appearances—large or small—Agnew consistently bids for votes in terms of detailed programs for state problems. . . . At coffee sessions and mass rallies alike, voters are asked by Agnew to support him for what he wants to do, not for a knack to excite the glands. Agnew's approach is crisp and businesslike. It is one, however, that prompted one observer to say that Agnew resembles a teacher more than a politician at times."

About three weeks before election day, Agnew and his advisors got the results of a private poll. "It terrified us," remembers Robert Goodman. It indicated that unless Agnew caught fire, Mahoney would win.

From that point, Agnew's strategy was to slam Mahoney personally and make him into the issue of the election. "We switched to the fear campaign," explains Goodman simply.

It wasn't often that a candidate had such a fat target to hit, although Agnew had drawn an equally easy mark in Mike Birmingham four years earlier. As a campaigner, Mahoney made virtually no impact since he seldom appeared in public after winning the primary. As an orator, he was so bumbling and inarticulate as to make Agnew look like William Jennings Bryan. On at least one occasion, his idea of campaign humor was to imitate a darky's accent.

Like Birmingham, Mahoney refused all challenges to debate Agnew, calling him a "nut" and a "big slob" and a captive of rich Greek shipowners. But on October 25 Agnew surprised Mahoney by accosting him at a testimonial dinner at the Chizuk Amuno Auditorium in Baltimore County. Mahoney hesitated for about thirty seconds before agreeing to shake Agnew's hand, but finally he did. Mahoney tried to pull away after an exchange of pleasantries, but Agnew wouldn't let him. "Let's talk about the issues, George," he challenged. "There are reporters here. Let's hold a press conference and discuss the issues. We can talk about education, taxes, and other important problems facing the people."

"Let's talk about your friends in New York who are giving you all that money," answered Mahoney, again trying to escape.

"Come on, George, I've finally caught up with you. You cannot keep running away from me forever," Agnew tossed back. "People want to know whether or not you are qualified to be Governor." Turning to the crowd, he asked, "Why is this man afraid to talk about the issues?"

"You run your campaign and I'll run mine," snapped Mahoney, who was then ushered away by an aide.

In the closing ten days of the campaign Agnew employed devastating innuendo: "Why were those Ku Klux Klanners wearing Mahoney hats at their rally two weeks ago? You remember all those cars with Mahoney bumper stickers on them when the National States' Rights Party nearly caused a riot in Patterson Park last summer? Well, it was all deliberate. It is nothing but bigotry that this man is appealing to." Without defending Mahoney, one might note that Agnew was blaming Mahoney for the Ku Klux Klan rally without offering a scrap of evidence of any connection. Four years later, the technique would be put to good use against the "radical liberals" in the Senate.

By election day, he made his campaign sound like a crusade to the Holy Land. His climactic sentence was: "This state must not be controlled by a devil that sits holding a two-pronged pitchfork of bigotry and hatred." What privately worried Agnew was not Mahoney but a nettlesome independent candidate, Baltimore City Controller Hyman A. Pressman, who had complicated his crusade by accusing him of conflicts of interest. The danger was not that Pressman might win, but that he might pull enough votes from Agnew to let Mahoney win. "I hate the bastard," Robert Goodman remembers Agnew saying about Pressman even after the election.

With the specter of Mahoney in the statehouse, the blacks and liberals could not afford to be squeamish about Spiro Agnew. From *The New York Times,* the Americans for Democratic Action, and the Rabbinical Association came frantic endorsements. In the earnest living rooms of Bethesda and Chevy Chase, liberal Democrats were ready to enshrine Agnew in their pantheon. On the last Sunday before the election, dozens of black ministers in Baltimore preached for Agnew from their pulpits.

One television network enlivened election night by projecting on the basis of a faulty computer run that Mahoney was the winner. It soon turned out that Agnew won by a stunning margin for a Republican running in Maryland. The official count was Agnew, 455,318; Mahoney, 373,543; Pressman, 90,899. A political scientist later calculated that Agnew had carried 72 percent of affluent Montgomery County and 70 percent of Baltimore City blacks with incomes of less than $3,000. He also ran surprisingly well on the Eastern Shore and in the mountains of western Maryland.

Now, for a moment at least, Agnew was a national celebrity. His forty-eighth birthday fell on the morning after the election, while the returns were still coming in. During a cake-cutting ceremony a guest asked him whether he now envisioned himself occupying a national role. That was hard for him to imagine, he replied disarmingly, "and I sometimes have difficulty imagining myself as a state leader."

The only sad part of the occasion was that his parents weren't there to see it. Only eight months before the election, he had to bury his mother. His father had died three years earlier, at the age of eighty-four.

9

"If you try to make it look like a dishonest transaction, there should be some investigation of your newspaper."

Portrait of a County Executive as Land Speculator

In a little real estate office across from the State Capitol building in Annapolis there hangs a color photograph taken in the fall of 1970 showing two hunters and their prize: a pair of dead Canada geese.

The man on the left, with creases in his hunting pants and his hair meticulously combed back, is Vice President Spiro T. Agnew. Under his right arm he is cradling a shotgun.

The man on the right, his pants baggy and his shotgun resting on his shoulder, is the suave land speculator and banker who operates from this little office. Although his boyish face and light wavy hair would not be recognized by one person in a million, he has been closer to Agnew for more years than anyone else outside his family. Yet up to now their mutual activities have never been fully exposed. His name is J. Walter Jones, Jr.

At the age of fifty, he has reached a bracket where he has

to discuss things like whether the inlays on his new yacht should be teak or mahogany.

Agnew and Jones. The story of their lives reads like two morning glories shooting up from the Maryland soil together, with stems and roots all intertwined. It begins soon after World War II when a lawyer and a land appraiser, both young men of modest means, happened to meet through the Kiwanis Club. For the next twenty years they got way ahead in the world—with each other's help.

And now, in one of the later scenes of "American Dream, Suburban Style," the two men are seen together at a splendid reception which the Vice President of the United States is hosting for Vice President Nguyen Cao Ky of South Vietnam. A *Washington Post* society reporter noticed this scene and wrote, "After everyone shook hands, the Agnews and Kys went off into one corner of the room while the rest of the guests stood at the other end. . . . The only guests to chat with the VIPs during the cocktail hour were Mr. and Mrs. J. Walter Jones of Annapolis, Maryland, personal friends of the Agnews."

Jones and Agnew. The story must also tell of their business deals while Agnew was County Executive of Baltimore County, about an unsecured loan, about no-bid appraising fees, about a rezoning Agnew forgot he made, and even about how the Governor's mansion got a wine cellar. A fraction of this tale surfaced during the 1966 and 1968 campaigns, but never enough to change Agnew's angle of ascent. The newspapers lost interest in Agnew's past business ventures after his election as Vice President, without taking the time to check the story out.

Now, enough evidence has turned up in dusty public documents and private interviews to warrant a long look at their tangled relationship. In my own opinion, the new facts should make the good citizens of Baltimore County wonder why they even have a conflict-of-interest law to regulate the private dealings of their public officials.

When I asked Vice President Agnew about his business dealings with Jones, he three times misrepresented important facts about the transactions. However, to be charitable, let's say these were simply gaps in the memory of a very busy man.

Neither Agnew nor Jones can see the slightest conflict of interest or impropriety in this or any other phase of the Vice President's past. Both patiently discussed their connections in a series of interviews with me in 1970 and 1971.

"On three or four occasions I have been challenged on this thesis of favoritism and special deals," said Agnew. "But it all comes tumbling down like a house of cards in the end." He added, "I think the disclosure of my assets is sufficient indication that this is a speculative exercise in nothing."

For his part, Jones said, "My word of God, there is no one I know in public life who has conducted himself more carefully and honorably." Or as he said on another occasion, "You can search until you're blue in the face and you won't find scandal. I know the man and what he does."

The two men offer differing interpretations of how close they have been over the years. In an interview *after* I had broached the conflict-of-interest question, Agnew told me, "I wouldn't call Walter a very close friend. He's not a person I see frequently—never has been. We've been friends. . . ."

"Never has been?" I asked.

"We've never been buddies, seen each other every day," he replied. "I've known him as a friend, well, from the time

I came back from World War II basically. I didn't really become closely acquainted with him until I moved my office to Towson. . . . When we moved to the Jefferson Building [in 1961] we occupied suites down the hall from each other. And I used to see him occasionally.

"Since I have been Vice President, I suppose I've seen Walter maybe seven or eight times, ten times or something like that. I wouldn't characterize him as a person I consult with on a regular basis."

Three weeks earlier, before I brought up the subject of conflict of interest, Jones sat in his Annapolis real estate office and told me, "The County Executive and I exchanged views very, very, very frequently. When he was County Executive he was at my office an awful lot. Every Friday he came over [so we could] sort of bring each other up to date on things. And then frequently during the week. And when he was Governor, he had constant communication by phone to this office. He was in my office, and I was in the mansion many times."

To jump ahead of the story, there seems no question that their relationship has tapered off in the Vice Presidential years. Occasionally Agnew works through Jones when he wants to keep his hand in Maryland politics. And Jones is known to have offered advice to Agnew about the tone of the rhetorical campaign Agnew was waging on behalf of Republican candidates in the fall of 1970. But their contacts are mostly social now.

The long story of Agnew and Jones started at the Kiwanis Club in Loch Raven, Maryland, back in the early 1950s. Jones belonged to the Kiwanis Club in Parkville, where he lived, but once in a while he would come over to Agnew's branch in Loch Raven to make up a meeting and preserve his attendance record.

From 1957 on, their paths often crossed in the third-floor hearing room of the County Office Building in Towson, where Agnew sat as a member of the Board of Appeals and Jones was a perennial expert witness on zoning cases. Agnew's recollection is that Jones appeared before him in about fifty cases, either on behalf of the rezoning applicants or the protesting neighbors. That would be about one out of every three cases Agnew heard.

In that time span Agnew was also struggling to develop his own little law office in Towson, handling mainly automobile negligence cases and out-of-town labor relations matters. The two men saw each other fairly regularly for lunch, and over the years Jones came to recognize unusual qualities in his friend.

"Many lawyers opening up offices spend time at various social organizations and Chamber of Commerce meetings, and anything to build up activity," he reminisced. "But Ted always seemed to be the sort of guy who would associate [only] with people whom he would like to be with. Maybe he liked to be with them because he thought they were people who could be of help to him, I don't know. But the fact remains, it wasn't the kind who would be bending his elbow over the Penn Hotel bar every afternoon the way so many of them do."

Over the years Jones became one of Agnew's two most important political fund raisers, although he was himself a Democrat until recently. When Agnew ran in 1960 for Circuit Court judge, Jones straddled—giving $100 to Agnew and $195 to the three sitting judges. Only nine other persons were listed in the official reports as giving any cash contributions at all to Agnew. Two years later, Jones helped finance Christian Kahl until he was defeated in the Democratic primary, then raised money for Agnew in the latter stages of the campaign. How much was not reported.

Jones says that they tentatively discussed the pros and cons of Agnew running for Governor as early as two years before the election, while they were attending the 1964 Republican Convention in San Francisco together. Sometime in 1965, according to Jones' recollection, Agnew asked him to devote full time to an informal fund-raising effort, and he accepted. When the formal finance committee was announced in 1966, Jones was not made the chairman, but he was one of its big producers.

While Agnew was governor, Jones was ubiquitous although he had no state job. Brad Jacobs, the savvy *Baltimore Evening Sun* columnist, wrote in 1967, "These days Mr. Jones is in steady if not daily communication with the Governor. . . . Mr. Agnew treats him as a sounding board, as a test of public reactions." Jones was also put in charge of raising a special political fund on Agnew's behalf called the Executive Assembly. The fund, which raised at least $35,000, was disbanded after Agnew was picked as Nixon's running mate.

There is a fascinating forgotten link between the two men: in 1960 while Agnew was on the Board of Appeals, he signed a rezoning decision that has made Jones rich. Curiously, no one has ever made an issue of the case. It goes back to the summer of 1959 when a three-man land company known as Opfer-Dickinson Co., Inc. bought a 159-acre piece of land next to an interchange on the heavily traveled interstate highway connecting Washington, Baltimore, and Harrisburg,

Pennsylvania. Although the land deed did not show it, Jones was a principal of Opfer-Dickinson with 15 percent of the stock.

The purchase was the opening move of a classic land coup. Because the property was zoned for houses, Opfer-Dickinson was able to pick it up for $2,600 an acre—$45,500 in cash and a mortgage loan from the sellers of $369,000. Jones and his associates next snapped up 46 adjacent acres of the gently rolling farmland, some of it in the name of a separate corporation.

The stage was now set to multiply the value of the land by transforming it into an industrial park. As a member of the Board of Appeals, Agnew was in a strategic position—he had to vote on whether to grant the needed rezoning to Jones' company. The petition to get the 159 original acres rezoned for light industrial use was filed on January 11, 1960. Although the land had been marked "residential" when the County Council revised the zoning map five years earlier, there was some unofficial thinking in the county Planning Board that the land ought to be rezoned for light industry. On the other side, some of the neighbors were violently opposed to any change. The case came before the Board of Appeals for a full hearing and review on March 31, after the Deputy Zoning Commissioner and the Planning Board had approved the petition.

One member of the board excused himself from the case, which left it up to two men, Agnew and the late Nathan N. Kaufman. A transcript of the hearing, which ran to more than a hundred pages, shows that Agnew actively questioned the witnesses. It was, after all, the fourth biggest tract which had come up for a rezoning in Agnew's four years on the board.

One of the most effective witnesses that day was J. Walter Jones, Jr., who identified himself merely as an expert witness for Opfer-Dickinson. On July 14, 1960, Agnew and his fellow board member Kaufman granted the rezoning. Evidently Jones' testimony had struck home because the board's three-page decision made a major point of his contention that the land in Baltimore County already zoned for industry was largely unsuitable for industrial development. As the decision put it: "If Mr. Jones is correct, and his testimony is uncontradicted in this respect, all the food set aside for the growing 1955 industrial baby is not digestible and additional food must be supplied to keep him healthy."

The opinion conceded that the new industrial tract would be an "industrial spot" bounded on north and south by residential land. But it would be "valid spot zoning" because it would benefit the public rather than merely the pecuniary interests of the owner.

Although the enrichment of Jones and his partners may not have been the intention of the rezoning, that was the result. The land which cost $2,600 an acre in 1959 was worth at least $10,000 an acre one year later. As soon as the Board of Appeals opinion was upheld by the local Circuit Court, Jones and his partners sold off 40 of their 205 acres for $474,000 in cash—thus paying off their original investment and leaving 165 acres for further dealing.[1]

Then, in January of 1962, they signed a merger agreement with McCormick and Company, an old-line Baltimore spice company which was anxious to diversify into the industrial park business. In the merger Jones and his partners traded their landholdings in exchange for stock in McCormick and Company, which is publicly traded, and in a new McCormick subsidiary for industrial parks. By 1971 the stock was worth more than $3,000,000—over fifty times the original cash investment by the Opfer-Dickinson partners. As for Jones' share, he put up $12,500 in cash in 1959 and received stock which was worth more than $600,000 by 1971.

The resulting tract, known as the Greater Baltimore Industrial Park, soon turned into the biggest and most successful industrial park in Baltimore County. It opened in 1962, and by 1968 it had grown into a nationally known complex with a country club, golf course, and convention center—all made possible by the original Board of Appeals rezoning.

There was nothing demonstrably wrong with Agnew's decision to grant the Greater Baltimore Industrial Park rezoning, provided he took no *quid pro quo* from the beneficiaries. That leads to the next question: did he?

To this Jones answered crisply, "Agnew has never made a penny out of the Greater Baltimore Industrial Park. Not one penny."

Not directly, anyway. That would be too unseemly, too stupid, too unethical for honorable men like Spiro Agnew and Walter Jones. But what did happen is that over the next six years Walter Jones cut Agnew in on some of the fanciest business deals Agnew had ever seen. They didn't make Agnew rich, but the meagerness of his profit tells more about his brilliance as a businessman than it does about his virtue.

During an interview on February 8, 1971, in his well-guarded office in the Executive Office Building, I asked the Vice President whether he didn't consider it a conflict of interest for him to have become a business partner in 1965 of someone who had benefited from his big Greater Baltimore Industrial Park rezoning in 1960. To my amazement he replied by denying that he had anything whatsoever to do with that rezoning. He repeated his denial four times.

"I didn't have anything to do with that," he said. "That was zoned before I went on the zoning board."

From that point the tape contains the following:

QUESTION: "You did not. . . ?"

AGNEW: "No, I did not participate in the Greater Baltimore Industrial zoning at all. That was zoned before I became a member of the Appeals Board."

QUESTION: "I am informed that, in fact—"

AGNEW: "Go look at the records and you will find out that was zoned before I took office. I had nothing to do with that at all."

He volunteered two more denials later in the interview.

After some rechecking I sent a photocopy of the rezoning decision bearing Agnew's signature to Victor Gold, the Vice Presidential Press Secretary. Gold telephoned thirty hours later to say that Agnew had experienced a "lapse of memory" during the interview—and would I like to see the Vice President again to get everything straight?

On February 16 I was ushered back into his office, to find the Vice President armed with a huge zoning map of Baltimore County. He had an ingenious explanation for his five flat denials of any connection with the original Greater Baltimore Industrial Park rezoning: Of course he had voted to rezone the Opfer-Dickinson tract, he said, but "I didn't recall" that it was part of the industrial park.[2]

The persuasiveness of his explanation diminishes when one visits the Greater Baltimore Industrial Park and sees that most of the original buildings are on the Opfer-Dickinson parcel, and that on three sides the industrial park still is bounded by main roads which were mentioned in the Opfer-Dickinson rezoning hearing. The industrial park is a ten-minute drive from Towson, and it is hard to believe that someone as professionally involved with the growth of Baltimore County as Agnew didn't know where it was. As Governor of Maryland, he knew enough about developments at the Greater Baltimore Industrial Park to issue a 23-paragraph press release when one of the tenants, Western Electric, added 300 jobs to its work force. "We are delighted with this expansion of a major Maryland industry," Agnew said in the press release. The name of the park was mentioned in the second and seventh paragraphs.

Later in the interview, he offered a more plausible explanation for his earlier denials: "My recollection was that it [the Opfer-Dickinson land] had been rezoned before I became a member of the Board of Appeals. And so I was wrong in that respect." And still later: "I had a very clear image that this Greater Baltimore thing was all accomplished before I went on the zoning board, and now I found out it really wasn't, and that surprised me."

The Vice President told me he didn't know that Walter Jones owned part of Opfer-Dickinson at the time he heard the case. However, he said he has known "for quite some time" that Jones had an interest in the Greater Baltimore Industrial Park. "I don't remember when I [became aware], but it was common knowledge that he was interested. I didn't know if it was as an employee or as an expert . . . or on his own behalf, but I have known he had an interest in it for quite some time."

It was also common knowledge in Towson, by 1962, that the industrial park was created out of land obtained from Opfer-Dickinson—and that Walter Jones was one of the owners of Opfer-Dickinson. Those facts were included in news stories in the *Baltimore Sun* and the *Towson Jeffersonian* announcing the creation of the Greater Baltimore Industrial Park in January 1962. For a county which had no big, modern industrial parks, it was an important story—one that could hardly have escaped the notice of someone about to run for County Executive. Then too, Agnew had a better chance of finding out the details than most people. During the first four months of 1962 the corporate office of the Greater Baltimore Industrial Corporation was listed with the State of Maryland as Room 404 of the Jefferson Building, Towson. Room 404 happened to be the office of J. Walter Jones Jr. Conveniently, his friend Spiro Agnew had his office next door, in Room 406.

After Agnew realized that his friend Jones was involved with the Greater Baltimore Industrial Park, he could have avoided any question of a possible conflict of interest by keeping clear of any joint business deals with Jones, especially those that promised rewards not generally available to everyday investors. However, that wasn't the course Agnew took.

Their first common investment was in stock in the Chesapeake National Bank in Towson, a new national bank which Jones and a few friends organized in 1963 while Agnew was County Executive. Before the bank opened its doors in January 1964, Agnew invested $10,000 in cash to buy 400 shares of Chesapeake National Bank stock. He was elected to the bank's board of directors at the outset and served until after the 1968 election. For part of that time, the bank letterhead listed him on top of its slate of directors as "Spiro T. Agnew, Governor, State of Maryland." Jones, who has been the bank's board chairman from the beginning, says it was he who originally asked Agnew to join the board. The reason had nothing to do with Agnew's role as a public official, said Jones: "He was a friend . . . there was nothing more to it than that."

Agnew got a rather unusual fringe benefit from the bank that up to now has been unpublicized. It turns out that on July 2, 1965, the bank granted Agnew an unsecured loan for $15,000, thus providing the County Executive with the cash he needed to join a syndicate of real estate investors speculating in an industrial park venture in neighboring Anne Arundel County.

The original bank ledgers, unearthed for me with Jones' authorization, indicate that on July 2, 1965, a personal note signed by Agnew for $15,000 was entered in Chesapeake's loan records. The original ledger card was marked to indicate that Agnew did not put up any collateral.

The president of Chesapeake National, Robert T. Baker, has taken the position that there was nothing unusual about the loan. "We have lots of unsecured loans," said Baker. "It depends on the financial net worth of the individual, his ability to repay us, and his deposit relationship with the bank." Asked whether it was extraordinary for bank directors to accept unsecured loans from their own bank, he replied, "As a matter of fact, directors normally prefer not to borrow money from their own bank." To be more precise, the Financial General Corporation, parent company of Chesapeake National, frowns on unsecured loans to directors, but they are legal.

On the day I saw Vice President Agnew to hear his explanation for the "lapse of memory" about the Opfer-Dickinson rezoning, I ventured to ask him also about the propriety of the unsecured loan. Again to my surprise, he didn't try to justify it. He simply denied that the loan was unsecured, despite what the bank records might say. "I had over $15,000 in my savings account in that bank," he told me. ". . . I had all my personal savings in that account. Their control over that money was certainly ample collateral for any loan. What better collateral could they have than having my money in their bank?"

As we talked, he buzzed his secretary and told her, "Would you get Mr. Robert Baker at Chesapeake National Bank in Towson, Maryland, for me?" Baker was unavailable so Agnew asked for a Mr. Bill Ryan. "Bill, could you do me a favor?" Agnew asked. The favor was to look up the records of his savings account "as quick as you can" and tell him how much money was in the account on the date the loan was granted.

"We ought to get this call back fairly quickly," he said a few minutes later, "because I think that is an important point, to show that there was no special favor advanced me by the bank."

Ryan called back in ten minutes with some unpleasant news. Although Agnew had just finished saying in a tape-recorded interview that his loan was fully secured by his savings account, he now learned that the savings balance was less than the loan. After several more phone calls that day, it was established that on the day he took out the $15,000 loan, his savings account balance was $10,327.40.[3]

"Well, generally everyone's loans are partially unsecured," was Agnew's immediate fallback position.

"I think the bank probably would have made a similar loan to a stranger on an equal basis if he was fairly reliable and looked like he was able to repay it. Certainly at that time, I was chief executive of the county, running for Governor. I guess a person in my circumstances in private life would be able to get a loan by securing 50 percent of it with collateral."

From a man who knew something about banking, it was quite a mouthful, but he said it with a straight face. If Agnew had been just a citizen, his chances of getting that loan on those terms would have been fairly close to zero. Only two years earlier, the Martindell-Hubbell Law Directory estimated his entire net worth at $10,000 to $20,000. And now here he was, a man about to embark on a dubious political venture, trying to borrow nearly a full year's salary with 50 percent collateral and no cosigners?

In fact, if the bank's records are accurate, none of Agnew's savings account was ever actually pledged to secure the loan. He repaid $5,000 of the principal on October 22, 1965, and retired the remaining $10,000 on December 23, 1968, after he was elected Vice President. Throughout that time Agnew paid six percent interest.[4] Baker said the loan committee which approved the $15,000 loan to Agnew consisted of himself, J. Walter Jones Jr., and four other bank officers.

The telephone operator at the bank answers all calls with a cheery "Chesapeake National, Best of All Possible Banks." Judging from the way it treated Agnew, it has to be the friendliest.

The venture for which Agnew wanted his $15,000 loan was a carbon copy of the Greater Baltimore Industrial Park coup which Jones had pulled off five years earlier, except in a different county. Once again, the man who put the deal

together was J. Walter Jones, Jr. Early in 1965 Jones heard
about a 106-acre piece of flat farmland near an express highway in Anne Arundel County, which adjoined Baltimore
County on the south. Perfect for another industrial park, he
thought, and the price was only $2,500 an acre.

Jones' first thought, he says, was to share his find with some
of his very good friends, including County Executive Agnew.
"This piece of land wasn't what you would refer to as a hot
piece of land, you know, one that you would buy for one price
and make a million dollars on it, but it was something that I
felt was a safe piece of land," Jones told me.

"If I'm going to buy something, I [usually] buy it myself
or get one partner. But [this time] I said, 'This is an opportunity where I'll get all my friends and let them have a little
piece of it.' And this is what I did."

The result was a syndicate of ten men who bought the
land in their own names in July 1965 for a total of $265,648.
There were eight full members, including Jones and Agnew,
and two others who split a share, meaning that Agnew personally owned one-ninth interest. The syndicate immediately
took out a $200,070 mortgage on the acreage, splitting the
debt among them. In addition, each full shareholder had to
put in $11,000 in cash for the down payment and other ex-
penses. Agnew's unsecured loan from Chesapeake National
more than covered his share of the down payment.

County Executive Agnew had no qualms about going into
business with Jones, the beneficiary of his Greater Baltimore
Industrial Park rezoning five years earlier, because the new
venture was not in his own county. In fact, he raised the
idea in the first place. As he described his reasoning to me,
"During the time I was County Executive I was complaining

about the fact that it was very difficult to do anything in a business sense because anything in your own county is prohibited. He [Walter Jones] said, 'Well, I've got an opportunity in another county, and certainly nobody can criticize you for owning a piece of land in another county.' I said, 'I guess not, I guess they can't do that.' "

On that he guessed wrong. When he announced his financial holdings in July 1966, during the gubernatorial campaign, the Maryland newspapers pointed out the fact that the land was on the probable approach route to a proposed new bridge across the Chesapeake Bay. "Mr. Agnew has got himself in the position of not being able to speak out on the bridge issue and let the voters know where he stands because of his private business stake in the outcome," the *Baltimore Sun* editorialized.

Stung by the criticism, Agnew decided to sell out. "Running on a record of integrity as a candidate for high office, admittedly afraid that some voters may not have the time to study the propriety of my position and may, therefore, be misled by the demagogues, I must reluctantly decide to sell this excellent investment at its cost to me," he declared.

In a moment of self-pity he added, "My friends know the truth—that I came up the hard way and am a person of modest means considering my age, position and former profession."

The Anne Arundel County land deal was scarcely mentioned during the 1966 campaign, but was revived in 1968 when *The New York Times* and other newspapers began combing his past for scandal. Agnew felt then, with considerable justification, that the proximity of the land to the proposed bay bridge was a red herring. He made a valid point when he said that the value of the acreage did not hinge on the creation of a new bridge, since the land was already near dual-lane highways to Baltimore and Washington.

The real issue was whether Agnew should have said yes to any fancy business deal with a man who had profited so grandly from a previous rezoning he had granted. Fortunately for him, no one knew enough of the facts to raise it.

The two friends joined in an even fancier deal on May 24, 1966, while Agnew was campaigning for Governor. On that day Jones and Agnew, along with ten other Marylanders, signed an agreement of limited partnership to develop what has become the largest condominium project on the island of St. Croix in the American Virgin Islands.

John W. Steffey, a Maryland State Senator who along with Jones was a general partner in the venture, said the profit projection originally supplied to all limited partners—including Agnew—was that they would double their money inside of four years. Actually, says Steffey, the profits have been lower because of building delays and carrying charges.

There is some confusion about the amount of money Agnew put into the so-called Christian View Limited Partnership (so named because it was near the city of Christiansted). The investment drew little attention during the 1966 and 1968 political campaigns because it sounded so small. "I do have a $1,600 interest in a condominium venture in the Virgin Islands which to date has shown a loss," he said as a Vice Presidential candidate. Two years earlier, he had valued his Virgin Islands interest at $1,650.

However, a certificate of limited partnership found in 1971 among the public land records in St. Croix states that when Agnew joined the partnership in May 1966 he agreed to contribute $15,000.

Asked to reconcile this apparent inconsistency, Agnew's personal lawyer, George W. White, Jr., told me that shortly after signing the original partnership agreement, Agnew took on two subpartners who invested $5,000 apiece in addition to the $1,658.33 in cash he put up himself. On the private books of Christian View Limited Partnership, Agnew's cash contribution was listed as $11,658.33, according to White. He identified Agnew's subpartners as Robert T. Mohre and Ernest C. Trimble. Both men were officers of the Chesapeake National Bank, and incidentally members of the loan committee which had granted Agnew the $15,000 unsecured loan. After explaining these details, White got tough. "If you try to make it look like a dishonest transaction, there should be some investigation of your newspaper," he told me.[5]

Agnew's memory seems to have played tricks on him in discussing his Virgin Islands venture, just as it did with the bank loan and the rezoning. Asked whether he ever had a written agreement with the two men who paid $5,000 to become his subpartners, Agnew told me on February 16, 1971, that he was "sure" he did. "I don't think these fellows would have put their money in there if they didn't have some kind of an agreement," he said. "Neither one of them were intimates of mine. They were both hard businessmen."

One of the subpartners, the bank's general counsel, Ernest Trimble, told me later there had been no written agreement, and a search by White confirmed this. "Why do you think you need a written agreement among friends?" asked Trimble.

As for his reasoning about the transaction, Agnew said, "I was the titular head of the subpartnership as they originally listed the thing. I suppose they just wanted my name on it more than the other guys', I guess. But I didn't have any $15,000 in it. . . . Perhaps I'd hoped that someday I might be able to put $15,000 into it, but I certainly wasn't going to do that at that moment."

Asked how this could have worked, he said, "Well, I suppose I would have had to buy somebody out if I wanted." He said he had no assurance that Mohre and Trimble would sell him their shares, but he did have the right to increase his investment from $1,658.33 to $5,000.

What all this suggested was an unwritten understanding to increase his stake retroactively, when he saw how the venture was working out. In other words, Jones had arranged for him an almost sure thing. As things turned out, Agnew never used his opportunity to increase his investment. In fact, when the costs of the project rose unexpectedly, the general partners did not insist that he live up to his original pledge to the partnership to put in $15,000. Of the nine original limited partners, Agnew was the only one who paid in less than his original $15,000 pledge.

When the results of Agnew's three joint investments with Jones are toted up, one has to sympathize with Agnew for having made so little money for all his trouble. He would have done better in savings bonds.

He paid $10,000 for his Chesapeake National Bank stock in 1964 and sold it in December 1968 for $11,200 after receiving no dividends or director's fees in five years. In 1967 he sold his interest in the Anne Arundel County land venture at what it cost him, $34,430. The closest he came to a "winner" was the Virgin Islands venture, where he put up $1,658.33 in 1966 and then sold out for $2,500 when he formally dropped out of the partnership on September 10, 1969. In addition to his $841 profit, he also enjoyed the benefits inherent in all good real estate tax shelters—he could deduct a total of $1,538.53 for "partnership losses" on his 1967 and 1968 income tax returns.

When he sold his interest in the Anne Arundel County acreage in 1967, he did not use the proceeds to pay off his unsecured loan at Chesapeake National. Instead he bought a $49,500 Virgin Islands condominium apartment unit from his own Christian View Limited Partnership, using $9,900 of the Anne Arundel County land proceeds as a down payment. The rest of the condominium unit he financed with a $39,600 mortgage held by his own Chesapeake National Bank. As Vice President, he has hardly used the condominium, and he figures he has lost $6,000 on the apartment in the two years, mainly in mortgage payments.

Summing up his dealings with J. Walter Jones Jr., the Vice President maintains, "I haven't gained a damn thing."

Even so, as a money saver he must have been a champion during the time he was in public office. In the 1962 edition of the Martindell-Hubbell law directory his net worth was estimated at $10,000 to $20,000—a range his law partner Owen Hennegan says was about right. In 1968, after six years on the public payroll, he announced that his net worth was $111,084, including $35,000 to $40,000 that had recently been given or bequeathed to him by his dead parents. After subtracting his parents' contribution, he had increased his own nest egg to $74,000. His 1968 list of assets, aside from real estate, included $36,621 in cash, $27,113 in stocks, and $10,000 in bonds. As Governor he got $25,000 a year in salary, and the state paid to maintain and supply the Governor's mansion. His County Executive's salary was $22,500.

Agnew may not have gotten rich from his deals with Jones, but that didn't automatically mean he should have made them.

The strict constructionist way of measuring the propriety of County Executive Agnew as capitalist is to refer to the conflict-of-interest section of the Baltimore County charter. These are the key sentences: "No officer or employee of the county . . . shall upon more favorable terms than those granted to the public generally accept any service or thing of value, directly or indirectly, from any person, firm or corporation having dealings with the county. . . . The provisions of this section shall be broadly construed and strictly enforced for the purpose of preventing those persons in public service from securing any pecuniary advantage however indirect from their public associations. . . . In order, however, to guard against injustice, the County Council may by resolution specifically authorize any county officer or employee to own stock in any corporation or to maintain a business connection with any person, firm or corporation dealing with the county, on full public disclosure of all pertinent facts to the County Council. . . ."

To an outsider Agnew's unsecured loan and the opportunities to join the Anne Arundel County and Virgin Islands land syndicates certainly look like "things of value." And accepted on terms "more favorable than those granted to the public generally."

So the issue of whether Agnew broke the law comes down to this: was Walter Jones, his benefactor, a "person, firm or corporation having dealings with the county"?

One could argue that the immensely profitable rezoning

signed by Agnew for the Greater Baltimore Industrial Park in 1960 made Walter Jones a "person . . . having dealings with the county." But that was five years earlier, and the conflict-of-interest section doesn't specifically cover people who "had dealings with the county" in the past.

Next question: was Jones still having any dealings with Baltimore County during the time he and the County Executive were business partners elsewhere?

The answer is yes, although he didn't get rich in the process. Records in Towson show that during Agnew's four years as County Executive he and his subordinates awarded about $2,500 a year in appraising fees to County Appraisers, Inc., a firm of which Walter Jones was the registered agent and main owner. Contracts for appraisals were awarded without bids. During Agnew's four years, County Appraisers averaged about three times as much in yearly fees as in the two years before and the two years after Agnew. Aside from its direct contracts, County Appraisers got another $14,000 from one subcontract for appraising work for the county in 1964. Though the amounts are small, the fees paid to County Appraisers appear to make Jones a "person . . . having dealings with the county."

When I showed Agnew the conflict-of-interest section and asked him whether he had violated it, he read it three times. No, he replied coolly, there was no conflict of interest. "County Appraisers didn't have any dealings with the county," he explained. "They were simply hired on a fee basis to perform a professional service." He went on to deny that any of his dealings with Jones involved accepting a "thing of value."

My conclusion: Although he'll probably never be prosecuted for it, there is a strong case for charging that Agnew violated the conflict-of-interest section of the County Charter. According to the language of the charter, those provisions "shall be broadly construed and strictly enforced" to prevent office holders from "securing any pecuniary advantage however indirect from their public associations." If Agnew had any doubts about whether the law applied to his deals, he could have filed a disclosure statement and left it up to the County Council, as the charter provided. But he didn't.

During an earlier interview in his little real estate office in Annapolis, Jones told about one further arrangement that he and Agnew enjoyed together: "I'm very fond of wines. And the Vice President—then the Governor—likes wines too. When he became Governor, there had never been a wine cellar in this old mansion down there, and you sort of think there should be.

"So I had them take a pantry and turn it into a cellar and put in an air conditioner. Then I contacted a number of his friends, and I made a list of the wines I thought he should have in the wine cellar. I had his friends buy the wine, you know—and none of them could buy more than three or four bottles. And he had an excellent wine cellar."

This is how the Vice President recalls it: "Walter sent me a case of wine here and there. And there was a little closet down there. He is somewhat of a wine connoisseur, and he came in and said the Governor ought to have a wine cellar where the wine can lie correctly, and he had these shelves built in."

Did he pay for it?

"Oh yes," replied the Vice President. "He paid for that, and as a matter of fact it is still in the mansion. It is not very big—about the size of an ordinary broom closet. When I left, I believe I left it there. As a matter of fact, we are not big wine consumers in my house."

On the morning after Agnew was elected Vice President, he invited seven friends to breakfast at the Governor's mansion. Six were members of his staff. The seventh was Walter Jones. What Agnew told him that morning, says Jones, was this: "I have two things to do. First, I want to get down to the Virgin Islands and get away from all this. And second, I want to get the wine out of the wine cellar."

The two men agree that somehow they didn't get it all out.

10

Governor Agnew—Embattled Liberal

For years, what went on in Annapolis was out of phase with the rest of Maryland. The balance of power in the state legislature belonged to Southern-style courthouse gangs in the rural counties that occupied most of the state. Maryland's spurt to the suburbs since World War II was not reflected in the division of legislative districts. In Annapolis, as in Albany or Tallahassee, legislative sessions came and went without much change in the status quo.

Through another link in his chain of good fortune, Spiro Agnew happened onto the scene just after the power in Annapolis had been radically redistributed courtesy of the United States Supreme Court's "one man-one vote" principle. He was still a Republican Governor meeting a Democratic legislature. But most of the old courthouse regulars had been plowed under by a new court-ordered reapportionment plan. In their place came men of the suburbs and the city, men who didn't mind shaking things up for a change. Ninety-seven of the 142 members of the House of Delegates were new faces, the most drastic turnover in years. As one observer put it, the courthouse crowd had been shouldered out by the Crabgrass Generation.

Central casting could have devised no more perfect symbol for the Crabgrass Generation than the incoming Governor, with his mortgaged colonial overlooking the Baltimore Beltway, his ping-pong table in the recreation room, his hi-fi stereo playing Patti Page and Carmen Cavallaro, his overweight spouse and her recipe collection, his golfing magazines, his season tickets on the twenty-yard line of the Colts games.[1]

The move to Annapolis made for an abrupt change in the Agnew family life-style. Judy Agnew, who had cooked all her life, now had a staff of eleven to serve all the meals and do all the housekeeping. But with all the luncheons and house tours and ladies' teas, there was little time to keep up with her Ki-Wives activities or the Swim and Slim classes at the YWCA. Their new home was a fifty-four-room neo-Georgian mansion known as Government House. Every dish, every piece of furniture, every wash cloth was provided. Originally built in the Victorian style in the 1860s, Government House was reconstructed on Georgian lines in 1935. Purists sometimes sniffed that the mansion's decor was a mélange of styles and periods, with few really distinguished pieces except for an Early American clock made by John Fessler of Frederick Town and a Rembrandt Peale portrait of Priscilla Dorsey Ridgely. Anyway, it was a step up from a little house beside the beltway.

After living in the mansion three months, the Agnews had to vacate the premises while new plumbing and wiring and a fire alarm system were installed. During the renovation the

Governor lived part of the time in the Governor's stateroom of the State of Maryland's 118-foot yacht and part of the time at a vacation cottage in the seaside resort of Ocean City, Maryland.

To relieve the formality of the mansion Agnew bought a ping-pong table and a pool table for the basement and wired in his hi-fi set. After dinner he liked to retreat to his bare-walled "Club Room" in the basement for a game with a guest or perhaps one of his State Police bodyguards. Another Agnew innovation was the sauna he paid to have built in a closet on the second floor. The sauna had been recommended by his doctor for arthritis, Judy Agnew once explained.

Among the old-timers in Annapolis, nothing much was expected from Governor Agnew. He was only the third Governor in fifty years who had not learned the mechanism of state government by serving as either Controller or Attorney General. He was only the fifth Republican Governor in the state's history, and clearly an accident. At the outset, some Democrats were talking about "cutting a new eyehole" for Agnew in the three-month legislative session that opened within a week of his inauguration.

His inaugural address, Kennedyesque in its tone, suggested a new brand of leadership, in which the Executive Branch would seek out problems to solve and improvements to make. "I speak of a new state of mind," he said, "and if it should be given a name, let us call it the Pursuit of Excellence.

"The Pursuit of Excellence does not promise the achievement of perfection—but does pledge the pursuit of it. It provides a discipline and a direction.

"It shall be the resolve of this administration to pursue a

course of excellence in its exercise of the duties of government. Each program, each statute, each appropriation will be measured to see that it achieves high standards of excellence. It shall be the hallmark of the new administration to exact excellence in program and service—through leadership and direction."

Skepticism was the quick reaction, typified by the remark of Democratic State Senator Roy Staten: "My God, he's endorsed excellence!" And soon an impression spread among the legislators that the new Governor was not as friendly, not as accessible as his predecessors. He would not be seen having lunch with the boys at the Maryland Inn, across the street from the State House. He would not run into the Hartford County delegate on the street and swap stories, the way other Governors often did in the clubby atmosphere of Annapolis.

Nonetheless, when the legislature finished its annual business in late March, the consensus was that the Republican Governor and the Democratic legislature were jointly responsible for the most productive session in years.

The central accomplishment was to raise and redistribute the state income tax, a goal Agnew had been promoting since his County Executive days. Although it wasn't called revenue sharing, the principle was similar to the federal tax-sharing program that Vice President Agnew would be assigned to merchandise to the states in 1971. Under Agnew's 1967 program in Maryland, the state would increase its personal income tax collections but turn back most of the new revenue to the cities and counties to alleviate pressure on the property tax.

Tax reform had bounced back and forth between Governor

Tawes and the legislature for eight years, always inconclusively. One of Agnew's first steps in 1967 was to name a study group to rejigger the tax plan developed by the Democrats and killed by the last legislature. Resisting a temptation to postpone the tax fight until his second year in office, Agnew endorsed a package very similar to the previous year's defeated bill. To replace the existing 3 percent income tax, Agnew proposed a graduated scale of taxes from 2 to 6 percent. The plan was designed to raise an additional $120,000,000 in revenue, of which $95,000,000 would be sluiced back to local governments. Among the changes Agnew put in the bill were tax credits for the elderly; state aid to local governments for law enforcement and kindergartens; and a special grant to slum schools.

After some minor modifications Agnew would later regret, the tax bill was nudged through the Assembly by the Democratic legislative leaders. The man who did the most to pass it was House Speaker Marvin Mandel, who would follow Agnew as Governor. The mail to Annapolis was so heavily against a tax increase that Agnew was unable to find a single taker for ceremonial pens after he signed the tax bill. But the newspapers called him statesmanlike.

In keeping with his Towson habits, Agnew was almost always willing to give in to the Democrats on questions of patronage, even when it meant that his friend and campaign treasurer Tilton H. Dobbin could not have the State Treasurer's job Agnew had offered him. At every opportunity he would say nice things in public about Speaker Mandel and the President of the State Senate, William S. James. Agnew's deference helped to bring about a legislative session that was low in rancor and relatively high in output. When the legislature adjourned a few minutes after midnight on March 29, its record of accomplishments included not only the tax bill but also a limited open housing law covering new construction and an authorization for new Chesapeake Bay and Baltimore Harbor crossings. The Senate defeated a proposal backed by Agnew to permit abortions where the health of the mother or child was involved, even though it had passed the House. Another casualty was a series of traffic safety bills which the Agnew administration had prepared and sponsored.

Despite his generally favorable press notices, the Governor found his new job dizzying at first, and later frustrating. "When I have a problem to solve, I like to reflect on it for at least two or three hours," he said after a month in office. "But often I felt I was flying by the seat of my pants." A week later, he was telling friends that he was frustrated by the fuzzy lines of control in the Executive Branch, which left him with less control of his subordinate department heads than he had exercised as County Executive. By August a Baltimore newspaper printed an apparently authoritative story that he had told his advisers he had "definitely decided not to seek a second term in office." He felt compelled to bat it down as premature, but admitted that he had indeed reflected some disappointments to his friends about achieving his goals quickly. He went on to insist that his disappointments were "far outweighed by a sense of accomplishment."

One source of his frustration was Maryland's curious constitution, which gave its Governors far less power than the chief executives of most other states. Maryland's Executive Branch, for which the Governor took the rap in the public mind, consisted of more than 200 agencies, commissions, and departments. Agnew found that his authority to merge or reorganize these bodies or even to install his own people was sharply limited. Another bothersome limitation in the constitution was the Board of Public Works, which was responsible for many of a Governor's normal administrative functions, such as selling state bonds, approving leases, letting contracts, selling state property, and approving the creation of unbudgeted jobs. The Governor was only one of three votes on the Board of Public Works. The other two members were Democrats—the Controller, who was elected by the voters, and the State Treasurer, picked by the General Assembly. Still another prickler in the constitution was that Agnew's chief legal adviser was an independently elected Attorney General, who happened to be a Democrat and an aspirant for the governorship.

To get a grip on the state bureaucracy Agnew delegated many of the Governor's management functions to a staff of professional "program executives," each responsible for supervising a cluster of existing state agencies. Compared to Governors McKeldin and Tawes, who had presided in Annapolis for the previous sixteen years, Agnew was a remote figure. Old-line bureaucrats complained that Agnew would not personally listen to their problems. In fact, Al Ward, the head of the state Department of Assessments and Taxation, served as one of Agnew's 200 department heads throughout his governorship without once meeting him. Agnew's new impersonal style of management depended for its effectiveness on the quality of his "program executives" and other personal aides he appointed. Even among Democrats, the consensus was that he tended to pick good people. When House Speaker Marvin Mandel succeeded Agnew as Governor, he kept many of the professional administrators Agnew had appointed, among them Health Care Administrator Dr. Neil Solomon, Police Superintendent Robert J. Lally, and Planner Vladimir Wahbe.

Early in his term a fundamental streamlining of the Executive Branch seemed possible when the legislature, after decades of study groups, finally voted to establish a Constitutional Convention to rewrite the hundred-year-old constitution. The Convention produced a draft constitution in January 1968 that would have reorganized the two hundred units of the Executive Branch into twenty main departments and would have allowed the Governor more latitude to make changes on his own. The constitution was heavily defeated in a referendum on May 14, 1968, and Agnew expressed "deep disappointment." Curiously, he did not commit his prestige in the referendum by any hard campaigning.

For someone who turned out to be a darling of the conservatives, Agnew espoused some stupefyingly liberal thoughts. In his first year as Governor he came out for abolishing the State Board of Motion Picture Censors; for lowering the voting age to eighteen; for liberalizing abortion laws; for abolishing capital punishment; and for a federal take-over of all state welfare programs.

Not the least of his heresies was his Ramsey Clarkish response to Baltimore City Police Chief Donald Pomerleau's request for legalized wiretapping to break the numbers racket. "I am 100 percent against it," declared Agnew in April 1967. "I am against wiretapping in any form." Later, after the police pointed out that Maryland already had a law permitting legal wiretaps in isolated cases, Agnew pulled back and said he supported the existing law.

One can readily visualize Vice President Agnew tearing

apart a speech which Governor Agnew delivered at the University of Maryland commencement in June 1967:

"I propose that we begin more positively to look at the idea of giving our finest minds a better chance to serve the people through government. We have a Peace Corps and a Job Corps. Why not, in Maryland, a Graduate Corps to bring our most promising young men and women into direct confrontation with the affairs and problems of state and local governments?"

His present-day Southern rooters might also find it hard to swallow his proposal in October 1967 that school boards should "explore such possibilities as both class and teacher exchange programs" between city, suburban, and rural schools. He added, "We cannot negate or neglect the truth that a certain segment of our society requires a better-than-average educational experience to compensate for a worse-than-average environmental background." When asked for clarification, he made his proposal sound less menacing by explaining that he meant voluntary exchanges, not mandatory busing to achieve racial balance.

Weird as it now seems, Agnew got into his mind during 1967 that his political future just might lie with Democratic President Lyndon B. Johnson. Agnew's old friend George White, who served as his campaign manager during the 1968 campaign, told me in 1971, "There was nothing definite about it, but I don't doubt that if Agnew had stayed on as Governor and Johnson had remained as President, Agnew would have been considered for a cabinet appointment." Asked whether Agnew himself believed Johnson might offer a high position, White replied, "In the back of his mind he felt this might be a possibility."

As a Governor, Agnew was invited to several large White

House social affairs and had at least one face-to-face meeting with Johnson. Later, Agnew told George White that Johnson had taken a liking to him, even to the extent of describing him as his favorite Republican.

Advertising man Bob Goodman remembers Agnew telling him, "Let's not knock Lyndon." In keeping with that decision, Agnew declared in July 1967, "It may not be the smartest thing I could say politically, but I'm not in accord with all the broad-based criticism of President Johnson, blaming him for big-city rioting. This criticism is to some extent a disservice to honest efforts to do something about urban areas." The only fault Agnew found was that the Johnson administration had "underfinanced and overprogrammed." Two months later he told a press conference that he was behind Johnson "100 percent" on Vietnam and urged Republican candidates to forget Vietnam as an issue. "I think he is a conscientious person who has the interest of the United States at heart," said Agnew.

Johnson's thoughts about Agnew, if there were any, are not available. Joseph L. Califano, who was Johnson's main domestic aide, does not recall that Agnew's name ever came up in any discussion about a possible high appointment, Cabinet or otherwise. However, Johnson did put Agnew on the Advisory Commission on Intergovernmental Relations, a not very important body, in July 1968. The framed certificate of appointment bearing Johnson's signature was resting on the floor of Agnew's Annapolis office at the moment Nixon chose him as his running mate in Miami Beach. Today some people who have stayed close to former President Johnson say he talks to Agnew from time to time on the telephone and that he has privately expressed some sympathy for Agnew's troubles with the press.

The high-water mark of Agnew's liberal period came after a year in office when he presented his first full legislative program to the new session of the legislature in January 1968. It was much more ambitious than his first-year offering, so much so that the Democratic-controlled legislature could not digest its most liberal features. One Agnew proposal that got nowhere was a state housing authority to provide technical and financial assistance for low- and middle-income housing projects, coupled with a state housing code that would set minimum health and safety standards. Other proposed innovations which the legislature refused to swallow included a rapid transit authority to develop a fast public transportation system for the Baltimore metropolitan area; a network of community mental health centers, mainly for alcoholics, financed by a 33 percent increase in liquor taxes; and a system of state loans to college students, replacing the existing college scholarship program in which state senators played a direct part in choosing the scholarship candidates.

The 1968 legislature did pass one important part of Agnew's package: a $129,000,000 water pollution control program to build sewer lines and treatment plants, using bonds as the financing mechanism. It was patterned on Governor Rockefeller's water pollution program for New York, as well as on a pollution program developed in the Maryland Legislative Council.

Agnew was plucked away from Annapolis after half of his four-year term as Governor. The sum total of his important accomplishments in that truncated tenure is four: he raised and revised taxes; he brought a more professional management style to the Executive Branch; he obtained a water pollution program; and he had no scandals.

To that list can be added some fractional pluses. One which comes to mind was his role in settling the tugboat and retail clerk strikes soon after he became Governor. "Unlike most politicians, Agnew was trying to get a settlement—not make political hay," enthused Retail Clerks chief negotiator Alvin Akman, a Democrat. Nor can one forget that Agnew ousted Vernon L. Pepersack as State Correction Commissioner to root out inefficiency and corruption in the state prison system. (Ironically, he replaced Pepersack with a prison administrator who later got into trouble with some legislators for being too permissive.)

Against that fairly impressive record of achievement must be posted two minuses: money and race.

Toward the end of his first year in office Agnew discovered to his horror that his pet tax program, which he considered his main accomplishment, was not pulling in as much new revenue for the state as he had expected. Adding to the problem, sales tax receipts were falling $12,000,000 short of the annual estimates. Suddenly he had to use a machete on departmental spending programs in order to produce a balanced budget, as was legally mandated in Maryland. His blade cut deepest into the budgets for health, welfare, and education, where he had hoped to develop a progressive image.

One of his unhappiest department heads was University of Maryland President Wilson H. Elkins, who submitted a request for an additional $9.1 million and had it cut to $4.1 million. "This is the first budget in my fourteen years at the university that fails to meet the reasonable requirements of the university," Elkins publicly lamented. Later, Elkins told legislators that he tried for fourteen months before Agnew would grant him an appointment.

Agnew's most drastic money-saver was an announcement in December 1967 that he was ordering a 10 percent cutback in the number of poor people receiving subsidized medical care under the state Medicaid program. The announcement meant 27,000 persons would lose their benefits. They got a reprieve the following month when the Governor discovered $5,000,000 in capital improvement money that could be used to keep the Medicaid program going temporarily. Six months later the state's money shortage worsened and he had to impose the cut in Medicaid after all. About 22,000 beneficiaries were actually dropped from the rolls. At the same time Agnew ordered the state payroll frozen and out-of-state travel by state officials restricted.

These moves were not nearly enough to haul the state out of its fiscal bog. Shortly after the 1968 Republican convention, Maryland's fiscal year ended with a deficit estimated at $9,000,000, one year after Agnew had raised the state income tax. When Agnew was leaving Annapolis for Washington six months later, the state's financial picture had deteriorated to the extent that a $35,000,000 budget deficit for the upcoming fiscal year was projected by the state Board of Revenue Estimates. The only way he could submit a balanced budget was to use a bit of gimmickry which allowed the state to get a one-shot $85,000,000 windfall by accelerating tax collections. In his final budget message, the Vice President-elect said this was "a one-time bonus" that did nothing to solve the problem of lagging revenues and growing government.

Because of Maryland's fragmented Executive structure it is wrong to pin the responsibility for the state's fiscal disarray on any one villain. Agnew said the crux of the difficulty was that in 1967 the state legislature had adopted his income tax program with rates varying from 2 to 5 percent, instead of 2 to 6 percent as he had proposed. Some of Agnew's aides complained that the Governor got a series of misleading revenue projections from the State Controller, who was a Democrat. To that, key Democrats in the state legislature reply that the main source of confusion was John Lauber, Agnew's budget aide, whom he imported from New York State.

Late in his first year in office Agnew promised not to ask for another increase in personal income taxes during his four-year term. But in a farewell interview in the *Baltimore Sun*, the Vice President-elect acknowledged that he would have to ask for another tax increase in 1970 if he stayed in Annapolis. Both the state income tax and the sales tax should be increased, he said.

Based on his short record of accomplishments, Agnew will go down as a good Governor. In an editorial just before he became Vice President the *Washington Post* judged him accurately: "He goes with a record that, on balance, marks him as one of the better Governors [of Maryland] in modern times but he leaves just when the most difficult part of his Administration would have begun." Even the Democratic National Committee's confidential study of Agnew in 1968 said, "Merely for self-defense, we ought to recognize that Agnew has accomplished some things during the year and a half he has been Governor of Maryland."

Nonetheless, if Nixon had picked someone else as Vice President, it is doubtful that Agnew could have been re-elected as Governor when his term expired in 1970. No Governor of Maryland in memory had dared to raise taxes twice in four years. And if that wasn't enough to defeat a Republican running in Democratic Maryland, he had also alienated his most solid bloc of supporters: Maryland's 700,000 blacks.

11

"We must draw the line between the
responsible leaders and the nuts."

Losing the Blacks

The image transplant is one of the rarer forms of political
surgery, seldom attempted because of its often fatal compli-
cations. Yet inside of his first eighteen months as Governor,
Spiro Agnew not only survived an image transplant but
emerged with new sources of strength because of it. Afterward, the blacks and liberals who combined to elect him were
jolted into the realization that they had mislabeled his approach to the race question. Some called him a chameleon
and a racist. But the "two Georges" voters, who went from
Wallace to Mahoney, began feeling that Agnew might be
their kind of man after all.

The paradox in his image surgery was that while the public viewed him as more and more of a racial conservative, he
was actually moving toward a more liberal position on civil
rights during his governorship. What made him come across
as a conservative was not the substance of his policies but the
tone of his increasingly strident language.

As late as January 1966, Agnew flatly opposed any open

housing legislation on constitutional grounds. But in that month, with the gubernatorial campaign approaching, Agnew budged a bit. Although holding onto his belief that home-owners should not have to sell or rent to anyone against their will, he now came out for legislation to guarantee that all future developments would be open to blacks. Mild though his proposal sounds in retrospect, it seemed sufficiently ven-turesome at the time for the *Baltimore Sun* to write a news story that "his positive stance on open occupancy . . . could well be said to have kicked off his campaign [for Governor]."

During Agnew's first two months in Annapolis, the Mary-land legislature debated and finally passed a limited open housing law similar to the one he had campaigned for. As Agnew would pridefully note, Maryland thus became the first state south of the Mason-Dixon Line to adopt any statewide fair housing legislation.

Even his liberal critics in the state legislature had to grant that Agnew lobbied effectively to secure passage of the limited open housing law. "I have to give him points for that," con-ceded Paul Sarbanes, a young liberal Democrat who has since graduated from Annapolis to the United States House of Representatives.

In retrospect, some black Baltimore legislators have criti-cized Agnew for not supporting their drive to get an unquali-fied open housing law through the 1967 legislature. While their stronger bill was pending, Agnew told a press confer-ence, "To me it is not politically salable at the moment. I'd like to put my weight behind a bill that I think has more than a fair chance of succeeding." To Agnew, it was better to feed open housing to the public with a small spoon rather than not at all.

By November of his first year as Governor, Agnew came to support the kind of broader open housing bill which nine months earlier he said was not "salable." He had undergone "a change in philosophy," he said, because of his increasing involvement in the problems of the Negro ghettos. As a result he promised to ask the next legislative session for an open housing law that covered all apartments.

"I was forced to a very hard decision," he explained to me in 1971. "Legally I still feel we are on very thin ground in open housing. My conservative Republican background says the private sector of the economy should not be imposed upon by government regulations. But socially the problem is of such overriding importance that after struggling with it a long time I finally came up with the idea that the lack of progress toward compatible mixing of people of both races with equal socioeconomic status was so harmful that the traditional safeguards to the private sector needed to be overridden.

"I modified my position and I have been for open housing in that [broader] sense ever since, even though I have some constitutional twinges about it in a pure legal sense. But I feel it's socially necessary to avoid a lot more difficult and horrendous problems."

Maryland's limited open housing statute, covering just new developments, never went into effect. A petition campaign against it popped up on the right and suddenly there were enough signatures to require a referendum. In March 1968 Agnew announced that he would lead the campaign to get the law approved. "I have been for open housing right along and my position is constantly liberalizing," he explained. Later that spring he urged the Maryland Congressional dele-

gation to vote for a broader federal open housing bill, covering resales as well as new houses. "The fact that it has wider
application than our limited state law makes it even more
desirable," he said. Ironically, the weaker Maryland law was
defeated in the referendum in November 1968, on the same
day Spiro Agnew was elected Vice President. But by that time
a federal open housing law was in effect.

Governor Agnew's gradual mind expansion on civil rights
was not limited to the issue of open housing. Actually, in
some ways he was more forthcoming on the race question
than all his Maryland predecessors.

He became the first Maryland Governor to appoint a black
to his personal staff. He reached that overdue milestone during his first month as Governor when he named Dr. Gilbert
Ware as his coordinator of the health, welfare, and human
relations program, a job that was supposed to include advis-
ing the Governor on race relations. Parren J. Mitchell, now
a liberal black Congressman and Agnew-hater, considered it
enough of a breakthrough at the time to call it "tremendously
exciting."

Agnew proceeded to name at least three black judges, including one on the conservative Eastern Shore, plus black
members on the Workmen's Compensation Commission and
the Board of Engineering Examiners. Seven of the first fifteen
vacancies on draft boards went to blacks. When there were
complaints that the chairman of the Board of Electrical Examiners was practicing discrimination, Agnew helped civil
rights leaders get him removed.

Open housing was not the only liberal race law that passed
the legislature with his support. The state's ancient anti-
miscegenation law, which Agnew called "a blot on Mary-

land's escutcheon for 306 years," was repealed in March of 1967. One year later the state's law against discrimination in public accommodations was significantly extended to cover taverns, which up to then had been exempt.

His catalog of civil rights achievements must also include Maryland's first state code of fair employment practices, which Agnew issued as an executive order in December of 1967. It directed all branches of the state government and all state contractors to abide by a nondiscriminatory policy in hiring.

Why was all of this not enough to keep his black constituency behind him? The kindest answer was that Agnew happened to turn up as Governor of Maryland just when America was rushing into the most accelerated phase of its racial revolution. Concessions which would have seemed radical three years earlier now had the look of tokenism. Blacks who had voted en masse for Agnew in 1966 found his responses to the changed situation not only outdated but coldly insulting.

It didn't take long for Agnew and the blacks to begin abrading each other. Three months after he took office, he remarked that black leaders were reducing the chances for civil rights legislation by their attacks against the Vietnam war. In particular, the Governor said he had completely lost confidence in the Reverend Dr. Martin Luther King, Jr.

This jelled a reaction among the leaders of the Interdenominational Ministerial Alliance, a black church-based committee that was responsible for much of Agnew's black turnout in 1966. "We were . . . disenchanted by the Governor's attempt to tell us what we can speak out for or against and how what we say will affect the progress of civil rights," declared the Reverend Marion C. Bascomb at a public meeting of the ministers' alliance.

Agnew responded with a fierce attack on Stokely Carmichael, coupled with syrupy praise for moderate blacks like Roy Wilkins and Whitney Young. "We must draw the line between the responsible leaders and the nuts," said Agnew. He called Carmichael "one of the most irresponsible people to have ever entered the national political scene."

All this preliminary bitterness might have blown away except for a night of rioting and burning in Cambridge, Maryland on July 24-25, 1967. Cambridge was one of the few racial disorders during that nightmarish summer where the facts supported an "outside agitator" theory. The shooting and fire bombing began about an hour after visiting black militant H. Rap Brown finished telling an outdoor rally, "It's time for Cambridge to explode, baby. Black folks built America and if America don't come around, we're going to burn America down. . . . You better get yourselves some guns. The man is out to get you."

Agnew was driven into Cambridge from his summer cottage in Ocean City, Maryland, before dawn on July 25 for an inspection tour. Five blocks of the black Second Ward were burnt out. Five persons, including a policeman, had shotgun wounds. Agnew was shaken, and with good reason. Twenty-three persons had been killed in the Newark riots two weeks earlier, and at that moment the news reports said Detroit was under siege, with a death list approaching forty-three. Would Baltimore go up next?

Governor Agnew impulsively blamed Cambridge 100 per cent on Rap Brown. "I hope they pick him up soon, put him away, and throw away the key," he said. "Such a person cannot be permitted to enter a state with the intention to destroy and then sneak away leaving these poor people with the results of his evil scheme." Brown, although wounded with a shotgun pellet during the previous night's violence, got away.

Faced with police intelligence reports of tensions extending into Baltimore, Agnew behaved like anything but a conservative ideologue. Forty-eight hours after Cambridge, a press release from the Governor's office announced that Agnew and Mayor McKeldin were creating a "state-city-financed program of created jobs similar to those of the Works Progress Administration (WPA) during the depression era." This reversion to New Dealism was to be accompanied by a "massive program by private industry to hire additional persons who can't find employment through regular state or city channels." The net effect, predicted the Governor and Mayor in a joint statement, would be "a comprehensive program in quick order that will benefit a large segment of our unemployed."

As it turned out, the program sounded grander than it was. About 600 unemployed youths were hired by the city a month to pick up debris from alleys and schoolyards, with the state paying the $200,000 cost through unexpended balances in previous budgets. Another 1,400 persons were placed in jobs with private companies. "The program accomplished what it was intended to do," says Donald C. Lee, a Westinghouse executive drafted by Agnew to run it. "But in terms of the numbers of unemployed people, it made no dent at all."

Two days after announcing the jobs program the Governor uttered the kind of pronouncement he might one day describe as hopeless hysterical hypochondria. Cambridge was a "sick city," he declared, and its leaders should speak out "militantly" for what they needed.

On July 30 Agnew swung his rhetorical course a few points back to the right. Feeling the need as he had in 1963 to issue a clear summation of his views on the race question, Agnew wrote a 450-word statement entitled "Civil Rights and Rioting." It was released to the newspapers almost word for word the way he wrote it, according to his speech writer Cynthia Rosenwald. The hard news in the statement was a threat by the Governor to have the police arrest speakers who were "inciting to riot" even before they finished talking. The full text is worth reproducing for what it reveals about how civil rights and civil disorders were interacting in his mind:

Our country is as much threatened by the lawless rioting in our streets as it is by our enemies abroad. In such a serious time, the people of a State are entitled to a clear and direct statement of their Governor's position. This is such a statement.

In the first place, it is evident that there is ample cause for unrest in our cities. There is still discrimination and, in too many cases, there are deplorable slum conditions. Our Negro citizens have not received, and in many cases are not receiving, equal educational, job, and housing opportunities. The gains recently made, while good, are not enough.

I believe that responsible militants within the Negro leadership should use every means available to place legitimate pressure on those in authority to break the senseless and artificial barriers of racial discrimination. But legitimate pressure—the power of the vote—the power of organized political, economic and social action —does not give any person or group a license to commit crimes.

Burning, looting, and sniping, even under the banner of civil rights, are still arson, larceny, and murder. There are established penalties for such felonies, and we cannot change the punishment simply because the crime occurred during a riot. The laws must be consistently enforced to protect all our people. If an angry man burns his neighbor's house, or loots his neighbor's store, or guns his neighbor down, no reason for his anger will be enough of an excuse.

In Maryland, rioting or inciting to riot, no matter what wrong is said to be the cause, will not be tolerated. There are proper ways to protest and they must be used. It shall now be the policy in this State to immediately arrest any person inciting to riot and to not allow that person to finish his vicious speech. All law-breakers will be vigorously and promptly prosecuted.

Acts of violence will not be later forgiven just because the criminal after a while adopts a more reasonable attitude. The violent cannot be allowed to sneak unnoticed from the war dance to the problem-solving meeting. No, the problem-solving conference must be reserved for those who shun lawlessness, who win their places at the conference table by leadership that builds rather than destroys.

The problem-solving must be done by constructive militants such as the Wilkinses, Kings, Youngs and Randolphs—not by the Carmichaels, Joneses and Browns. But it should include the younger responsible leadership as well as older, more established leaders. Responsibility is the yardstick.

It shall continue to be my firm policy to do everything possible to provide jobs, good housing and better educational opportunities for the poor and underprivileged, both Negro and white, in Maryland. I will meet with any responsible leaders to discuss the problems that confront us. I will not meet with those who engage in or urge riots and other criminal acts as weapons to obtain power.

In conclusion, I commend the citizens of both races who have continued to conduct themselves with intelligent restraint in spite of great pressure. I share the sorrow of those who have suffered and who continue to suffer from the reckless acts of a few. For the confused and weak who seek to excuse, appease and rationalize for the criminals who threaten our society, I have only pity.

It was a warning that blacks in Maryland must work through the system, equally weighted with an acknowledgment that their cause was just. The cutting edge of the statement was his threat to seize speakers in mid-speech.

Three weeks later the Governor decided he must issue a clarification to square his arrest policy with the First Amendment. In a somewhat ambiguous letter to State Police Superintendent Lally, he insisted that "it was never my intention to impose any type of 'prior restraint' on the speech of anyone." The new test for arresting speakers, he said, was a "clear and present danger" of violence.

The first challenge of his tough-mouth Cambridge pronouncement arose nine months later at Bowie State College, a small, predominantly black campus between Baltimore and Washington, D.C. The Governor's office got its initial warning of trouble on March 25, 1968, when Dr. Samuel Myers, the new president of Bowie State, telephoned to say that there was "potential unrest" on the campus. The main grievance, Myers said, was that a popular history instructor named Virginius B. Thornton had been denied tenure.

The next day the students began drafting a list of further grievances, which wasn't hard to do at Bowie State. There were peeling paint, falling plaster, bad food, and a shortage of laundry facilities and vending machines. Its student body had tripled in three years, overloading the shabby old facilities that survived from the days of legal segregation. Aside from the legitimate grievances, Bowie State happened to be located thirty miles from the campus of Howard University, where black power disruptions were at their peak. When Dr. Myers called the Governor's office that second day, he reported that although the campus was orderly, the Bowie student leaders were now in touch with a group of Howard University students.

The news got worse when Dr. Myers called the third day. Now the Student Government Association had approved a boycott of classes. Fifty Howard University students were on the campus. And to complicate matters, Myers said that he was in sympathy with the students on their demands for improving the college's physical facilities. The only way to keep the outside influences from controlling the campus was for Agnew to meet with a student delegation, Myers insisted. He put the point so strongly that it sounded like a demand.

In his Cambridge pronouncement Agnew had promised to "meet with any responsible leaders to discuss the problems that confront us," so long as they hadn't taken part in rioting. A few months later he had gotten favorable notices by meeting Danny Gantt, the director of CORE in Baltimore, to plan for the relocation of 1,800 blacks displaced by an expressway. However, Bowie State was a different kind of problem to the Governor and his staff. As they saw it, Bowie State was not a racial question. No, Myers was told by an Agnew aide, the Governor would not meet with any student delegation.

Privately, Agnew had decided early that year to be very tough the first time there was a campus disruption in Maryland. In the presence of Herb Thompson, his press secretary, Agnew had sworn that the type of student rebellion that had dotted the map between Columbia and San Francisco State would never be tolerated in his state. Part of being tough, apparently, was staying aloof.

At a press conference on the fourth day Agnew had little sympathy for the protesters. "Students always have objections to the way colleges are run," he said. "I doubt if we'll ever change that. Our problem is to make certain that we properly assess their objections and make changes where they are indicated, but don't overreact in this case." He made clear that he wouldn't meet the student leaders personally, although his aide Charles S. Bresler had been dispatched to the campus.

On the evening of Friday the 29th, one day after Agnew's icy press conference, the students seized Bowie's administration building with the help of a cadre from Howard University. In comparison to some student takeovers it was relatively undestructive, despite rumors that water faucets were turned on and the telephone switchboard "liberated" for the benefit of anyone who wanted to make long-distance calls. Police sources reported to the Governor's office that the takeover was engineered by Kenneth Brown, a field coordinator for the NAACP.

Dr. Myers, who had been off campus giving a speech when the administration building was occupied, admitted to Bresler at 1 A.M. Saturday that matters were out of his control. Among other things, the students had prevented him from entering his own campus. In the early morning hours he agreed to a suggestion from the Governor's office that he ask for state aid in putting down the disorder. At 3 A.M. he telephoned the formal request to Herb Thompson, who woke up Governor Agnew three hours later.

According to Thompson, Agnew immediately called the State Police duty officer and ordered him to retake the campus as soon as possible. Thompson says he heard Agnew telling the State Police official: "I don't want to see any head cracking or anything else like that going on, unless it is necessary to defend yourself. Use a minimum amount of force."

With that kind of orders the State Police could have marched in with billy clubs before breakfast. Instead, police commanders on the scene held back to give the students time to withdraw. By 5 P.M. the student leaders marched out voluntarily.

Agnew countered with a statement that was anything but soothing. At the time of Cambridge nine months earlier, his statement tried to balance two sentiments: sympathy for the rioters' grievances and contempt for those who riot. Now the sympathy was reduced to a parenthetical phrase and the threats were in the first person singular:

Today's events at Bowie State College should amply demonstrate that this Administration has no intention of yielding to the demands and threats of those who would take matters in their own hands and attempt to run the State government.

It is unfortunate that students, who no doubt have legitimate grievances, came under the spell of outside agitators and sought to redress those grievances through occupation of the college administration building and denial of access to the campus even to the college president. This was an intolerable situation—to the college administration, to the Board of Trustees, and to me. I am glad that it has been relieved without the use of force. But force was present in the State Police that I sent to the campus today and force would have been used had the need arisen.

I also was prepared to issue a proclamation closing down the college indefinitely had that become necessary. I am glad it wasn't necessary, but I would like it clearly understood by the students and by the general public that I am prepared to take such action should further trouble erupt.

After the students have returned to normal campus life, including the end of their boycott of classes, I will then—and only then —consider discussing their grievances with them. Some reports that are being aired and published to the effect that I am planning to meet with them Wednesday are totally false.

It is time that public officials in this country stop yielding to pressure and threats and intimidations by those who would take the law in their own hands. I certainly don't intend to yield to such pressures, and I hope that this is clear from today's events at Bowie.

By his truculence Agnew shoved the students into a choice of either throwing in the towel or escalating. Some did decide to go back to classes. But a more aggressive faction decided to take their grievances to the Governor's doorstep. On Thursday, April 4, more than 200 Bowie students trooped into the main corridor of the State House demanding to see Agnew. Told he was unavailable, they voted to stage a wait-in and promptly sat down in the corridor.

State Police Superintendent Lally, who was in touch with Agnew throughout that afternoon, recalls that the Governor "really agonized" over the student sit-in. He grasped the validity of many of their complaints, according to Lally, but saw little that could be done about getting more money for Bowie with the legislature out of session. Also, the Governor had an instinctive feeling that he could not be put in a position of being forced to hold a meeting.

Agnew settled on a strategy of massive retaliation. Step one, he decided to have all the students arrested for trespassing if they remained in the building past the 5 P.M. closing time. Step two, he decided to close the whole Bowie State campus. "I don't know whether you should use the word retaliation," Lally told me, "but he had let the student leaders and the president of the college know that if they took this action [the sit-in], he would be forced to close the college."

When closing time came at the State House, 227 students chose to stay and be arrested. The State Police passed out 3-

by-5 cards for names and addresses and then put the students in school buses for a trip to the Anne Arundel County Detention Center. Meanwhile, Lally led a contingent of troopers south toward Bowie to evict the remaining students from the campus.

Over his car radio Lally heard a news flash: Martin Luther King Jr. had just been shot in the head on a balcony in Memphis.

Back in Annapolis Agnew heard the news soon after his press conference to justify the Bowie State arrests. He had just finished saying, "My refusal to knuckle down to the demands [of the] students is not a point of personal pride with me, but pride and respect for this democracy and the office of Governor of this great state."

According to Herb Thompson, Agnew never gave any consideration to whether, in light of King's assassination, he should rescind his order to close the Bowie campus. To Agnew, Bowie was still not a racial matter.

It was pouring rain when the State Police arrived at Bowie and began evicting the students. On the spot, Lally decided that he could not leave them sitting on their suitcases in the downpour. Those who had no rides were allowed to stay on campus an extra day or sometimes two. "The Governor was amenable to this," Lally later explained.

After Cambridge, Agnew got a notion anchored in his mind that the only way to get the whites of Maryland to swallow open housing and other racial reforms was to isolate the black power militants from the moderate black leaders who helped elect him. Several times in the fall of 1967 he met with small groups of black moderates, including members of the ministerial alliance or political leaders like State Senator

Verda Welcome. His pitch was that the black moderates must denounce the militants in order to win the confidence of the whites. To set the tone, the Governor would play a tape recording the State Police had obtained of Rap Brown's incendiary speech in Cambridge.

Agnew got more and more disappointed at their response. "I expected that they would be incensed at the setback to what we were trying to accomplish caused by Cambridge," Agnew said later. "Instead they were very protective of Rap Brown—they would say things like 'We don't agree with what he did but his motives were good.'" Out of his disappointment came a speech that would shatter and then re-create his image on race relations as though he had hired a plastic surgeon.

The message had been forming in his mind for several months when he announced on April 6, 1968, that he would meet in five days with "prominent Negro leaders" in Baltimore for a "frank and far-reaching" discussion. At least two external developments were part of his calculation to hold the meeting. Clearly the most important, Martin Luther King had been assassinated two days earlier. Baltimore was intact but restless. However, 45 miles down the parkway a riot was burning corridors of destruction through Washington.

The second external development in Agnew's equation was the stinging editorial in the *Baltimore Evening Sun* had carried after Bowie State. It called him "stiff-necked" for not meeting the student leaders and accused him of "trying to make problems go away by decree." To Agnew, it was like a slap in the face.

Like a hundred other American cities, Baltimore did not stay intact for long. Beginning that evening, streets in many black neighborhoods belonged to looters, fire bombers, police, the National Guard, and finally paratroopers. Within 72 hours Baltimore suffered 6 deaths and at least 300 injuries, 420 fires, and 550 looted stores.

The Governor kept his distance from the tactical problems of riot control once he had summoned the National Guard and later asked the White House to send federal troops. He saw it as his role to compose a speech that would impart to the black moderates enough backbone to take a stand against the extremists. In seclusion, he wrote the speech himself in longhand on yellow legal pads while the Baltimore riot was tapering down.

Once he finished writing, he tested his draft on at least two aides, Herb Thompson and Charlie Bresler, and perhaps others. He also took Walter Jones into his confidence during an evening cruise on the Chesapeake Bay aboard Jones' yacht. The morning of the speech he called in Cynthia Rosenwald, his speech writer, and handed her a typed copy. "I took this thing, I looked at it, and you know, I started to sweat," she remembers with a shudder. "But I could understand, in a way, you know." Among them, Thompson, Bresler, and Mrs. Rosenwald toned down Agnew's draft somewhat. Several of the Governor's more extreme phrases were edited out, and someone composed an upbeat conclusion that was tacked onto the end. But with these exceptions the final text was all Agnew.

Somehow Agnew managed to omit from the consultations the one black man on his staff, the one whose function it was to advise him on his dealings with blacks. "Poor Gil Ware never really knew about the speech until the day the Governor came to Baltimore to deliver it," allows Cynthia Rosenwald. Horrified when he finally saw the text, Ware told the

Governor that it would insult the black leaders who heard it and quite possibly add to the tension in the ghettos. Lally added his private opinion that the speech might kick off another disturbance in Baltimore. Agnew listened but he would not pull back.

There was in Baltimore an informal circle of about a dozen of the most influential black moderates who called themselves, with a sense of irony, the "Goon Squad." When the Governor announced the April 11 meeting, the Goon Squad got together one night at the home of Parren Mitchell, then an aide to the Mayor of Baltimore, to plan for what would obviously be a pivotal session with the Governor. The result was a list of twelve proposals for better race relations, including a suggestion that the Governor make an appearance in a black neighborhood. "Everyone I talked to said this [the April 11 meeting] is great, maybe this will be a breakthrough," recalls Mitchell.

When the hundred "prominent Negro leaders," including most of the Goon Squad, arrived at the State Office Building to see Agnew on April 11, they were ushered toward a conference room on the eighth floor. Once their invitations were checked by uniformed State Policemen, the one hundred blacks entered a room big enough for fifty people to sit in comfort. Although they came expecting a closed meeting, they found the pencil press and a battery of TV cameras waiting inside to capture the proceedings.

Agnew was twenty minutes late. As everyone waited, Charlie Bresler gave a little impromptu talk in which he touched on the virtues of pulling yourself up by your bootstraps, the way Agnew did. Some blacks in the room found it patronizing, which got things off to a bad start.

Meanwhile, Agnew was delayed by two unscheduled appointments. The first was with Lenny Moore and John Mackey, two black Baltimore Colts whom he had invited to the meeting with the "prominent Negro leaders." Politely the two athletes declined, saying they could be more effective out in the streets if they did not get tied to the power structure. The second unscheduled appointment was a staff meeting to consider fresh rumors picked up by police intelligence that the rioting in Baltimore would break out again over the weekend.

The restless black leaders got their first glimpse of Agnew as he walked briskly toward the front of the room in the company of Major General George M. Gelston of the National Guard, Superintendent Lally, and Baltimore City Police Commissioner Donald Pomerleau. The unfortunate first impression of the Governor flanked by his martial legions was compounded when Gelston, with his starched fatigues and jump boots, laid his swagger stick on a table in front of the audience. Seeing no place cards at the front table, the three white riot control officials sat down beside Agnew in places that had been meant for civilians in charge of health and welfare.

In his calm, flat voice Agnew began reading phrases that lashed his listeners and then stung the wounds. Even if the meeting had been choreographed to perfection, with no unfortunate symbols like Gelston's swagger stick, the speech itself was enough to produce rage.

"Hard on the heels of tragedy come the assignment of blame and the excuses," Agnew began. "I did not ask you here to recount previous deprivations, nor to hear me enumerate prior attempts to correct them. I did not request your presence to bid for peace with the public dollar.

"Look around you and you may notice that everyone here is a leader—and that each leader present has *worked* his way to the top. If you'll observe, the ready-mix, instantaneous type of leader is not present. The circuit-riding, Hanoi-visiting type of leader is missing from this assembly. The cater-wauling, riot-inciting, burn-America-down type of leader is conspicuous by his absence. That is no accident, ladies and gentlemen, it is just good planning. And in the vernacular of today—'that's what it's all about, baby.' "

To many in the audience, it already sounded as if the Governor was trying to split all black leaders into two categories—agitators and money-grubbers. After setting his listeners on edge, he proceeded to insinuate that they were cowards.

"Several weeks ago," the Governor said, "a reckless stranger to this city, carrying the credentials of a well-known civil rights organization, characterized the Baltimore police as 'enemies of the black man.' Some of you here, to your eternal credit, quickly condemned this demagogic proclamation. You condemned it because you recognized immediately that it was an attempt to undermine lawful authority—the authority under which you were elected and under which you hold your leadership position. You spoke out against it because you knew it was false and was uttered to attract attention and inflame.

"When you, who courageously slapped hard at irresponsibility, acted, you did more for civil rights than you realize. But when white leaders openly complimented you for your objective, courageous action, you immediately encountered a storm of censure from parts of the Negro community. The criticism was born of a perverted concept of race loyalty and inflamed by the type of leader whom I earlier mentioned is not here today.

"And you ran. You met in secret with that demagogue and others like him—and you agreed, according to published reports that have not been denied, that you would not openly criticize any black spokesman, regardless of the content of his remarks. You were beguiled by the rationalizations of unity; you were intimidated by veiled threats; you were stung by insinuations that you were Mr. Charlie's boy, by epithets like 'Uncle Tom.' God knows I cannot fault you who spoke out for breaking and running in the face of what appeared to be overwhelming opinion in the Negro community. But actually it was only the opinion of those who depend on chaos and turmoil for leadership—those who deliberately were not invited today. It was the opinion of a few, distorted and magnified by the *silence* of most of you here today. . . ."

Everyone in the room knew what the Governor was talking about. Earlier that year the head of the Baltimore City CORE chapter, Robert Moore, had irritated some black moderates by a blast at the police as "the enemy of the black community." One of the prominent moderates, State Senator Clarence M. Mitchell III, responded on the Senate floor with a statement accusing Moore of bigotry. Then came a black unity meeting and an informal agreement among the moderate and militant factions to refrain from criticizing each other in public.

When Parren Mitchell heard Agnew say the words "And you ran," he jumped to his feet. "I am not going to listen to any more of this crap!" he interjected. Then he walked out the door. Others followed, singly and in clumps. Out in the corridor someone yelled, "Black caucus, black caucus." Before long, seventy of the hundred black leaders had walked out on Agnew.

The Governor kept on reading in his calm newscaster's voice, apparently oblivious to the walkout. "I publicly repudiate, condemn and reject all white racists," he intoned. "I call upon you to publicly repudiate, condemn and reject all black racists. This, so far, you have not been willing to do.

"I call upon you as Americans to speak out now against the treason and hate of Stokely Carmichael and Rap Brown. If our nation is not to move toward two separate societies—one white and one black—you have an obligation too.

"I submit to you that these men and others like them represent a malignancy out of control; that they will lead us to a devastating racial civil war. I submit to you that there can be no winner from such a conflict and that the heaviest losers will be the Negro citizens of America. . . ."

Eventually, he came to the conciliatory conclusion that his aides had written for him: "So let us begin to rebuild now—to rebuild our city and to rebuild the image of Baltimore. Let us work together—not as black or white—but as responsible citizens of Maryland who uphold the law: as concerned citizens who are united in their dedication to eliminate prejudice and poverty or any conditions which create hopelessness and despair. . . ." After what he had said already, the conclusion scarcely made a difference.

When he finished, Mrs. Juanita Jackson Mitchell, the lawyer for the state NAACP, rose to deliver a philosophical reply about the nature of violence, concluding that the body politic moves only when there is violence or the threat of violence.

"It's going to stop being the history of this country or

we're all going to be dead, every one of us," Agnew cut in. "Are you willing, as I am willing, to repudiate the Carmichaels and the Browns? Answer me! Answer me! Do you repudiate Rap Brown and Stokely Carmichael? Do you? Do you?"

"We don't repudiate them as human beings," answered Mrs. Mitchell in a quavering voice.

"That's what I was afraid of," snapped Agnew.

Later, a reporter asked him what he would have done if all one hundred of the leaders had walked out. "I would simply be faced with a situation where I would have to find other Negro leaders," said the future Vice President.

It stretches the imagination to think that any white politician would arrange to tongue-lash a black audience in front of TV cameras immediately after a riot if he hoped to promote better understanding between the races. But that is exactly what Agnew now contends he was trying to accomplish. "I didn't go there expecting that there would be trauma and arguments and recriminations," he recently explained. "I went there expecting that there would be a purging, an exchange of ideas, and a better understanding." [1]

If he really had wanted those results, it is hard to see why Agnew took the unusual step of bringing TV cameras and newspaper reporters into what had originally been planned as a private meeting. Agnew's subsequent explanation is not flattering to him, nor is it totally persuasive.

"I considered the idea of just going over it privately with them," the Vice President told me in 1971. "But I thought that because some people in that group would disseminate the information in a warped or twisted sense, I had to have a public airing of it to protect myself." He said his decision to invite the press was reached only after the riots in Baltimore.

But if his only motive was self-protection, why not keep the meeting closed and later release a copy of his speech? Or a transcript of the meeting? Or why not minimize the impact of press coverage by inviting the pencil press but no TV cameras?

The answer is simply that Agnew had decided to go over the heads of the hundred black leaders and reach a mass audience on the evening news. As he made clear on Walter Jones's yacht the night before, his aim was to reach whites as well as blacks.

He did. The confrontation between Agnew and the black leaders got a strong play not only on local television but on the network news. Within twenty-four hours his office had logged in 1,039 telegrams and 298 phone calls favoring his speech. Only 63 telegrams and a few phone calls were counted as critical. "I would like to congratulate you for standing up for the average middle-class American citizen when no one else did," read a typical communication from one Maryland suburbanite. Messages flowed in from as far as California, some going so far as to urge Agnew to run for President. It was the biggest splash he made since getting elected in 1966.

In the long run, race relations in Maryland weren't much helped or harmed by the brief governorship of Spiro Agnew. Originally perceived by the public as more of a liberal than he really was, he nevertheless began to develop a more progressive record on race than he had ever built in Towson. But later he destroyed his good will with the blacks by ill-timed insistence on exorcism of militant devils. On balance, his performance on civil rights as a border state Governor came out slightly on the plus side of zero.

More permanent than what Agnew did for race relations is

what race relations did for Agnew. The lessons he learned in two short years in Annapolis would bias his thinking long after he got to Washington. Lesson one: racial disturbances can be started by outside agitators. Lesson two: campus disruptions are often the fault of weak administrators; they can be stopped by firm police intervention. Lesson three: one way to mobilize the white conservatives is to berate the black militants.

And yet he was enough of a pragmatist to react differently the next time he ran into an incipient Bowie State. It was only a month later when the students at Maryland State College, an almost all-black institution, began demonstrations about discrimination by the local businessmen in the nearby town of Princess Anne. It was red-neck territory on the Eastern Shore and Agnew knew it. Acting before the student protests reached a crescendo, he called in a delegation of sixteen students and some faculty members and talked with them for an hour and a half. As if by magic, the student leaders called off their protests, saying, "We have achieved our goals."

To Agnew, it was vital to make everyone realize he was not giving in to threats when he summoned the students from Maryland State. If he were faced with another Bowie State, he insisted, "I'd do the same thing over again."

12

Miracle in Miami Beach

Richard Nixon, who was well acquainted with literally thousands of public figures, somehow decided that Spiro Agnew was the best one to be his Vice President. No one has put Nixon on a couch and dug out his inner motives for picking someone so ordinarily gifted. So the question haunts the rest of us: how did it happen?

The usual beginning of the story is that Nixon never met Agnew until 1968, the year he made him famous. Actually, Agnew first flickered across Nixon's field of vision about four years earlier, while Agnew was a hustling County Executive and Nixon was practicing law. One day a letter arrived at Nixon's law office. The letter, from Agnew to Nixon, will presumably turn up someday in a Presidential library, dated sometime in 1962 or 1963. Agnew's executive assistant at the time, Dutch Moore, says the thrust of the message was approximately this: Despite everything that has happened, you should run for the Presidency again. If you do, you have enough potential support to win.

No reply came from Nixon for about a month. "He won't even acknowledge his mail!" the County Executive was heard to grouse. Then, two weeks later, a letter from Nixon finally arrived. Although noncommittal, it was warm and open. "The County Executive was tremendously elated," recalls Dutch Moore.

Did the notion enter one of the compartments of Nixon's mind that someone out there with the unlikely name of Spiro Agnew was a pretty perceptive fellow? It would have been only natural. Having been whipped in his race for Governor of California in 1962, Nixon was not being deluged with fan mail from potential delegates.

The story of how the two men met for the first time has never gotten into print, possibly because the occasion turned out to be a bit embarrassing for Nixon. That first encounter took place at a political cocktail party on June 9, 1964, at Fife Symington's rolling estate in Lutherville, Maryland. Symington, still no pal of Agnew, felt constrained to invite him to his house along with two dozen important Maryland Republicans for drinks before a big Republican fund-raising dinner in Baltimore County. Nixon, the dinner speaker, was a guest at the cocktail party too.

Believing he had been called on to say a few words, Nixon stood up on Symington's porch and began a little speech on the virtues of holding an "open" convention in San Francisco, i.e., a convention that was not sewed up in advance by Senator Barry Goldwater. To the host and hostess, who worshiped Goldwater, this was heresy. Marsie Symington, the Foxcroft debutante and Frick heiress, broke in and demanded that Nixon stop. "We don't want to hear from you at all," she is supposed to have said. Painfully, Nixon obeyed and stopped talking.

It may surprise President Nixon to learn how a Baltimore newspaper columnist happened to print something about his embarrassing confrontation with Marsie Symington. The story was leaked by none other than Spiro Agnew.

They had nothing more to do with each other until four years later, when they were both deep in Presidential politics—on opposite sides.

Agnew had hardly gotten settled in the Governor's mansion in early 1967 when he got a visit from Leonard Hall, the chief political agent for front-runner George Romney of Michigan. When Hall fished for a commitment, Agnew fended him off with humility. The real powers controlling the 1968 Maryland delegation, said Agnew, would be Congressmen Rogers Morton and Charles M. Mathias.

By April of 1967 Agnew had shed his reticence. During an appearance at Yale to address the Young Republicans Club he announced that he would encourage New York Governor Nelson Rockefeller to run for the Presidency. "If he wants to run he ought to get into the race now and not wait like Bill Scranton," said Agnew.

Like most of the newly elected Republican Governors, Agnew was interested in erasing many of the labels the GOP had accumulated in losing the last two Presidential elections. His speech at Yale, written for him by his advertising man Bob Goodman, suggests that inside of four months as Governor he had conquered his difficulty in envisioning himself on the national scene.

"We must correct the impression," he said, that Republicans "regard big government as at all times bad, or massive spending as in every instance evil. We must refuse to tolerate the role of a minority party, the yesterday party, the protest party, the white Anglo-Saxon party, the rural America party, the stand-pat party. Once we are cleansed of undeserving images we may set about purifying American society. And the very first thing we must do is to make a sacred covenant with the people that we will tell the truth, the whole truth, and at all times the truth. Never before in our history has leadership had its credibility so seriously questioned or its integrity so nakedly challenged. . . ."

Except for sporadic statements from Tom McCall of Oregon, Agnew was the first of the twenty-six Republican Governors to begin stirring up a draft-Rockefeller movement. Once he was out ahead of the pack, he did not give up easily, even though his Yale statement was outdated before he ever made it. When he got back to Annapolis the next day, he was greeted by the disconcerting news that Rockefeller had just written a letter to Governor McCall declaring that he would not run. Agnew acknowledged to the statehouse reporters that he had been caught off base by Rockefeller's decision but went on to insist that the New York Governor could still be persuaded.

Agnew had been drifting on the liberal side of the Republican mainstream ever since he got into politics. In 1963 his first choice for President was not Rockefeller, but Senator Thomas Kuchel, soon to be defeated because he was too liberal for California. After reading of Kuchel's attack on right-wing extremists, Agnew drove to Washington to meet him in June 1963. "He's terrific," said Agnew later. "He talks like I think."

When Kuchel failed to ignite, Agnew moved behind William Scranton, the reluctant Pennsylvania Governor, in plenty of time to vote for him as a delegate at the San Francisco convention. Neither Goldwater nor Rockefeller enthralled him in 1964. "I have the feeling there are masses of Republicans who can't adjust their thinking to either Goldwater or Rockefeller," he said before the convention.

When Goldwater became the Republican nominee, Agnew came close to committing an error that would have killed his chances of being Nixon's Vice President. "I cannot endorse Senator Goldwater's brinkmanship posture on foreign affairs, nor can I endorse his reluctance to support legislation aimed at removal of discrimination in public accommodations," Agnew said in July 1964. But given the choice between Goldwater and Lyndon Johnson, he held his nose and backed Goldwater.

After the Johnson landslide Agnew turned his affections to Rockefeller for 1968. As an official of the National Association of Counties, Agnew had been exposed to an array of Rockefeller programs for New York State. And once Agnew was elected Governor, he sometimes tapped the Rockefeller staff for aid in recasting a New York program, such as water pollution, to be used in Maryland. As 1968 approached, he was convinced that Rockefeller had a far better chance of winning than either Romney or Nixon. It did not offend his liberal instincts to call for an ideologically balanced ticket. His real preference, he said, was a Rockefeller-Ronald Reagan combo.

Rockefeller would not oblige. "I'm not a candidate, I'm not going to be a candidate, and I don't want to be President," he remarked in October 1967. He made the comment in surroundings guaranteed to produce the maximum political echo—a National Governors' Conference aboard a chartered ocean liner en route to the Virgin Islands.

The reporters left Rockefeller on the sun deck and sought

out his booster-in-chief, Spiro Agnew, to flesh out their stories. "That's pretty definite, but I still say if he's drafted it would take a pretty emphatic individual to turn down a genuine draft," replied Agnew doggedly. "Indeed, I cannot conceive of it."

His judgment about the decisiveness of Nelson Rockefeller could not have been sharper. A month later Rockefeller zagged back toward candidacy by acknowledging that in the unlikely event of a genuine draft, he would "have to face it." That was several shades different from saying he did not want to be President. Once again Agnew leapt into action. After several visits to Rockefeller's office, Agnew made a formal announcement on January 9, 1968, that he was starting a draft-Rocky movement in Maryland.

Just when the Rockefeller movement began to look plausible, Agnew chanced into his first substantial conversation with Richard Nixon. The meeting was arranged by one of Nixon's wealthy admirers in Maryland, State Senator Louise Gore, whose family owns the Jockey Club, one of Washington's fancier restaurants. As President, Nixon made her the United States representative on the UNESCO executive board.

"I wanted to do something special for the women who worked in my campaign," she told me. "So I arranged to take them up to the National Women's Republican Club luncheon in New York. Then I called Mr. Nixon's secretary, Rose Mary Woods, and told her that the one thing my girls would like to do is meet Dick Nixon. It was arranged that he would drop over and see us at the apartment of Mrs. Edmund C. Lynch, Jr. Then I heard that Governor and Mrs. Agnew were in New York for the same luncheon, and so I invited them to come by too. I admired both of them tremendously and I thought they should meet each other.

"Dick Nixon arrived with Dwight Chapin around fifteen minutes before the Agnews. One of my campaign workers got Mr. Nixon talking about some pretty serious questions right away, and the conversation stayed in that vein after the Agnews arrived. For the next two hours Nixon and Agnew got so engrossed with each other's thoughts that they almost forgot we were in the room." Nixon discoursed about the capture of the U.S.S. *Pueblo* by North Korea. Agnew held forth on urban problems and pollution.

While Louise Gore was walking Nixon to the elevator, she noticed that he was deep in concentration, forgetting the usual small talk about what a nice party it was. Finally, as the elevator door was closing, he told her, "Louise, you should see that your Governor speaks out more. He has a lot to say."

Agnew was impressed too, although not about Nixon's Presidential prospects. "He'd make a great Secretary of State," Agnew told a friend back in Annapolis. As far as he was concerned, the GOP needed a forward-looking image to win and Nixon would look slightly shopworn.

As long as George Romney was still campaigning, the Rockefeller camp never gave Agnew any authorization, even covertly, for his draft-Rockefeller noises. But neither did Rockefeller go out of his way to get Agnew, his most vocal supporter among the Governors, to pipe down. In Annapolis, the Governor and his political advisors read this as a green light. "He [Rockefeller] did not discourage us from acting, and in politics if somebody doesn't stop you, you keep on going," explained Agnew's man, Charlie Bresler.

As the New Hampshire primary drew closer, George Rommey's private opinion polls showed him losing to Richard Nixon by an unbelievable ratio of 6 to 1. Romney threw in the towel on February 29, two weeks before the primary.

That left the next move up to Rockefeller, and two days later he announced at a Governors' Conference in Washington that he would run for President if the Republican Party wanted him, although he would not "create dissension" by contending for the nomination. In the corridors, the two Governors who maneuvered the hardest to line up their uncommitted brethren behind Rockefeller were still Agnew and Tom McCall of Oregon.

For the next three weeks Nelson Rockefeller and his advisors tried desperately to massage a draft. On March 8 George Hinman telephoned Al Abrahams, a young war-horse who had run the Rockefeller headquarters in Washington in 1964. A national draft-Rockefeller organization was about to be created with Bill Scranton of Pennsylvania as chairman, Hinman explained. Even though Rockefeller had not made up his mind to run, there was a need for some independent organization to organize the would-be Rockefeller drafters around the country. Would Abrahams be willing to come to New York at 9:30 A.M. the following Monday to talk with him and Scranton about taking a job as the executive director?

Abrahams showed up in Hinman's office Monday but ex-Governor Scranton did not. Instead, a message had arrived the night before that Scranton's plane was fogbound at Harrisburg, Pennsylvania. Soon it became clear that the fog was a Scrantonesque way of saying no to the whole idea. After hearing initially from Hinman, Scranton had decided to check with his successor, Governor James A. Rhodes, before committing his name to any pro-Rockefeller movement. Rhodes was cool enough to the idea to get Scranton to decline.

With Scranton out of the picture, Hinman urgently needed someone with a name to preside over the Rockefeller committee while Abrahams actually did the work—someone who would not impale himself on a spear if Rockefeller decided against running, as Abrahams later put it. Hinman's first thought was J. Irwin Miller, the head of Cummins Engine in Indiana. "The Governor thinks a lot of Miller," observed Hinman. But Abrahams interjected a caveat: since Rockefeller had only two weeks to decide whether to run in the Oregon primary, wouldn't it be better to pick somebody who was already a figure in national politics?

"What about Agnew?" asked Abrahams, who knew the Maryland Governor slightly.

It says something about Agnew's standing with the Rockefeller inner circle that the idea of making him chairman of a draft-Rockefeller movement had not spontaneously occurred to George Hinman, even though he had been Rockefeller's Old Faithful in every meeting of Governors. But now that Abrahams happened to mention it, Hinman settled on Agnew with a snap of his fingers. When Hinman telephoned, Agnew accepted the assignment with alacrity.

In his elation Agnew apparently got the impression that his part in Rockefeller's design was grander than it really was. One Maryland newspaperman recalls Agnew telling him off the record that he had been asked by Rockefeller to run his whole Presidential campaign. "He was very excited about it—it was as if he had reached the big time at last," the newspaperman said later.

The creation of the National Rockefeller '68 Committee was announced by Agnew himself at a press conference in New York on March 14, two days after Nixon's sweep of the New Hampshire primary. The committee would coordinate the draft-Rockefeller activities spontaneously springing up around the country, Agnew said. According to his press release, the Committee would set up an office in Annapolis (P.O. Box 864), and he would serve as temporary chairman.

The first and only puff of wind generated by the Agnew-Abrahams committee was a conference of Rockefeller partisans from fifteen states at the Mayflower Hotel in Washington a few days later. At one session Agnew asked all the participants to gather around him so he could tell them a "real secret." After directing his contingent of Maryland state troopers to check for reporters behind every curtain, he told his secret: Rockefeller could not declare his candidacy right away, or else he would be forced to run in the Nebraska primary, which he would certainly lose to Nixon. Evidently Agnew did not know that his "real secret" had appeared in that morning's *New York Times*. Predictably, the conference ended with a statement calling on Rockefeller to announce his candidacy "without delay."

Agnew's impression that he was a linchpin in the Rockefeller apparatus was reinforced when Rockefeller flew to Washington the next day. By invitation, Agnew met the New York Governor at the air terminal and drove with him in a limousine into the city. Later that day, after Rockefeller had appeared with Agnew at an AHEPA dinner, the two Governors sat in their parked limousine for fifteen minutes outside the Washington Hilton going over the prospects.

Until that day, Agnew had been given no assurance that

Rockefeller would actually decide to run. He had accepted the assignment from Hinman with the understanding that the odds were no better than 50-50. In the limousine, however, Rockefeller said something which Agnew interpreted as a signal that Rockefeller would not pull out. According to Rockefeller's later recollection, he tried to convey the impression that he was still undecided. "But," said Rockefeller, "he really wasn't paying too much attention." Whatever Rockefeller told him, Agnew got out of the car believing that there were just two possibilities: Rockefeller might openly declare against Nixon, or he might stay out of the primaries while deliberately encouraging a draft.

That conversation infused Agnew with the warm feeling of being an insider all through the next three days as speculation multiplied about what Rockefeller would announce at his special press conference at 2 P.M. on Thursday, March 21.

Thursday happened to be Agnew's normal day for holding press conferences in Annapolis. On the morning of the twenty-first his young Assistant Press Secretary Jack Surrick threw out an idea: why not sandwich Agnew's press conference around the TV broadcast of Rockefeller's announcement from New York? That would allow the Governor to get the Maryland-related questions out of the way before the Rockefeller announcement and then give his views about national politics right after the Rockefeller TV broadcast. Surrick's idea appealed to Agnew, who envisioned his ten months of persistence about to be honored.

One man in Annapolis could have told Agnew otherwise. Just after noon that day, George Hinman had telephoned Al Abrahams at the national draft-Rockefeller headquarters a block away from Agnew's office. Bluntly Hinman told

Abrahams there was no point in keeping the office operating because Rockefeller would announce that he was pulling out of the race.

"What about Agnew, have you told Agnew?" Abrahams asked.

Hinman, the total professional, had thought of that. "The Governor called him himself this morning," Hinman assured Abrahams. Even so, Abrahams put in calls to Charlie Bresler and Art Sohmer, his contacts on the Agnew staff. They were out to lunch. Unhappily nobody had told Abrahams about Agnew's plans for a press conference tied in with Rockefeller's New York announcement. If someone had told him, he could have sprinted to the Governor's office in three minutes. Instead he waited for Bresler or Sohmer to call back, but they didn't.

When Hinman said that Rockefeller had called Agnew that morning, he was almost right. A list of nine "must" phone calls to important backers had been placed in the Governor's hands, and one of the names was Agnew. At 10:30 A.M. Rockefeller's personal secretary telephoned Mrs. Alice Fringer, Agnew's personal secretary, to say that Rockefeller would call Agnew between twelve and one. But Rockefeller made the mistake of listening to one of his young public relations aides, about Jack Surrick's age, who told him he must use his last hours before the press conference to get ready for the TV cameras. The call list was pushed aside. At 1:30 P.M., just as Agnew's press conference opened, Rockefeller's secretary called back Mrs. Fringer to say that the Governor could not speak to Agnew before going on TV.

Thus it was that Spiro Agnew got trapped in the humiliating position of having to learn of Rockefeller's decision from a television set with the whole Annapolis press corps watching and snapping pictures.

And thus it was that the interim chairman of the National Rockefeller '68 Committee began migrating toward Richard Nixon.

Considering the pain, Agnew carried off the rest of his press conference with extraordinary composure, although the reporters noted that he shook his head grimly as Rockefeller spoke. "I confess that I am tremendously surprised," he said when the television clicked off. "I also frankly add that I am greatly disappointed. . . . I felt there was a good chance that he could enter the campaign actively without becoming devisive to the party. Apparently he doesn't feel that way. . . ."

Agnew's conversion to Nixon was far from instantaneous. At the continuation of his press conference he made no effort to climb off Rockefeller's falling limb. "Whatever the case may be, I haven't changed my position about the Governor. I think he is clearly the best possible candidate the Republican Party could offer to the electorate in November," he maintained.

Asked whether he would actively support Nixon if he became the nominee, Agnew replied with less than an encomium: "Yes, I certainly would. I have indicated even during the time that I have been most outspoken for Governor Rockefeller . . . that Mr. Nixon is a very acceptable candidate to me and in fact said on several occasions that he may be my second choice."

Still wondering if they had heard properly, Agnew's staff contacted New York to see if the draft-Rockefeller headquarters should be kept operating on a covert basis. The word came back—chop up all the stationery, pay the secretaries severance, break the lease, and close up shop no later than next Wednesday. When Agnew finally heard from Rockefeller that night, he got the same message.

Campaigning in Wisconsin, Nixon coolly decided against an all-out blitz to tie up every Rockefeller delegate. Instead, he let it be known that he would seek appointment with all twenty-six Republican Governors, "to discuss the issues."

Agnew was the first of the pro-Rockefeller Governors Nixon saw. For two hours they talked alone in Nixon's Manhattan apartment over luncheon on March 29, eight days after the Rockefeller statement. Whereas in January Nixon dwelled on foreign issues, now Agnew drew him out on urban policy. Before parting, Nixon voiced an interest in hearing more about some of Agnew's programs in Maryland and they agreed that a Nixon staff aide would soon visit Annapolis. Agnew was impressed but unconvinced. On his way out he told reporters, "I am not ready to announce my support of Mr. Nixon at this time. I have a high regard for him. He's the front-runner." He also told them that he still believed Rockefeller was the best candidate.

His conversion from Rockefeller to Nixon might never have taken place except for the trauma of the Baltimore riots in early April. His speech writer Cynthia Rosenwald, who was privy to his thoughts as they developed, explains, "I think the event that changed his philosophy was the riot, not Rockefeller pulling out. . . . His consistency broke with those riots, right there. Crash. That was it. I think those riots scarred him and changed him from being, for the want of a better phrase, a New Deal Republican. They completely shattered his faith."

More cynical Agnew watchers believed that what really

transformed him into a potential Nixon man was the flood of plaudits from conservatives which followed his April 11 speech to the black leaders. Along with the outburst of conservative approbation came word that some of Rockefeller's advisors were embarrassed by his April 11 performance.

In any case, Agnew never came out for the Rockefeller team after the Baltimore riots. When the same old Draft Rockefeller faces gathered in Washington in mid-April to sound another summons, Agnew stayed away. When Rockefeller finally did get into the race on April 30, two planeloads of politicians and businessmen were airlifted to Albany for the grand event. The original Rockefeller drafter, Spiro Agnew, was in Hawaii helping his friend Bud Hammerman dedicate a new hotel in which he had an interest.

By that time, Agnew had decided that the only way to avoid a contentious state primary over convention delegates was to project himself as an unpledged favorite son. To implement this, Charlie Bresler met with Louise Gore and Rogers Morton, the resident Nixon agents, and they agreed to work out a deal on splitting the delegates. As part of the arrangement, Bresler had indicated that Agnew would keep an open mind about which candidate he would eventually support.

While their deal on delegates was being struck, Agnew found himself more and more attracted intellectually to what Nixon was saying. Toward the end of April he happened to spot in *Time* magazine a half-page excerpt from a radio speech by Nixon on the plight of blacks living in the slums. Nixon's answer was an idea Agnew had toyed with in the past: developing black capitalism, instead of pouring additional billions into government programs. So struck was

Agnew by Nixon's logic that he paraphrased part of the *Time* clipping in his next speech.

As for Rockefeller's just-announced plan for huge government programs to assault the problems of the slums, Agnew had a pungent critique. "It's just more of the same shit," he remarked to Bob Goodman. Nor was Agnew happy about Rockefeller's new dovish tendencies. "I read Nelson's statement on Vietnam, and I don't know what it says," he told a reporter.

Once Rockefeller became a candidate, his brain trust used every tactic in the book to recapture Agnew's favor. At one point his brother David Rockefeller, President of the Chase Manhattan Bank, even contacted fellow banker J. Walter Jones to explain just how Agnew got no telephone call on March 21. Jones passed along the message, but Agnew did not melt.

Another repair mission was attempted on May 17 when Rockefeller himself flew into Baltimore and delivered a public apology for "having gone the wrong way at the psychological moment" during the stage when Agnew wanted him to run. Later the Rockefeller forces arranged to have their candidate appear with Governor Agnew at a cocktail party in hopes that a tête-à-tête might deevlop. Dejectedly, they watched Agnew edge over to the side of the room, as far as possible from Rockefeller. "I've never seen him talk to more little old ladies," recalls one fellow guest. On their way out the two Governors spoke some pleasantries to each other, but that was all.

Rockefeller flew back to Baltimore on July 12 to play a final overture. This time he brought along the late Spyros Skouras, the seventy-two-year-old former President of 20th

Century-Fox Film Corporation, who had contributed the moderate sum of $1,000 to Agnew's campaign for Governor. Skouras tried over luncheon to rekindle the ashes for Rockefeller but got nowhere.

Richard Nixon, who knew a thing or two about ploys and counterploys, chose to dangle the Vice Presidential nomination in front of Agnew's nose the first time Rockefeller was on his way to Baltimore. Having been briefed on Rockefeller's planned trip, Nixon told *Washington Post* political reporter David Broder on May 16 that Agnew was among the men he had his eye on as possible running mates. The story was the freshest piece of gossip in Baltimore on the day Rockefeller arrived.

The following day Nixon told the rest of his press contingent that he was currently considering five men for Vice President: Senator Percy of Illinois plus Governors Schafer of Pennsylvania, Romney of Michigan, Rhodes of Ohio, and Agnew of Maryland.

When he got to Agnew's name, Nixon paused and added, "There is a man who has gained strong support because of his stand on cities." It was only a casual phrase, but it is suggestive of Nixon's original calculations about Agnew's attractiveness.

Over the next few months, the idea of Agnew as Vice-President grew on Nixon, particularly as he sharpened his private definition of what he wanted in a running mate. Intuitively, Nixon anticipated difficulties in working with anyone in the superstar category. "He wanted someone who was capable of working with him in a number 2 spot, and that is difficult to find in politics," is the way one of Nixon's strategists put it. Nixon's intuition was bolstered by some private polls by Opinion Research Corporation which showed him running better with no running mate than with any of the glittery combinations the staff could think up. Well before Miami Beach, Nixon decided that if he could manage it, he would rule out all candidates who would tend to polarize the party on any regional or liberal vs. conservative axis.

What Nixon was looking for was a center-of-the-center Republican who had demonstrated his pulling power in Democratic precincts. If possible, he should be a Governor or former Governor, to balance Nixon's own background in Congress and foreign policy. He must have good health, a distinguished manner, and the right age. Obviously he had to be scandalproof.

Naturally, Nixon also gave a lot of thought to how his number 2 man would perform if, as he antiseptically put it, "the need arose."

Nixon could have picked any one of twenty-five men who suited his minimum political requirements and would have sounded as plausible to the outside world as Spiro Agnew. During the spring and summer of 1968, he was thrown together with most of them in the course of his campaign, both in public and in private. Out of this crowd of potentials, Spiro Agnew was one of the few new faces who happened to make a stunningly positive personal impression.

Nixon was no doubt giving an honest playback of his own mental processes when he said, at a Key Biscayne cocktail party for the press immediately after the convention, "There can be a mystique about a man. You can look him in the eye and know he's got it. This guy has got it."

That impression began to coagulate in Nixon's mind at

their first two meetings, one in January courtesy of Louise Gore and the second in March thanks to Nelson Rockefeller. Although Nixon's aides made nothing of it at the time, later they would recall little remarks by Nixon about what a helluva guy Agnew was. They saw each other twice more before the convention—once on June 20 in New York and then on July 17, when Nixon came to Annapolis to dine at the Governor's mansion with the Maryland delegation. To Nixon's mind, Agnew was an imposing figure. And when he started talking about federalizing the welfare system or developing new towns, he seemed to know just what the problem of the cities was all about.

In his mawkish paean "Why I Chose Ted Agnew" written shortly after the convention, Nixon told why he had concluded that Agnew had the courage, character, and intellect to be President. "There is a quiet confidence about him," Nixon wrote. "In this atomic age the President is constantly facing the threat of nuclear war. Ted Agnew is the one in whom I would have confidence to face that threat." For someone whose only experience in international affairs was handling a tugboat strike in the port of Baltimore, that was quite a compliment.

On the basis of their four meetings Nixon could also write, "I know Ted Agnew well. We have had long and tough discussions. We have examined each other's ideas, debated issues, and tested each other. He has real depth and genuine warmth. . . ."

So Nixon came to Miami with a personal attraction toward Agnew as a human being. Beyond that, Agnew was in control of one of the three largest uncommitted delegations at a time Nixon was seeking desperately to pin down a first-ballot nomination. With hindsight, it is obvious that Agnew jumped the right way at the right time while the other uncommitted leaders switched to Nixon too late.

Throughout June and July, Agnew played the role of an uncommitted favorite son, saying he could live with Rockefeller, Nixon or Reagan. But as early as June 22, when the Maryland Republicans held their state convention in Annapolis, Nixon headquarters knew that Agnew was in the bag. Robert Ellsworth, who flew to Annapolis to represent Nixon's interest during the state convention, remembers knowing at the time that Agnew was committed. In retrospect, it seems quite possible that Agnew made his pledge during his two-hour unannounced talk with Nixon on June 20 at Nixon's Manhattan apartment. It is interesting that when reporters asked Agnew on June 20 whether he would consider taking a job in a Republican administration, he wouldn't say flatly no. "I would feel a responsibility to complete a major portion of this term," he said. ". . . So I suppose what I am saying is you have to hedge a little bit."

Nixon sensed great drama in the conversion of this one-time leader of the draft-Rockefeller movement. As the convention approached, he would sometimes remark to Senator John Tower of Texas, his Southern commander, that Agnew was a "real find." Perhaps due to a shortage of other last-minute converts, Nixon decided about a week before the convention to ask Agnew to deliver his nominating speech. It didn't take Agnew long to say yes.

Unaware of this, Rockefeller paid one last visit to Agnew in Miami Beach, but to no avail. On Monday, August 4, as Nixon was landing in Miami to take charge of his troops during convention week, Agnew made public his conversion.

Nixon remained aboard his plane for ten minutes so that his arrival would not cut into the TV coverage of Agnew's announcement.

Late that night, as Agnew worked on his nominating speech, he received a confidential visitor from high in the Nixon entourage. The visitor was Nixon's dour campaign manager, John Mitchell. For about an hour they talked alone in Agnew's suite at the Eden Roc and then Mitchell left without being noticed by anyone. His message, as it filtered down to Agnew's inner circle, was that Nixon was very high on Agnew as a possible running mate and he wanted to know whether Governor Agnew would accept.

When Agnew was asked at a press conference on January 9, 1968, whether he would accept the Vice Presidency, he categorically said no. "I am not under any circumstances a candidate, [and I] would not accept such a nomination if it were offered," he declared. "I guess that lays it to rest completely." [1] Nonetheless, when the cup was passed to him by the midnight emissary, his ambition wouldn't let him say no. His visitor hinted at one possible hooker that could spoil his chances: it was vital for Nixon to win on the first ballot, and that might have to mean a deal with Governor Rhodes of Ohio. At that point Rhodes' candidate for Vice President was New York Mayor John Lindsay.

Jim Rhodes, of all people. It was enough to provide some comic relief during the next two and a half nervous days of waiting. The Sunday before the convention opened, Agnew and Rhodes had been on the fourth hole of a golf game in Miami when an attendant ran out to say that Nancy Dickerson and an NBC crew were on the way to do an interview. "Rhodes reacted as if he had just placed his hands on a hot griddle," Agnew told the story later. The Ohio Governor, loath to be photographed on a golf course, tried to escape through the clubhouse, with Agnew tagging along behind.

Finding the camera crew was already there, Rhodes hustled Agnew into an electric cart and they drove the wrong way down the ninth fairway until they reached an eight-foot wire fence. Standing on the golf cart, Agnew hoisted one leg over the top. But the other one wouldn't make it—panic, he was stuck. Only after someone found a ladder were Agnew and Rhodes able to get away. "Nobody in Ohio knows I golf yet," Rhodes told Agnew later. (One wonders whether Nixon would have picked Agnew if Nancy Dickerson's crew had caught him stuck on the fence.)

Agnew's nominating speech on Wednesday evening was no better or worse than the average for its genre. "When a nation is in crisis and when history speaks firmly to that nation that it needs a man to match the times—you don't create such a man; you don't discover such a man; you recognize such a man!" he intoned. For what it was worth, Nixon thought it was a brilliant performance.

All Wednesday evening and into Thursday morning, nominating speeches were followed by seconding speeches which were followed by "spontaneous" floor demonstrations. It was nearly 2 A.M. when Nixon learned for sure that he had won on the first ballot, without any help from Rhodes. The crises had passed and now came what he recognized in his book *Six Crises* as the moment of maximum peril: "the period immediately after the battle is over" when "there is an increased possibility of error because [an individual] may lack the necessary cushion of emotional and mental reserve which is essential for good judgment."

Even so, there were certain party customs that he thought

could not be bypassed or delayed. One of them was the formal convening of party leaders to jaw-jaw about the Vice-Presidency. Eisenhower had called such a meeting in 1952, at which the leaders picked Nixon out of a list of names submitted by Eisenhower. In 1960 Nixon presided over the post-midnight gathering of thirty-five top Republicans who recommended, almost to a man, that he pick Henry Cabot Lodge—his private choice all along.[2]

In Miami Beach the ritual of consultations began at 2:00 A.M. and ended ten and a half hours later, after not one meeting but four. First came a forty-five-minute gathering of about twenty-five key Nixon campaign workers, men like John Mitchell, Peter Flanigan, Frank Shakespeare, and Maurice Stans. The next meeting went from about 3:00 A.M. to 5:30 A.M., after which Nixon took a break for a few hours of sleep. A third meeting lasted from 9:00 A.M. to midmorning. The second and third meetings were for the permanent party establishment, minus nearly all liberals and Rockefeller backers. Senators Dirksen, Tower, Fannin, Goldwater, Mundt, Thurmond, Miller, and Fong were all there. But Senators Javits, Goodell, Percy, Aiken, Brooke, and Cooper were not. The list also included an assortment of Republican State Chairmen, Governors, elder statesmen, and Congressmen. And, for some reason, Nixon's friend the Reverend Dr. Billy Graham.

After hearing the inputs, Nixon assembled six men in his penthouse suite at midmorning to make the decision: H. R. "Bob" Haldeman, John Mitchell, Robert Finch, Robert Ellsworth, John Tower, and Rogers Morton. The participants in the fourth meeting made up the top command of his campaign organization.

The four discussions that morning turned out to be like

sifting gravel through a series of screens, each with successively smaller mesh. The larger particles—Lindsay and Reagan—were the first to be eliminated. Lindsay was nixed by Thurmond and Goldwater. Then Thurmond's candidate, Ronald Reagan, was blocked by objections that he was too controversial or wouldn't run.

The next-size mesh filtered out Percy (the Illinois delegation was mad at his defection to Rockefeller), Hatfield (too dovish), Romney (unpopular with the Southerners and considered a lightweight by the press), and Tower (a liability in the North).

Once the superstars and even the lesser lights were out, there were six men who still had a chance. One indication of Nixon's strategic thoughts is that four of the six who passed through the initial filtration process were from the Southern border states. From Tennessee came freshman Senator Howard Baker, who was Everett Dirksen's son-in-law. From Texas there was Representative George Bush, whose father had been a Senator from Connecticut. And from Maryland, which had never before had a Vice President of any party, there were two finalists: Agnew and Rogers Morton. The two others still in contention were Nixon's personal friend Robert Finch, who was Lieutenant Governor of California, and John Volpe, the Governor of Massachusetts.

As it came down toward the point of decision, Nixon went around the room calling on his advisers one by one with his index finger. The final choice was so close that if anyone had said something damaging about Agnew and his land deals, he would not have been picked. As it was, all the finalists had accumulated a certain number of negative comments during the night, and the minuses almost balanced out. Bush was only a Congressman. Baker had been in the Senate only two years. Morton was only a Congressman. Finch was too close to Nixon, so it would look like nepotism. Volpe was from Massachusetts, and everyone knew the Republicans could never win Massachusetts. Agnew was unknown.

About noon it came down to a choice between Agnew, Volpe, and Finch. When Nixon finally made a move, it was oddly elliptical: he offered the job to his old friend Bob Finch. The curious part is that Finch had told him ahead of time that he would not take the nomination unless Nixon flatly commanded him to accept. As they talked it over that morning, Nixon's words to Finch amounted to an offer—but not a command. As Nixon was nearly sure he would, Finch turned it down.

That left Volpe and Agnew, the two ethnics. In Nixon's mind Volpe's Italian Catholic background was a strong plus, in keeping with his private theory that the Italian vote would be the next ethnic bloc to swing over permanently to the Republicans. Volpe's problem was that he was Governor of the wrong state. And there was some question among the Nixon advisors of whether he had the Presidential image.

For reasons he keeps to himself, John Volpe was certain that Nixon was going to pick *him* that morning. When he was told that Agnew had been chosen instead, he was "floored." Even after joining Nixon's Cabinet, Volpe once wistfully remarked, "I guess there is nothing sure in life until you have a written contract."

Nixon made the final selection himself without taking a vote. The ten and a half hours of meetings had sifted all the others out and he was left with Spiro Agnew, someone he had liked from the start. When he tried that day to explain why to one advisor, he dwelled on his observation that Agnew was a real *man*. "You mean he is a *mensch?*" asked his aide, using the familiar Yiddish word. Nixon did not know what a *mensch* was. But when the aide explained it, he said, "Yes, that's it!"

Only a few in Agnew's entourage at the Eden Roc shared the secret of his midnight visitor from Nixon's headquarters three nights earlier. On Tuesday Walter Jones and Agnew had talked quite casually about where they could get away to play golf for a few days after the convention. With Agnew's assent, Jones made reservations for a golfing weekend at the Lucaya Beach Hotel in the Bahamas, known primarily as a gambling spa. They had planned to fly across that morning, even before the Vice Presidential nomination, but at 8 A.M. Agnew called Jones to say there would be a slight delay because he was still one of the ten men under consideration. At 9:30 A.M. he called Jones back to say he should come over to the room because it was down to four names.

In Agnew's suite everyone was watching TV and trying to be casual. "No news is good news," Bob Goodman told the Governor hopefully. Nixon's publicity men had promised a decision by 11 A.M., but the hour passed with no development. On television, the reporters were filling time trying to put together clues on Nixon's thinking, and they weren't assigning Agnew much chance.

At 12:22 P.M. the telephone rang. It was Rogers Morton on the phone, asking for the Governor. "Ted, are you sitting down?" Morton asked him. "Here's a friend who wants to talk to you." The friend was Richard Nixon.

Watching Agnew's face, Agnew's aides saw no hint of elation. Herb Thompson thought it was simply a courtesy call to a losing candidate, even when Agnew said into the mouthpiece, "I'm deeply honored." The way Agnew broke the news was to turn toward Judy and form two silent words with his lips: "I'm it."

13

"It's just that I've stayed still while literally thousands of
people have rushed past me in a wild dash to the left."

The Proper Usage of
a Household Word

What we have all come to love—or hate—about Spiro Agnew is his mouth.

Take Debbie Stepanovitch, for instance. "I just love him—
there is a certain fire and rage about him," exclaimed the
nineteen-year-old Miss Indiana College Republican of 1970.
"I admire him because he stands up for what he believes
even though I don't agree with him about everything."

Or take "L.P.," the former New Deal Democrat who wrote
to the *Washington Star:* "Mr. Agnew—bless his plainspoken
heart—is articulating the precise feelings of us taxpaying, non-
squawking, law-abiding, out-of-patience squares."

Or listen to black Congressman William Clay, a Democrat
from St. Louis: "Apparently Mr. Agnew is an intellectual
sadist who experiences intellectual orgasms by attacking, humiliating, and kicking the oppressed."

Or consider the words of the late Democratic Secretary of

State, Dean Acheson: "I get a great deal of pleasure out of Agnew. I don't agree with him. I know him fairly well, and I've protested to him that he would do better to do less of this [criticizing the press], but I don't feel this is McCarthy at all."

Never in history, except possibly when Henry Wallace was in office, have so many Americans gotten so stirred up about their Vice President. A man who was picked out of nowhere at the 1968 Republican Convention has become not only a household word but a playroom word. By the Christmas of 1971 the toy industry had given us the Spiro T. Agnew American History Game, the Spiro Agnew jigsaw puzzle showing him in a Superman suit, and the miniature drag racer called the "hard hat hauler" with Agnew's picture engraved on one wheel. Like the Kennedys, Spiro Agnew is no longer a mere politician but a part of our pop culture.

To get a sense of the man's impact on our political life one should follow him to one of his least dramatic performances, the kind one would never see on Walter Cronkite. For instance, the Vice President's visit to Indianapolis on September 23, 1970.

As campaign stops go, it was pretty dull stuff for the national press corps. From touchdown to takeoff, Agnew spent less than eight hours in Indianapolis, most of it in his hotel room. He stopped for four minutes at a cocktail party for $1,000 contributors and he gave one speech at a sweaty indoor rally. What he had to say, to quote a local columnist, was "pretty ordinary politicalese, unworthy of so grand a gutfighter." And yet the cumulative effect of his rather drab appearance was awesome.

The reason Agnew went to Indiana was Republican Senate

candidate Richard "Roudy" Roudebush, a colorless conservative Congressman who looked a bit like Mayor Daley. The polls showed Roudy slightly behind the incumbent Democrat, Senator Vance Hartke, a cautious liberal whose campaign manager had just gotten him to lose some weight so he would look more like a Senator.

The mere announcement of Agnew's visit precipitated a decision that probably would not have been made for any previous Vice President. With only slight coaxing from Roudebush's television consultant, four Indiana television stations and twelve radio stations decided that Agnew's political visit was such a newsworthy event that they would arrange to broadcast his entire speech as a special news program. In Indianapolis, Agnew was important enough to preempt "The Beverly Hillbillies."

The speech Agnew read at the rally was a blunt instrument, devoid of alliterative gems. To some at the dinner, it sounded just like the stuff Roudebush had been saying in his own campaign speeches. This was no coincidence. L. Keith Bulen, the Indiana Republican National Committeeman, had passed the word to the Agnew plane that the Vice President should come down hard on a few simple issues, like law-and-order, big spending, and loyalty to the President. To Bulen's professional eye, it was a fine speech. "We didn't need any cute sophisticated clichés in here," he said.

The next morning at Roudebush's advertising agency, a media expert calculated what one drab visit by the Vice President had meant. It meant that without any cost to Roudebush, 53 percent of the homes in Indiana were within viewing distance of Agnew's full speech. Probably 500,000 of the state's 2,600,000 registered voters watched him denouncing Hartke as a radical liberal, according to the media man's estimates. That did not count people who saw only film excerpts on regular news programs. If Roudebush had been forced to buy the half-hour slot on four stations as a paid political announcement, the bill would have been only $2,880, cash in advance, plus another $2,000 to rent a "remote truck." But the audience would undoubtedly have been smaller because news specials almost always outdraw paid politicals.

The Republican dinner drew 4,207 customers at $100 apiece. "This is the most successful fund-raising dinner in the history of Indiana," Earl Butz, Citizens Finance Chairman (who would become Secretary of Agriculture), told his fellow guests. "There are many ways to value you, Mr. Vice President, but those of us on the finance committee think you are worth a great deal." (Across town, the Democrats held a fund raiser for their Senate candidate the same night. With no national luminary, the gross was $450 in cash plus $650 in pledges.)

The day after Agnew and his entourage had flown on to Washington I stood on a street corner in downtown Indianapolis and asked 100 people whether they had heard or watched the speech; 24 said yes. For those who missed it, Roudebush headquarters proceeded to edit the tape of Agnew's speech into 20-second, 30-second, 60-second, and 5-minute commercials to be broadcast straight through election day.

Hartke countered by demanding equal air time. The request was granted, and the Democrats used their free half hour for a rebuttal by Senator Birch Bayh that made little reference to Agnew. "We feel Agnew hurt us, despite the free time," said Hartke's campaign manager, Jacques LeRoy, after the campaign. "If someone calls you names, a certain percentage of the people are going to believe it."

In the end, Roudy Roudebush lost by 4,283 votes despite another jet stop by Agnew, two visits by President Nixon, one by Mrs. Nixon, and half a dozen assorted appearances by Cabinet members. His loss didn't negate the curious fact that on September 23, 1970, a Vice President materialized on an estimated 500,000 Hoosier picture tubes even though he had nothing special to say.

The interplay between Spiro Agnew and the media forms one of the arresting paradoxes of his life. Few politicians in American history have owed so much of their prominence to the media. And yet no national leader has ever devoted as much effort and prestige to castigating the electronic and pencil press.

Agnew sincerely believes that there are liberal elements in the media that are hell-bent to destroy him. "They will pick up one phrase, strip away its qualifications, and attempt to use it as a hammer to drive you into the floor with," he told an English TV audience in 1970. What's more, he said, whenever he gave a speech that was bland and positive, the story was trimmed down and printed back with the obituaries.

In the same interview Agnew gave his British listeners a remarkably candid glimpse at his psychology of prominence. "In a desire to be heard," he said, "I have to throw them what people in American politics call a little red meat once in a while, and hope that in spite of the damaging context in which those remarks are often repeated, that other things that I think are very important will also appear."

In the early years of his political career Agnew nurtured

a symbiotic relationship with the venerable *Baltimore Sun* and its stepsister the *Evening Sun*. He freely admitted that as a minority party politician, he would be dead without the *Sun* papers. As County Executive he made a practice of holding a long lunch at Sabatino's, his favorite Italian restaurant, every couple of months with the local editorial writers of the Baltimore papers. Seldom would he make an important announcement without trying to sniff out the reaction in advance. Dutch Moore, then his confidential secretary, contends that Agnew sometimes would drop an idea just because the editorial writers didn't like it—or even latch onto something because it would win him a positive editorial.

The enemies Agnew made in the press were mostly among the weekly newspapers. His hottest feud was with the late Paul Morgan, owner of the *Reisterstown Community News* and the *Catonsville Herald Argus*. Angry at Morgan for what he considered one-sided journalism, Agnew retaliated by smiting him in the ledgers. "I probably control half of all the county's legal advertising," Agnew said in October 1965. "As it stands now, none of that is going to Paul Morgan's papers. . . . It's not a personal vendetta. It's because he consistently goes beyond the bounds of correct reporting. He never carries our side of the story. He never will print our replies to charges he has aired."

Although Agnew was sometimes criticized by the press during his Towson phase, he never had to cope with teams of investigative reporters boring into his questionable dealings. When potentially damaging stories popped up in the normal course of covering the county, the papers published them. But because Agnew seemed cleaner than the average local politician, the *Sun* papers and the Hearst-owned *Baltimore*

News-American often let stories die without investing the effort to check out all the angles. Agnew's move to dump Charlie Steinbock from the Board of Appeals (see Chapter One) is one example. Six months before Steinbock's public charges that Agnew had intervened in a zoning case and then dumped him when he wouldn't go along, Steinbock told the same story privately to reporter Stuart Smith of the *Baltimore Sun*. Smith passed the information to his city desk, but the story was killed without a full investigation because Steinbock was reluctant to be quoted.

Another story the Baltimore papers did not vigorously investigate was Baltimore County's so-called "broker of record" controversy. In November 1965 the Democrats on the County Council discovered that early in his term as County Executive, Agnew had written a letter to three loyal Republicans naming them as "brokers of record" to handle group insurance for county employees. Gleefully the Democratic Councilmen forced Agnew to rescind his commitment on the ground that all contracts of more than $25,000 required Council approval. "Yes, it's patronage," Agnew finally conceded. "But bear in mind that these are not just people picked to be recipients of political largesse. These are full-time insurance people."

When he was finally forced to cancel the insurance commitment, Agnew charged that the newspapers had "victimized" him. Actually, it now appears that their coverage was not aggressive enough. Looking back now, the former County Solicitor, Scott Moore, and his brother Dutch recollect that Agnew's "broker of record" letter was written to fulfill a commitment he made *before* the 1962 election. If that is true, the County Executive may have violated a section of the state election law dealing with preelection promises. But in 1971, the trail is too cold to say so with certainty. One of the three brokers, Everett Hay, says Agnew made no preelection deal on insurance business. Another broker, Agnew's old friend Clarke Langrall, says Agnew did make a commitment—not to him, but to Everett Hay. One thing is clear: back in 1965 the scent was ripe to be followed, but the papers failed to pursue it. Nor did they follow the smell of Agnew's Anne Arundel County land deal during the 1966 campaign.

Agnew's intimacy with the media began to fade after his first six months as Governor. Reporters covering the statehouse began getting irate early morning calls from Agnew when he didn't like their stories. One statehouse newspaperman says Agnew called him "the worst fucking reporter in the state of Maryland."

After six years of generally favorable editorials, Agnew was mad and upset when the *Evening Sun* printed an editorial criticizing his handling of the campus disruptions at Bowie State in April 1968. "That was the beginning of the end as far as his relations with the *Sun* papers went," says his friend George White. "I will always claim it was like a lover's quarrel. Agnew was their boy, and then he disappointed them. Brad Jacobs [editor of the *Evening Sun*] was in love with Agnew before that. Afterward he was just like a jilted lover."

Over the next few months the newspapers pictured him as growing more conservative, but Agnew disagreed.

"It's just that I've stayed still while literally thousands of people have rushed past me in a wild dash to the left," he said in a month before he was nominated for the Vice Presidency. "And I believe this is happening particularly with regard to certain of the news media. I think the media are involved in a headlong rush to the left—great numbers of them."

What convinced Agnew the liberal press was trying to crush him was the treatment he got during the 1968 campaign, starting with the "fat Jap" incident. One day in September as the Vice Presidential campaign jet was leaving Las Vegas, the candidate walked back through the aisle of the rear cabin to exchange what he considered a little masculine humor with the traveling press corps. "What's the matter with the fat Jap?" he asked Dick Homan of the *Washington Post* about Homan's seat partner, Gene Oishi of the *Baltimore Sun*.

"Did he say what I think he said?" asked Mike Weiss of the *Evening Sun,* leaning over his seat when Agnew walked away.

After a while Oishi woke up from his nap and heard from the other reporters what Agnew had said. Apparently the point of Agnew's jest had been that after an evening in wide-open Las Vegas, Oishi looked exhausted. Oishi's immediate reaction to hearing himself described as the "fat Jap" was to let the remark pass. Homan and some of the other reporters wanted to file something on it, but Oishi thought his own editors would be upset if a *Baltimore Sun* reporter became a participant in the news. Mainly out of deference to Oishi's feelings, nobody wrote the story that day. Instead, Homan tossed off a mock press release calling Agnew a "squishy soft Greek." [1] When it was passed forward to Agnew's compartment, the candidate wrote across the top, "If the fat Jap would lay off those TV dinners, he'd become a flat Jap."

Later in the week, Oishi felt less and less amused by the

"fat Jap" label, particularly after getting his wife's angry reaction on the telephone. When the *Time* correspondent, Charles Eisendrath, asked Oishi for permission to include the incident in his weekly file, Oishi finally said yes. Hearing that Eisendrath had written it, Homan got Oishi's permission to mention something in the *Washington Post,* so he wouldn't be scooped. As it happened, *Time* didn't print a word, but Homan's brief account ran as he wrote it at the end of his column-and-a-half story.

One reader who was not amused when he read the *Post* story was Democratic Representative Spark Matsunaga of Hawaii. When he walked into his office that morning, he had already written out a two-hundred-word statement in long-hand. As soon as it was typed he hurried over to the Capitol and was given permission to address the House out of turn. Matsunaga made the point that both "Polacks" and "Japs" are derogatory words,[2] and Agnew "should be instructed that one does not make friends by insulting people of other racial background, particularly through mouthings of racial preju-dice." Unhappily for Agnew, the story broke while he was campaigning in Hawaii, of all places, where 28 percent of the population is of Japanese origin. Suddenly all sorts of suspicions darkened the minds of Agnew and his traveling staff. All along there had been bitterness against Oishi and the other Annapolis reporters for not giving the rest of the national press more favorable fill-ins on Agnew's achieve-ments. Now, it looked as though Homan and Oishi had am-bushed them by holding back a nasty story for two days just to multiply its impact. Later, that rumor was discovered to be unfounded, but a second suspicion replaced the first: that Homan had not wanted to file the story but the *Washington*

Post's national editor, Richard Harwood, insisted on putting it in the paper. That wasn't true either, but it helped to set Agnew's mind about the editors of the *Washington Post*. If that wasn't enough to prejudice him, the *Post* editorialized that his selection as a Vice Presidential candidate was "perhaps the most eccentric political appointment since the Roman Emperor Caligula named his horse a consul."

The New York Times joined the *Washington Post* on Agnew's list of hate objects ten days before the election when it published a six-paragraph editorial headlined "Mr. Agnew's Fitness." In retrospect (see Chapter Nine), the editorial was on the mark in its central allegation: "It now develops that as a Zoning Board member, as Chief Executive of Baltimore County and as Governor of Maryland, Mr. Agnew has been the political ally and financial partner of a group of wealthy land speculators. These businessmen have made sizable fortunes out of developing land in suburban Baltimore over the past fifteen years, in part because of favorable zoning and government decisions, and Mr. Agnew's financial net worth has also risen sharply. . . ."

What could have been a disaster for Agnew turned out amazingly well. Over the next week it developed that the *Times* lacked the hard evidence to document its allegations, even though its reporter Ben Franklin had parked in Towson for days investigating Agnew's past. Agnew and his lawyers were able to seize on two factual errors in the *Times* editorial.

First, the *Times* suggested that Agnew was in conflict of interest because he was a director of the Chesapeake National Bank at the same time he was responsible as Governor for supervising banks in Maryland. The trouble was Chesapeake National was a national bank, and Governors only supervise state banks. Second, the *Times* suggested that Agnew sold his land on the probable approach route to the Chesapeake Bay Bridge only after he became Governor and after he participated in the decision to approve the bridge route. As Agnew was only too happy to point out to the *Times,* he actually disposed of the land through an irrevocable trust before he was elected Governor.

Although no one realized it at the time, the *Times'* real mistake was in not pouring half a dozen investigative reporters into Maryland as soon as Ben Franklin found his first interesting clues. A team of reporters would probably have discovered Agnew's unsecured loan, his forgotten rezoning, his silent partners in the Virgin Islands, and perhaps a few other nuggets no one has yet found. As it was, the *Times* had a weak case.

Instead of turning against his running mate, Richard Nixon accused the *Times* of "the lowest kind of gutter politics." In the face of Agnew's threat of a libel suit, the *Times* issued several clarifications but would not back down. However, the *Washington Post* and the *Baltimore Sun,* which had both endorsed the Democratic ticket, handed Agnew an apparent vindication by writing stiff editorials charging that the *Times* was off base.

Even after the election, the mood toward the press in Agnew's inner circle was a mix of hurt and hatred. One bit of evidence I happened to overhear personally. Fifteen minutes after Richard Nixon's victory statement at the Waldorf-Astoria in New York, about twenty Nixon and Agnew advance men gathered in the littered but empty ballroom for their last meeting. Nixon's chief advance man, John Ehrlichman, opened the session by congratulating them for "the most consummate job in the history of American politics." Then he delivered the happy hint that he would soon see many of them in Washington. The next speaker was Roy Goodearle, Agnew's chief advance man and now his senior assistant for national affairs. "Why don't we all get a member of the press and beat them up?" Goodearle suggested. "I'm tired of being nice to them."

Agnew kept his own emotions hidden not much longer than Goodearle did. At a closed meeting of Republican Governors in December, the Vice President-elect attacked *The New York Times* and *Newsweek* as "executionary journals." There were other publications, he said, that were "fit only to line the bottom of birdcages." A few weeks later he disclosed in a television interview that at one point in the campaign he thought of quitting, after one press comment he considered particularly unfair. But, he said, "I began to think, 'If you can't develop a little skin—enough to take a few reverses, you can't handle this job.' And from that time on I had no trouble."

Although his ego was scarred during the campaign, he had no inclination during his first months as Vice President to make a public issue of his complaints against the media. His earliest press strategy, in fact, was to become blander and less direct about stating his convictions. As he told interviewer Mike Wallace three weeks before Inauguration Day, "I think that I can tell [my critics] what kind of a person I am in a different way, a more careful way, a less frank way." When Wallace asked him whether he thought frankness in politics was dangerous, Agnew replied, "Exactly. Total frankness in politics—where there's not a chance to see the person in the context of the entire situation—is dangerous because a flick of a picture, a part of a statement without the modifications that go with it, can be terribly damaging." [3]

Agnew recognized that he came into office with an image problem of horrendous proportions. "Six months ago I was a fairly popular and successful Governor," he grumbled. "Now I'm being called the village idiot." The remedy he adopted was to work with visible diligence at learning his new job, and it worked. Within his first two months in office his village idiot image began to wither. In its place a revisionist view took root among the Washington press corps that was capsulized by a *Wall Street Journal* headline on March 14: "Agnew Treads Softly, Works Hard to Ease Inept Campaign Image; He Does Homework, Makes Contributions in Meetings, But Says Little in Public; Still a Question Mark to Some."

Then, at the annual dinners of the Gridiron Club and the White House Radio and Television Correspondents Association, the Vice President unleashed an unsuspected talent for self-deprecating humor. "I deeply appreciate the fact that the President has ordered that I be issued my own plane," he deadpanned. "It's *Air Force 13*—and it's a glider." He followed with a string of one-liners about his thorough policy briefings ("Right now I'm studying the AMB"), his access to the White House ("I can only come in with the tours, but still it's wonderful"), and his service to Nixon ("This morning I served his sweet rolls and marmalade"). *Time,* in a story headlined "Agnew Ascendant," called his assortment of gags "some of the best political punchlines heard in a long time." [4]

Agnew the tough-mouth social critic reappeared for the first time on June 7, 1969, at a commencement speech at

Ohio State. "A society which fears its children is effete," he declared. "A sniveling, hand-wringing power structure deserves the violent rebellion it encourages. If my generation doesn't stop cringing, yours will inherit a lawless society where emotion and muscle displace reason." The story made page one of the *Washington Post,* but any excitement soon passed.

As the Vietnam protests rose toward their autumn crescendo during the Moratorium and the New Mobe, it fell to Agnew to trumpet back the Administration's countermelody in his own way. Most of the Administration reacted in muted tones to the outpouring of peace sentiment on Moratorium Day, and Agnew's ghostwritten text for his speech four days after the Moratorium was similarly bland. But for Agnew this was a moment to unsheathe his old shrill flair with words. When he finished reworking the draft of his October 19 fund-raising speech in New Orleans, he had written 80 percent of it himself—including a razor phrase about "an effete corps of impudent snobs" that would nick a national nerve.

Sometimes, it appears that we are reaching a period when our senses and our minds will no longer respond to moderate stimulation. We seem to be approaching an age of the gross. Persuasion through speeches and books is too often discarded for disruptive demonstrations aimed at bludgeoning the unconvinced into action.

The young—and I don't mean by any stretch of the imagination all the young, I'm talking about those who claim to speak for the young—at the zenith of physical power and sensitivity, overwhelm themselves with drugs and artificial stimulants. Subtlety is lost, and fine distinctions based on acute reasoning are carelessly ignored in a headlong jump to a predetermined conclusion. Life is visceral rather than intellectual, and the most visceral practitioners of life are those who characterize themselves as intellectuals.

Truth to them is "revealed" rather than logically proved, and the principal infatuations of today revolve around the social sciences, those subjects which can accommodate any opinion and about which the most reckless conjecture cannot be discredited.

Education is being redefined at the demand of the uneducated to suit the ideas of the uneducated. The student now goes to college to proclaim rather than to learn. The lessons of the past are ignored or obliterated in a contemporary antagonism known as the generation gap. A spirit of national masochism prevails, encouraged by an effete corps of impudent snobs who characterize themselves as intellectuals.

That final bit of verbal arrhythmia was the lead-in for his denunciation of the Moratorium kids.

Thousands of well motivated young people, conditioned since childhood to respond to great emotional appeals, saw fit to demonstrate for peace. Most did not stop to consider that the leaders of the Moratorium had billed it as a massive public outpouring of sentiment against the foreign policy of the President of the United States. Most did not care to be reminded that the leaders of the Moratorium refused to disassociate themselves from the objectives enunciated by the enemy in Hanoi.

If the Moratorium had any use whatever, it served as an emotional purgative for those who felt the need to cleanse themselves of their lack of ability to offer a constructive solution to the problem. . . .

Only once before, when he took on the black leaders of Baltimore, had he evoked such passion with something he meant to say, and this time the waves spread nationwide. As in his first experience with high-voltage reactions, the formula for making electricity was shrillness multiplied by timing. In the next few emotional weeks, Agnew continued his Soccit Tuum performances against the "merchants of hate," the "parasites of passion," the "ideological eunuchs," not to mention those who "treat the South as a punching bag."

The media's revisionist view of Agnew as a quiet, hard-working, self-spoofing learner now had to be revised once again. Here obviously was a figure to be reckoned with, if not feared. "He is emerging as a kind of *mahdi* of Middle America," declared *Time* in a cover story. ". . . Armored in the certitudes of middle-class values, he speaks with the authentic voice of Americans who are angry and frightened by what has happened to their culture, who view the '60s as a disastrous montage of pornography, crime, assaults on patriotism, flaming ghettos, marijuana, and occupied colleges."

For the first time in years, a Vice President was beginning to create his own magnetic field. Lined up on the left were the *Washington Post,* which called on Nixon to "repudiate the excesses of his Vice President or silence him or—ideally—do both," plus various columnists such as Michael Harrington, who called him "the Joe McCarthyite spokesman for an administration which once pretended it wanted to bring the nation together."

There were anomalies in the lines of force toward the right. To columnist William S. White, "Agnew is day by day becoming Mr. Conservative." To his fellow conservative columnist James J. Kilpatrick, Agnew "will emerge from the hustings as a national hero."

But to the guru of the thinking right, William F. Buckley Jr., what made Agnew worth a column was that his celebrated line about "impudent snobs" was a case of inelegant writing. "It was careless, silly, and analytically indefensible,"

Buckley pronounced, adding, "Agnew is not skilled in polemics, and therefore should not engage in them without help."

To the mildly conservative *Washington Star,* the problem with Agnew's semantics was not the craftmanship but the wisdom. Recalling Nixon's inaugural address, the *Star* editorial complained that "Agnew raised his voice in a manner calculated to widen the gulf that exists on the question of how and when to wind up the Vietnam war."

On the night of November 13, 1969, a group of Republican contributors gathered in the staid elegance of Washington's Sulgrave Club expecting to see the Vice President, but they were in for a disappointment. "He was called away," Mrs. Judy Agnew informed them, "to make another one of his famous speeches."

Although she didn't say so, her husband had grave qualms about the speech he would deliver that evening at a meeting of the Mid-West Regional Republican Committee in Des Moines, Iowa.

Planting all those banderillas into the backs of liberals, drug users, students, social scientists, and black militants had been his idea. But now President Nixon wanted him to get into the ring with a far more devastating creature: the media. Although he had no lack of antagonism against liberals in the press, he wondered about the political wisdom of starting what would be a ritual combat. But a tough draft of the speech had been written by Patrick Buchanan, Nixon's conservative in the White House speech-writing shop, and checked with Nixon's chief of staff, Bob Haldeman. Haldeman left no doubt in Agnew's mind that the President himself wanted the assignment carried out. Agnew's relationship with the President was such that he probably could have declined. He weighed the implications and finally decided to go ahead, after junking certain parts of Buchanan's draft which troubled him the most and adding some words of his own.

Columnist Kevin Phillips, the one-time assistant to Attorney General John Mitchell, has disclosed that on the day he gave the speech Agnew told his advance man, "Well, they really ****** me this time. After this speech, I might as well give up. I can never run again. The media will kill me."

From the viewpoint of Nixon and Haldeman, what necessitated the Des Moines speech was a round of unfriendly television commentaries immediately following Nixon's Vietnam address ten days earlier. Among the more galling offenders were Marvin Kalb of CBS, who questioned the President's interpretation of a letter from Ho Chi Minh, and Frank Reynolds of ABC who said, "There was in his speech no new initiative, no new proposal, no announcement of any more troop withdrawals, and, in short, Mr. Nixon has taken a hard line. . . ." ABC added to its sins by inviting Averell Harriman to join its panel of commentators.

So it was that Vice President Agnew let himself be nudged into the most important and lasting action of his public life. It was a meaty speech he gave in Des Moines. Not only did it deplore the "instant analysis and querulous criticism" served up by "a small band of network commentators and self-appointed analysts," but it also struck at the whole system of network television news.

"A small group of men, numbering perhaps no more than a dozen 'anchormen,' commentators, and executive producers, settles upon the twenty minutes or so of film and commentary that is to reach the public," Agnew read. By their power they can "elevate men from local obscurity to national prominence within a week" or create doubts about a government policy "with a raised eyebrow, an inflection of a voice, a caustic remark."

And who belongs to this "tiny and closed fraternity of privileged men, elected by no one and enjoying a monopoly sanctioned and licensed by government?" To a man they live and work in New York City or Washington, they read the same newspapers, they draw their political and social views from the same sources, they reinforce their shared viewpoints by talking constantly to each other.

His solution was not censorship but public pressure for "responsible" news. "The people can register their complaints on bias through mail to the networks and phone calls to local stations," he helpfully suggested.

The speech ended with some bait to draw the networks into maximum coverage. "Whether what I have said to you tonight will be heard and seen at all by the nation is not my decision," he said, "it is not your decision; it is their decision." Advance texts had been delivered to the networks by Herb Klein's office in Washington, and the bait worked. All three networks felt compelled to broadcast the Des Moines speech live during prime time, giving Agnew an audience of perhaps 40,000,000.

It was the kind of speech everyone could react to, and did. Lines to the networks, the stations, and even the White House were clogged with messages, mostly pro-Agnew. In Congress, the sentiments of nearly everyone but the liberal Democrats was summed up by Senate Republican Leader Hugh Scott of Pennsylvania, who said "the networks deserve a good goosing." Senator Stephen M. Young, the eighty-year-old Ohio Democrat, said it for the liberals: "I thought it was a scurrilous speech."

From the networks came sounds of pain. "An appeal to prejudice," NBC President Julian Goodman called it. Frank Stanton of CBS said it was an unprecedented attempt "to intimidate a news medium which depends for its existence upon government licenses." At ABC, President Leonard H. Goldenson said his network "will continue to report the news accurately and fully, confident in the ultimate judgment of the American people." Privately, broadcasters worried what Agnew meant by his pointed reference to a recent Supreme Court decision that gave radio and TV newscasters less Constitutional protection than newspapers.

The gush of newspaper editorials contained some that made delightful reading for the Vice President. The *Chicago Tribune* spoke of his "temperate and reasoned appraisal of some lopsided emphasis by network news reporters and commentators." The *Newark News* declared that "Mr. Agnew wasn't raising the hobgoblin of censorship." And the *Pittsburgh Press* offered the opinion that his criticism may have "a beneficial effect by prompting all concerned to try harder and do better." Numbering among the others who liked it were the *Washington Star*, *The State* (Columbia, South Carolina), and the *New Orleans Times-Picayune*.

The lineup of viewers-with-alarm included Agnew's old friends the *Washington Post*, *The New York Times,* and the *Baltimore Sun*. But some of the angriest yells emanated from elsewhere. "On balance, Agnew has overstated his case and raised the dangerous spectre of government intimidation. . . ." warned the *Charlotte Observer*. According to the *Louisville*

Courier-Journal, Agnew's criticism "strikes an ominous new note in American politics." The *Miami Herald* synthesized what many felt: "Some of what Spiro Agnew said . . . is true, has been said before, and needed to be said again. But not by the Vice President of the United States. . . . The suppressive power of federal authority is mighty and dangerous. Mr. Agnew is toying with this dynamite as no other federal official in modern times."

Although he needed Presidential prodding for his first thrust against the media, it was his own idea to keep on thrusting. His next swat was aimed at the doyens of the press establishment, the *Washington Post* and *The New York Times*. The words and the angle of attack were again conceived by Pat Buchanan, but this time Agnew was an eager collaborator. Before the outcry from the first speech faded, Agnew flew to Montgomery, Alabama, and delivered a second speech hitting "the concentration of more and more power over public information in fewer and fewer hands." His only example was the Washington Post Company, owner of the *Washington Post, Newsweek,* and a TV channel and an all-news radio station in Washington. "All," he claimed, are "grinding out the same editorial line and this is not a subject you have seen debated on the editorial pages of the *Washington Post* or *The New York Times.*"

As for the *Times,* he suggested it had "grown fat and irresponsible because of the collapse of its competing papers in New York. "I offer an example," he said. "When 300 Congressmen and 59 Senators signed a letter endorsing the President's policy in Vietnam it was news—big news. . . . Yet the next morning *The New York Times,* which considers itself America's paper of record, did not carry a word. Why?" [5]

It was shortly after his first two media speeches that the Gallup organization took the poll that resulted in the amazing conclusion that Agnew was the third most admired man in the world, behind Nixon and preacher Billy Graham. The poll was published within a fortnight of the equally incongruous finding by the International Press Institute in Zurich that Agnew's attacks on the media were 1969's "most serious threat to the freedom of information in the Western world." [6]

The media issue was one which the President was content to let Agnew grab for himself, and Agnew milked it as if it was his only issue. To the delight of fund-raising audiences, he would read quotation after quotation from editorials castigating him and Nixon, then denounce them all as wild, hot rhetoric. "Nothing would be more pleasing to some of the editors and columnists I have quoted tonight than to have me simply shut up and disappear," he said in a Texas speech in May 1970. Although he announced at one point that he was calling off his onslaught against the networks and the newspapers, he has revived it so often in 1970 and 1971 that some image-conscious politicians in the White House whispered that he was becoming one-dimensional. All too often for those on the receiving end, however, there were painful elements of truth in what he said. For instance, when CBS broadcast its documentary on military flackery entitled "The Selling of the Pentagon," Agnew flayed it as a "disreputable program" on the legitimate grounds of deceptive film editing.

There is little question that the Vice President's performance as the A. J. Liebling of the Nixon administration has made some difference in the way he and Nixon have fared in the media. From Nixon's viewpoint, the clearest gain has been that television commentators have tended to be a bit blander and less picky in their remarks following Presidential addresses. It was a conspicuous exception when a network correspondent in October 1970 referred to Nixon's new plan for peace in Indochina as a "big bucket of mush." Far more typical was the blandly objective remark that Nixon "had presented a plan which Hanoi would find difficult to dismiss out of hand."

From Agnew's perspective, the most measurable fallout has been the unprecedented attention the press corps paid to the utterances of a man who is, after all, just the Vice President. As columnist Marquis Childs put it, "Agnew was saying, in effect, that if you don't fully report my attacks then you're proving what I say about the power you have to keep the truth from the American people. It worked."

Agnew wasn't the first national figure who felt aggrieved by the press. Woodrow Wilson told of being "so accustomed to having everything reported erroneously that I have almost come to the point of believing nothing I see in the newspapers." Harry Truman complained that "the press is controlled by big business" and Dwight Eisenhower railed against the "sensation-seeking columnists and commentators." Even during Agnew's political career John Kennedy canceled his subscription to the *New York Herald-Tribune* and Lyndon Johnson insisted that the Eastern press was trying to make him out as "an irresponsible hick."

The difference was that Spiro Agnew transformed his grievances into a crusade. If he does nothing else, that alone will guarantee him his niche in the history of twentieth-century America. A more tangible by-product was his near-canonization by the conservatives in the Republican Party. The sins of the media have long been a passionate subject among today's conservative politicians, many of whom came to maturity as followers of the late Robert A. Taft. When their hero was defeated at the 1952 Republican Convention, they bitterly agreed with his statement that "four fifths of the influential newspapers in the country were opposed to me continuously and vociferously and many turned themselves into propaganda sheets for my opponent." When Agnew allowed himself to be nudged into his gladiator's role, he inherited deep and tenacious support among bedrock Republicans and conservatives. One of his newfound admirers in 1970 was William Buckley, who happily forgot his semantical quibbles to observe that there had been twenty-five years of complaining about the press but only Agnew had mobilized public sentiment on the issue.

Even after everything Spiro Agnew has said in public about "this little cabal that revolves around the networks, the *Times,* and the *Washington Post,*" he still has pools of bitterness unseen by the public. To get a fascinating reflection of these hidden feelings, one should drive to Towson and look up his old buddy from the Loch Raven Kiwanis Club, insurance man Clarke Langrall, who served as his finance committee chairman when he ran for Governor. Langrall tells the following story, which Agnew's office will neither confirm nor deny:

A month or so after the 1970 midterm elections, he and Agnew got together to chew the fat about old times. Before long the conversation turned to the media and its horribly unfair treatment of the Nixon administration and of Agnew himself. The liberal media were so unfair, said Agnew, that he had decided to do something about it. Why, only the other day he had privately advised a group of top businessmen in

New York to assemble enough capital to buy up newspapers and television properties and break the liberal media monopoly.

Apparently they didn't take his suggestion. Sadly, he later told interviewer Allen Drury: "I wish there were some way to create a conservative newspaper in New York and also a conservative television and radio network. It is very hard to get people who have the money to cooperate with each other. It is an example of the difficulty of getting people on the conservative side to organize to combat this intensive liberal drive all the time on the other side."

For a politician who thought eight years earlier that he would be dead without the backing of the *Baltimore Sun,* he had come a long way.

14

"I try not to burden him with too many requests for conferences
because I think he's got plenty that requires his attention."

A Source Not Close to the President

Between convention and inauguration Spiro T. Agnew absorbed a dizzying burst of signals about what it would be like to be Vice President under Richard Nixon.

The ones that turned out to be the least accurate were the grandiose designs that Nixon released to the public. As Eisenhower's Vice President, Nixon felt so encapsulated that he later called the Vice Presidency "a hollow shell—the most ill-conceived, poorly defined position in the American political system." After living in that shell for eight years, Nixon talked as though Agnew would function as a sort of Deputy President for Internal Affairs, leaving him free to worry about the rest of the world.

In his little campaign essay "Why I Chose Ted Agnew," Nixon went so far as to say, "I will ask him to be my chief mediator in jurisdictional disputes—between federal and state governments, between the executive and legislative branches, within the various departments of the federal government. I will ask him to help me and my Cabinet in mediating disruptive strikes that seriously endanger the strength of the nation."

If Nixon conceived of Agnew as the mean gunslinger of the Republican Party, he gave no sign of it in "Why I Chose Ted Agnew." In fact, he made a special point of saying that Agnew "will campaign in a way that will not jeopardize our ability to unite the country."

The signals Agnew got from the Nixon-Agnew headquarters in New York were less grandiose but more prophetic. During the campaign he heard almost nothing directly from Nixon. His daily political guidance came in the forms of memos teletyped to his campaign plane from middle-echelon operatives at Nixon-Agnew headquarters named Sherman Unger and Joe Hillings, plus some running commentary by John Sears, a Nixon man delegated to the Agnew plane.

The Unger-Hillings memos, which up to now have been unpublished, were supposed to prepare Agnew for each town along his itinerary. Some of the contents were routine reminders that any national candidate in the jet age needs—things like "Reported that you spent first night of honeymoon in nearby Waynesboro [Virginia]," or "Do not get photographed eating grapes, which has become a tactic of Max Rafferty," or "Don't use Spanish unless you have good pronunciation." While these daily memos didn't purport to describe what Agnew would be doing after the campaign, they were much more than simply an Emily Post of local politics. The first and most important section of each memo was an advisory on what issues Agnew should plug hardest.

Leafing through a file of the memos teletyped to Agnew, one is struck by the way Nixon-Agnew headquarters usually kept accentuating his hard-liner image and downplaying his background in urban problems that so impressed Nixon in the first place. Excerpts from these teletyped memos trace the way he was eased into his now familiar role as a conservative heavy hitter:

Roanoke Virginia—"HHH. Hit Hard. Again use good humor and smile. National issues all of interest. These people are predisposed toward you. Feel you didn't have to back up on what you said about HHH. Consider you strong and forthright."

Nashville, Tennessee—"Law and Order. Crime in the streets. Disrespect. Civil Disorder. Hit hard with feeling. No. 1, Enforce the law. Liked your position in Baltimore."

Fort Wayne, Indiana—"People are glad you're coming—you have the real Republican 'stand up and be counted' image."

Midland, Texas—"Law and Order. Full blast. These are highly educated people so you may want to give a little more substance but don't diminish the velocity. Wallace has support here. Like your stand up and be counted attitude in Baltimore. . . . Fiscal Responsibility, High Taxes, Unbalanced Budget, Inflation, Big Government, Corruption, Conservative. Proper Balance of Government."

Bakersfield, California—"Law and Order. Make it strong. Wallace has about five per cent of vote (it is decreasing) since many area residents originally from Oklahoma, Arkansas and Texas. Area in recent years has gone from Democratic to rather conservative Republicans. Fairly big pocket of Birchers. Hate Ramsey Clark."

Only occasionally would Agnew be sent before a big-city audience with a mandate to talk about urban problems. One of these exceptions was his October 22 trip to hopelessly

Democratic Boston. For this stop the Unger-Hillings memo suggested a quieter tone: "Solving the problems of our cities. Intellectual discussion, understanding, compassionate, return of domestic tranquillity (not law and order here—seems to be anathema)." Even with that, the memo warned him, "Your ethnic remarks have lingered in this highly ethnic state."

A few days after winning the election, Nixon summoned Agnew to Key Biscayne, Florida, for a long talk. Afterward they walked out to the microphones which had been set up on Bebe Rebozo's back lawn and Nixon made clear that he was symbolically drawing Agnew to his bosom by assigning him an office a few doors from the Oval Office. With his penchant for making historical precedents, Nixon said that Agnew would be the first Vice President in history to have his office in the White House. As it turned out, Agnew was assigned the sunny office in the West Wing which Sherman Adams occupied during the Eisenhower administration. Nixon also announced that he and Agnew would share a single staff, meaning Agnew would have no aides of his own except for a few at the Senate.

The changes Nixon announced in Key Biscayne were meant to symbolize a brand-new status for the Vice President within the Administration. Although all Agnew's duties weren't filled in, it was clear among the top Nixon aides that he would be an intimate of the President and an important gear in the White House machinery. He would become, as one of those aides remembered it, the second most important man in the United States.

After four years, no one around the White House claims that Agnew's role within the government has turned out the way Nixon projected it. Clearly Agnew isn't one of Nixon's intimate advisors and he isn't an important gear in the White House machinery. In fact, he has gone off on his own within the Administration just as he has gone off on his own in public. While the President has never said why he preferred to keep a distance between him and Agnew, a friend of both men suggests that Nixon's rigid staff system doomed any intimate relationship from the start. Nixon is, as this friend put it, a person who deals personally with only about four aides.

One overt development which mirrored the collapse of any special relationship was the steady growth of Agnew's staff, which soon exceeded the entourage of any previous Vice President. Although Nixon once believed Agnew should have no aides except a few at the Senate, there were seventy-nine names in the Vice Presidential staff telephone directory by April 1971. And that count did not include his Secret Service detail. Most of his assistants are people with gut loyalties to him personally rather than to Nixon or to the Republican Party. At first he relied on a Towson-Annapolis crew. His first Chief of Staff was C. Stanley Blair, the lawyer and gentleman farmer he had made Secretary of State of Maryland in 1967. Art Sohmer, his factotum from Towson and Annapolis, began as his top political aide and later moved up to Chief of Staff when Blair left to run for Governor of Maryland.

To the disgust of some of the White House political types, three of Agnew's principal aides were registered Democrats. There was Press Secretary Herbert Thompson, the longtime Associated Press bureau chief in Annapolis who began as his Press Secretary in Annapolis. There was his science and technology advisor, Jerome Wolff, who had been Agnew's road builder in Towson and Annapolis. And there was speech writer Mrs. Cynthia Rosenwald, a thirty-one-year-old Baltimore housewife and onetime Wellesley student who had researched and written drafts for him since 1966, including one speech in Maryland in which he quoted H. G. Wells, Walter Lippmann, Voltaire, William Ernest Hocking, George Wallace, Descartes, Nicholas Murray Butler, and Charles de Gaulle. Mrs. Rosenwald, the wife of a Baltimore executive, quit the staff early in 1970 because of a seriously ill child. (When she left, Agnew wrote her what must be a remarkable letter. Baltimore advertising man Robert Goodman, who has seen it, says the Vice President told her, among other things, that there were many times when he was fixed in his ideas and she was the one person who could turn him around. "It was almost like a love letter," claims Goodman. "It was sensitive, it was warm, it was human.")

The important staff members who weren't in the Maryland mafia tended to be technician types rather than old Nixon hands. Army Colonel (later Brigadier General) Michael Dunn, a sophisticated intellectual with a Ph.D. from Princeton, was assigned as his military aide. A foreign service officer, Kent Crane, became his foreign affairs advisor. C. D. Ward, a man Agnew knew as counsel to the National Association of Counties, was hired as his top assistant for domestic affairs. And Walter Mote, a minority staff member of the Senate Rules Committee for eleven years, became his legislative advisor at the Capitol.

As the staff grew, the relative importance of the Maryland contingent diminished. But for the most part the outsiders were Agnew men first and Nixon men second. Among the newcomers were Press Secretary Vic Gold, a onetime Goldwater campaign aide who replaced Herb Thompson when he became a speech writer, and Peter Malatesta, a nephew of Bob Hope, who became Agnew's personal aide (and frequent golfing partner). The one old Nixon man in their midst was Roy Goodearle, who was put in charge of "national affairs," the euphemism for politics.

Time widened the distance between Nixon's staff and Agnew's. Throughout 1969, when Stan Blair was Agnew's Chief of Staff, he regularly attended Bob Haldeman's 8 A.M. staff meetings so that the Vice President would be wired into all the day-to-day developments within the White House. In 1970 and 1971, when Art Sohmer was Chief of Staff, he attended Haldeman's staff meetings only by special invitation. Inevitably, the gap between the two staffs sometimes became personal as well as organizational. "Man for man, he just doesn't have as good a staff," sniped a young Nixon aide. Meanwhile, an Agnew intimate vented his bitterness about the men around Nixon. "I don't know what those guys think they are doing," he said.

Along with the disengagement between the two staffs, there came a symbolic separation between Agnew and the seat of power. One day in 1969 it was quietly disclosed that Agnew had given up Sherman Adams' old office in the White House and would conduct his affairs on the second floor of the Executive Office Building. When Agnew moved out, Bob Haldeman moved in. Although nobody at the White House said so, the separation between Agnew and Nixon was more than geographical. The more he became a national power distinct from the President, the less he was used as an advisor and deputy. "The Vice President is a personality in his own right, and the President can't quite relate to him the way he relates to a Bob Haldeman," explained one Nixon aide. "You don't call up the Vice President and tell him to get the hell over here because we've got a problem to solve."

The White House makes something of a mystery of how often Nixon and Agnew ever talked man-to-man, but the impression was very seldom. Staff people recall that Nixon saw Agnew privately just before the 1970 election campaign, and before Agnew's several trips abroad. There have been other private talks, but apparently not many. In fact, it is quite possible that Agnew had more frequent heart-to-heart conversations with Nixon in the eight months before his nomination than he has since Miami Beach.

Usually the only times Agnew gets to see the President is when there is a meeting of the Cabinet, the Domestic Council, the National Security Council, or the Congressional leadership. If he's asked about the way Nixon has set up his machinery, he tried to avoid leaving the impression that he feels isolated. "I think the President has found that the closed two-person conference is a very inefficient device in the complexity of modern government," he said late in 1970. "He's much better off, if he's going to have an exchange with me, to do it at a table like this with other people who might be affected made aware of what we're talking about and having a chance to chime in their objections. If he talked to me privately and then talked to them, he's got to come back to me and tell me what they say. It's a question of efficiency."

While acknowledging that his main contact with Nixon has been at formal committee sessions, he insists there were informal meetings too. "There are times," he said, "when I've not asked to see him that he'll just ask me to come over and we'll sit down for three-quarters of an hour and we'll talk generally about Administration policy. Or if I need to see him, I can generally see him on the same day, if I ask to see him. I try not to burden him with too many requests for conferences because I think he's got plenty to do that requires his attention."

Agnew shows no such bashfulness about speaking up at National Security Council or Cabinet meetings. When Nixon was Vice President, he was often called upon by Eisenhower for a summation of what had been said by others, but Nixon wasn't expected to inject many of his own thoughts. Agnew's role is different. To a degree that few people even inside the Administration realize, Agnew has made himself the voice of dissent in the highest councils.

Although he has the image of Nixon's house conservative, there seems to be no ideological pattern to the disagreements and objections he has thrown up to the President. Both the left and the right may be upset to hear that Agnew was one of the few members of the National Security Council—perhaps the only member—who expressed much reluctance about proceeding with the Anti-Ballistic Missile system in March 1969. After hearing high officials from the Pentagon argue their case for an ABM system to protect missile sites, each NSC member had a chance to expound his views to Nixon. When it was Agnew's turn, he argued that instead of building a highly controversial ABM system, the Defense Department could just as well expand its fleet of forty-one missile-firing Polaris and Poseidon submarines. As he saw it, the United States could buy as much deterrence with submarines as with the ABM, and at less political cost at home. Nixon listened, but ultimately ruled against that option, in part because more Poseidons could cause the Russians to build more of their own offensive missiles.

If the ABM was Nixon's first really important policy decision, welfare reform was the second. Once again, Spiro Agnew came down hard against the policy the President would finally adopt. As Governor of Maryland, Agnew had told everyone who would listen, including Nixon, that the solution to welfare was full federal financing and uniform benefits in the fifty states. As vice chairman of Nixon's new Urban Affairs Council, he saw for the first time just how much of a dent that would put in the federal budget. In the early months of internal debate over welfare, Agnew was eager to serve as the honest broker between Presidential Assistant Daniel P. Moynihan's radical-sounding scheme for a guaranteed income to all poor families and Presidential Counselor Dr. Arthur Burns' far more limited plan for increased federal financing of state welfare programs.

The compromise Agnew seized on in May 1969 was a hybrid. Under his proposal, the federal government would provide a guaranteed income to four categories of welfare recipients: the elderly poor, the blind, the permanently disabled, and the poor but "intact" families with dependent children. However, there would be no guaranteed income for the largest category of welfare families, the broken homes receiving Aid to Families with Dependent Children. For those, Agnew's compromise would keep the existing welfare system, sweetened with federal payments to the states based on a matching formula. All the new payments were tied to work incentives for welfare recipients.

Although Nixon had originally envisioned Agnew as his internal mediator, he turned instead to his Labor Secretary, George Shultz, and his White House counsel John Ehrlichman, to fit together a final welfare proposal from the pieces created by the Burns and Moynihan factions. On August 6,

1969, three days after returning from his trip to Rumania, Nixon called his Cabinet to Camp David for a briefing and a discussion of the welfare plan he had tentatively okayed.

After hearing the details, Agnew was upset about the tremendous cost of adding coverage for the "working poor," which would double the number of welfare recipients to more than twenty million people. As the discussion moved around the table, Nixon heard objections from more than half of his Cabinet, including George Romney of Housing and Urban Development, David Kennedy of Treasury, and Counselor Arthur Burns.

After most of the Cabinet had spoken, Agnew weighed in on the side of Burns and Romney. "His objections to the program were keyed around its political drawbacks," remembers one participant at Camp David. "He pitched quite hard against it." While arguing that some elements of the Family Assistance Plan were too ambitious, he also pushed hard for adding a new foster care provision to help dependent children.

Agnew had to leave Camp David early. Back at the Senate, the roll call on the ABM was coming up that afternoon, and Agnew was needed in case there was a tie vote. "How do you know which way I will vote, Mr. President?" asked Agnew with a parting smile. His vote to save the ABM wasn't needed, but he cast it for the President's program anyway, making the roll call on the amendment 51-50.[1] When Nixon went on television to announce his welfare program two days later, it was the Moynihan-Shultz-Ehrlichman package with no trace of Agnew's dissenting views.

Agnew hadn't been totally ignored, however. At the next Governors' Conference he disclosed that Nixon had agreed to ask Congress for a new federal program to underwrite the cost of adoptions of dependent children or their placement in foster homes. Under Agnew's prodding, Health, Education and Welfare sent up a $155,000,000 foster care program in the fall of 1970.[2]

Agnew has never bothered to hide his disagreements with Nixon over welfare, although he has publicly supported the President's proposal as a vast improvement over the existing system. "I've been more liberal on welfare than the Administration has since the beginning," said Agnew in March 1970. Despite his liberal self-perception, he also said that some of his ideas on welfare were less liberal than the Administration view. "I'm not the President," said Agnew. "I'm the Vice President, and it's up to me to get these programs through."

Of the Administration's main domestic initiatives, the one Nixon assigned to Agnew to promote across the country was revenue sharing. Within six months of its designation as one of the great goals of Nixon's "New American Revolution," Agnew appeared before thirteen state legislatures from Olympia, Washington, to Columbus, Ohio, seeking to build a pressure on Congress for revenue sharing. What very few of his listeners realized was that Agnew opposed one of the main features of the package he had been assigned to sell. Agnew's objection was that the bill contained nothing to stop the states and localities from using their "general revenue sharing" checks to cut local taxes instead of providing more services. At one meeting of Cabinet officials, Agnew told of a practical lesson he learned in Annapolis about sharing tax revenues with local communities: no sooner had he shepherded his 1967 tax-sharing bill through the Maryland legislature than the Democrats in Baltimore used the proceeds to cut property taxes on the eve of a city election. As he saw it, revenue sharing should be designed to avoid that trap. President Nixon viewed things differently and decided to stress the possibility of local tax cuts under revenue sharing. Although Agnew offered his objections, his aides insist that he made no real fight against revenue sharing.

The first time Agnew is known to have angered Nixon with his dissenting habits is over China. His sin wasn't heresy but publicity. What Agnew said at a meeting of the National Security Council in the spring of 1971 was safe Republican dogma: that the government mustn't shift its policy too fast toward embracing Peking at the expense of the Taiwan government. Specifically, Agnew was dubious about having the American ping-pong team accept an invitation to visit the Chinese mainland.

Talking out of school is something National Security Council members just don't do, but Agnew violated the vows of silence in one of the strangest episodes of his Vice Presidency. The day after the ping-pong team's return from China, Agnew flew to Williamsburg, Virginia, to attend the Republican Governors' Conference. On the way down in his jet, Agnew told Vic Gold to get him a list of the reporters covering the session because he might want to see some of them for an off-the-record talk. From the list he later picked out nine reporters he knew and directed Gold to bring them to his room. He made up his mind so late that at least one reporter had to be hustled out of bed and another from the bar. From 12:30 A.M. to 3:30 A.M. on the morning of April 19, Agnew chatted over drinks with the nine reporters, the way he used to at Governors' Conferences when he had been Governor. Before they all went to bed, Agnew had informed the reporters that he thought the United States took a propaganda beating on the ping-pong team's visit. Part of it he blamed on the press for glorifying the Chinese hosts. But he also blurted out his belief that the United States government had been trapped by the Chinese invitation, and that it had been a mistake to accept it. When someone asked him whether he had made his feelings known in Washington, he acknowledged that at one meeting of the National Security Council he had indeed argued against some facets of the new China policy. This was dynamite. Within hours, one of the nine reporters violated the off-the-record ground rules and leaked the story to David Kraslow and Jules Witcover of the *Los Angeles Times,* two reporters Agnew had not invited.

When the story hit the front pages, Agnew allowed Ron Ziegler, Nixon's Press Secretary, to assure everyone that "there is no difference of opinion" between him and the President on the government's recent trade and travel initiatives toward China. As for the ping-pong team's visit, Ziegler said as little as possible. But it was too late to undo the damage. Nixon, who was trying to court China without enraging the conservatives at home, let it be known that he was surprised and unhappy at seeing Agnew's criticisms in print.

Over the next six months Nixon made two of the most momentous turnabouts of his Presidency, and both times he very visibly left Agnew out in the cold.

At the time of Agnew's Williamsburg gaffe, Nixon was already making preliminary contacts with the Chinese government that were leading toward a secret trip to Peking by his National Security Advisor, Henry Kissinger. In the evenings the President would meet Kissinger and Secretary of State Rogers in a sitting room upstairs in the White House to plot out Kissinger's visit. Agnew was never brought in on the secret. Three months after the contacts with Peking began, he woke up one morning in the Congo to learn that Kissinger had been to Peking and had arranged a summit meeting between Nixon and Chou En-lai. When Agnew heard the news, it had already been announced by Nixon on television. Although Agnew apparently had an inkling from a previous National Security Council meeting that there would be contacts with the Chinese at some point, he was totally unprepared for what he heard. Vic Gold initially left the impression with reporters that the Vice President had been aware in advance of the Kissinger mission. Gold was promptly cut off at the knees when a White House source disclosed at a background briefing that Kissinger, Rogers, and the President were the only senior officials with any foreknowledge of the mission. It came out later that the source who held the backgrounder was Kissinger himself.

During the next twenty-four hours, as he mulled over the news, the Vice President prepared one of the most bizarre and seemingly self-destructive statements of his career. Once having written it, he deliberately avoided showing it to his advisors, knowing they would try to talk him out of it. As soon as his jet took off for Madrid, he strode back to the press compartment to read his handiwork. It was a gratuitous lecture to "most" of the black leadership in the United States that they had much to learn from Emperor Haile Selassie, President Jomo Kenyatta, and other leaders he had met in Africa. The quality of their leadership, he said, "is in distinct contrast . . . with many of those in the United States who have arrogated unto themselves the position of black leaders, those who spend their time in querulous complaint and constant recriminations against the rest of society." A transcript of the occasion shows it took the reporters four pages to get around to asking about China, and then Agnew said, "No comment." If one could burrow around in his psyche, it would be fascinating to learn whether he would have made such a corrosive statement about American black leaders if he had not just been jolted by the China announcement. One theory, suggested to me by one of Agnew's most perceptive friends, is that Agnew was deeply upset about China but couldn't say anything about it, so his mind lashed out at the most convenient target.

When Agnew returned to Washington, he did make one remark that could be construed as a knock at Nixon for keeping him uninformed about China. When Godfrey Sperling Jr., of *The Christian Science Monitor* asked him whether he knew anything of the Kissinger mission while he was abroad, Agnew at first repeated his refusal to comment. Then he added a puzzling sentence: "But I don't think it's reasonable to expect a person in my position to be uninformed on a direction by the President."

Exactly a week after the quotation was published, Nixon helicoptered to Camp David with ten of his top advisors for the critical weekend of conferences that produced the wage-price freeze and the 10 percent import surcharge. Unlike the messy debate at Camp David over welfare in 1969, the sessions on the economy were described as surprisingly harmonious. One man was conspicuously absent: the chairman of the Cabinet Committee on Economic Policy, Spiro T. Agnew. While the most important economic decisions in thirty years were being made, he was spending a quiet weekend at his apartment at the Sheraton-Park Hotel in Washington. Like all Cabinet members except Treasury Secretary Connally, Agnew hadn't been invited. After the decisions were wrapped up, an aide called him shortly before the President went on television to tell him what had happened.

The frequency with which Agnew gets to contribute to global policymaking has gradually diminished, if only because Nixon uses the National Security Council less and less. During his first year, when all old policies were being reexamined, there were thirty-seven NSC meetings. The Council met twenty-two times in the second year of the Administration, and by the third year there were ten meetings in the first nine months. Of those first sixty-nine meetings, Agnew attended fifty-one.

Increasingly, Agnew has had to occupy himself with the alluvium of lesser duties that have over the years been deposited on the Vice Presidency. As all other Vice Presidents have found, the functions assigned to the office give him not much leverage within the government. What little he has, he's tried to exert from time to time, with mixed consequences.

His only Constitutional duty, as long as Nixon breathes, is presiding over the Senate. He is the first Vice President since 1945 who hasn't previously served in the Senate. As soon as he was elected, he began reading up on its rules and procedures because, as he put it, "I don't want inadvertently to do anything that will be considered gauche or impolite." In the early months he would sit through at least an hour a day of other people's speeches, far more than Hubert Humphrey or Lyndon Johnson did in their time. Several days a week he would invite groups of four or five Senators to lunch, and sometimes he would even be seen eating in the Senators' dining room alone.

All this effort to cozy up to The Club abruptly ended in the summer of 1969 when he overreached in his eagerness to get the Administration's income tax surcharge bill through the Senate. At a meeting of the Senate Republican Policy Committee on July 29 he enraged the late Senator Everett Dirksen of Illinois, the Minority Leader, by bluntly rejecting Dirksen's suggestion that the White House accept a compromise on the surtax. The word got back to the White House that the reason Dirksen later decided to vote with the Democrats on a key test vote two days later was that he was still infuriated with Agnew. Even so, Agnew's willingness to stand up to Dirksen won him admiration at the White House. Agnew had gotten his marching orders in a radiotelephone call from Nixon, who was visiting Thailand.

On July 31 he made his fatal error. As the roll call on the surtax approached, Agnew walked out on the floor of the Senate to the desk of Len Jordan, a seventy-two-year-old Republican Senator from Idaho whom he had gotten to know fairly well. "Are you with us, Len?" asked Agnew. If he had posed the question inside his own office forty feet away, no one would have thought twice about it. On the Senate floor, it was a violation of a protocol that supposedly goes back three centuries to the great struggle between Charles I and the British Parliament. The tradition is that Vice Presidents, like Kings, must not interfere with what occurs on the floor. When Agnew asked him the question, Jordan exploded. "Don't twist my arm," he told the Vice President. Later, at a meeting of the Policy Committee, the Senator promulgated what became known as the Jordan rule: Any time the Vice President lobbied him for his vote, he would automatically vote the other way.

One year earlier, Nixon had talked of making Agnew his chief mediator in jurisdictional disputes with Congress, but now any hope of that went out the window. After the Jordan blowup, the Administration never tried to use Agnew in any of its dealings with Congress. He began appearing much less in the Presiding Officer's chair, and his contacts with Senators even of his own party dwindled nearly to zero.[3] One can talk to a dozen Republican Senators and not find one whom Agnew has talked to on the telephone on a piece of legislation in the last three years. In fact, he rarely talks to Senators about anything. The only phone call of any kind I know he's made since 1969 was to Republican Senator William B. Saxbe of Ohio. One day when Agnew was presiding, Saxbe walked up to greet him, only to find that Agnew didn't seem willing to shake hands. Later Saxbe complained to Walter Mote, Agnew's legislative aide, about this apparent slight, and subsequently Agnew telephoned Saxbe to apologize.

When Nixon was Vice President, he had to cast tie-breaking votes repeatedly. Lyndon Johnson, who was Democratic Majority Leader during the Eisenhower years, told Vice President Agnew much later that the Democrats deliberately set up tie votes when Nixon was out of town. Oddly, although the Senate has had a succession of cliff-hanger votes in the last three years, Agnew has not once had to break a tie. The only time he voted was in 1969 on the ABM, and in that case the tie vote would have sustained the Administration's position without his vote.

The one time Agnew did something that mattered as President of the Senate came in January 1971, when he was asked to make a parliamentary ruling in the Senate's biennial debate about changing the filibuster rules. At the start of nearly every Congress, Senate reformers tried to change the rules in order to reduce the number of Senators needed to cut off a filibuster. The sticking point was that proposals to change the filibuster rule are themselves subject to a filibuster. The only way the reformers got around that obstacle was to contend that at the start of each new Congress the Senate had the Constitutional right to make its own rules by majority vote. For their strategy to succeed, they had to win a favorable parliamentary ruling by the Vice President. In a similar situation in 1957, Richard Nixon had ruled in favor of the reformers and so had Hubert Humphrey in 1959. However, Spiro Agnew in 1971 refused to issue the needed ruling, and the filibuster reformers lost their fight. Agnew reached his decision by himself, with no orders from downtown.

Outside of the Senate, Agnew's most important responsibility has been supervising the Administration's liaison with the Mayors and Governors. Nixon created this job for him at the start of the Administration, giving him his own little agency with a twelve-man staff to handle the details, known as the Office of Intergovernmental Relations. The former Republican Governor of South Dakota, Nils Boe, was hired to manage day-to-day business, and Agnew was expected to provide the vision and the clout to get things done. Three years later, the Governors, the Mayors, Agnew's staff, and the White House all agreed that the Office of Intergovernmental Relations hasn't worked. "A disappointment," says an important Agnew assistant. "A failure," is the way a White House official puts it. "A joke," says a Democratic

Governor. At the National Governors' Conference in Puerto Rico in September 1971, Agnew privately offered to move in as the Governors' day-to-day liaison man instead of Boe, who had been appointed to the federal bench. The Governors accepted, but with little confidence that Agnew would work out any better than Boe.

Agnew's problem is that he tries to be a liaison man one day and a political Rocky Marciano the next. Over the months, a lot of local and state governments have preferred to go around Agnew, either through their Senators or directly to the White House staff. While he hasn't become a stunning success as ambassador to the state and local governments, he has scored some isolated triumphs for which he is not often credited. Early in the Administration, it was Agnew who got the President to reverse a Treasury Department proposal to end the tax-free status of municipal bonds. Then, when Presidential Counselor Arthur Burns convinced Nixon to impose an anti-inflationary cutback on federal construction, Agnew was able to win the Governors an all-important loop-hole for highway construction. Early in 1971 Agnew went to bat for the Mayors and won White House promises that money for the Model Cities program would continue to flow until special Revenue-Sharing legislation takes effect. This meant undoing part of Nixon's newly announced budget, which provided no more Model Cities funds after January 1, 1972.

Another important bureaucratic duty Nixon assigned to Agnew was the chairmanship of the Cabinet Committee on Education in February 1970. The idea was to implement the Supreme Court school desegregation decisions in the least disruptive way by establishing biracial citizens committees in every Southern state. Given Agnew's popularity in the South and his hankering to work on something important, it was no surprise that he accepted the chairmanship with what he called "a great amount of enthusiasm." However, for reasons that were never announced, Agnew stopped functioning as chairman after five months and was replaced by George Shultz, now the director of the new Office of Management and Budget. One White House source offered the explanation that Agnew couldn't find time to attend all the meetings because of his increasing schedule of political appearances in 1970.

Aside from the duties Nixon gave him, Agnew inherited from past administrations half a dozen committees to chair: the President's Council on Youth Opportunity, the President's Council on Indian Opportunity, the President's Council on Physical Fitness and Sports, the National Aeronautics and Space Council, the National Council on Marine Resources and Engineering Development, and the Peace Corps Advisory Council.

Space became his first fascination. After watching the Apollo 9 blast-off, Agnew stepped into the foreground as a special pleader for the space program. "I will lend whatever thrust I can to nudge the President into an awareness of what I consider of overriding importance," he said. "I'm afraid I am going to be a regular nuisance about the space program." Four months later Agnew came out for a space budget big enough to put a man on Mars by the year 2000. "I think it [a man-to-Mars goal] is something that creates enthusiasm among the average persons in the street," he said. "The average person is interested in that kind of simple but very heady attempt to do something extremely innovative and ambitious." To his regret, he was almost alone in the Administration in pushing a Mars landing and the project was soon sidetracked.

Lately, he has cared less about space and more about the Indians. President Nixon's new policy of offering "self-determination" to Indian tribes grew out of a meeting of Agnew's Indian Council in January 1970. When self-determination was announced six months later, it was clear that the two senior officials at the White House most responsible for its development were Agnew and Leonard Garment of the White House staff. In practice, self-determination meant asking Congress to grant each tribe an opportunity to take over programs run for them by the federal government. Agnew met four times in the next year with the eight Indian representatives on his Council, and more than once he enjoyed the satisfaction of knowing he had done something tangible to help. At a meeting with the Indian representatives in March 1971, the Eskimo member, Mrs. Laura Bergt, intrigued him with her arguments about the unfairness of the bill being prepared by the Administration to settle the Alaska native land claims. Four days later Agnew was able to sit Interior Secretary Rogers Morton and George Shultz down in Washington with Don Wright, the eloquent leader of the Alaska Federation of Natives. The upshot was that the Administration sent up a new bill offering the Eskimos forty million acres of land to settle their claims, quadruple the Administration's original offer. Two other bureaucratic scuffles he fought on behalf of his Indian constituency involved the upgrading of the Administration's proposals for Indian health and housing.

When all his bureaucratic achievements are totaled, it is

painfully obvious that he has not a great deal to show for his efforts—little, that is, beyond the public side of his Vice Presidency. That side has made him famous but hasn't made him happy. Spiro Agnew is still the same man who said during the 1968 campaign that there were a lot of things he didn't like about traveling around the country as a national figure. Hotel rooms, for instance. "Despite the fine accommodations, they're still hotel rooms," said Agnew then. "Because of the crowded schedules and constant meetings, we eat a lot in the room. Everything is beginning to look alike." And although he was always moving from city to city, "it's a sedentary life and it could easily turn a person into gelatin."

Four years of traveling between hotel rooms have not made him love the political circuit any more. Unlike a Hubert Humphrey or a Richard Nixon, he simply doesn't like shaking hands in a crowd or making small talk with the party hierarchs of Onondaga County. And he has made no effort during his travels to build up his own network of political contacts the way Richard Nixon did so feverishly when he was Vice President.

Part of the job he does relish is the chance to board the big jet with "United States of America" on the side and zoom overseas on a good-will mission. Those who know him say he feels more on his own when he is halfway around the world from Washington. It is commonly assumed that when Agnew visits Athens or Kinshasa or Madrid, he does so because the President or the State Department thought there was a specific foreign policy reason for the visit. Some of Agnew's travels, like his 1971 visits to Korea and Iran, did originate with the President. But after getting an assignment to travel, Agnew is relatively free to expand the itinerary to please himself. It turns out that the reason he visited Spain in July 1971 was that when he had escorted Prince Juan Carlos to the Apollo 14 launching, the Prince had invited him to visit Spain. Agnew's stops in Ethiopia, the Congo, Kuwait, and Saudi Arabia also came about because foreign potentates on official visits to the United States met Agnew and invited him to drop by someday. Having nothing better to do, Agnew seized the chance. And late in 1971, on the way back from representing the United States at Iran's 2500th anniversary celebration, he was allowed by the White House to make an official visit to his ancestral Greece. There he happily accepted Greece's highest honor, the Grand Cross of George I—the Greek king whose allegiance his father had renounced when he became an American citizen sixty-two years earlier.

Perhaps it is in the nature of the office that all Vice Presidents are condemned to boredom and frustration. The first one, John Adams, lamented, "My country has in its wisdom contrived for me the most insignificant office that ever the invention of man contrived or his imagination conceived." Thereafter, Vice Presidents have vied with each other to see which one could leave behind the most pungent expression of their frustrations. Thomas R. Marshall, who served under Woodrow Wilson, said the Vice President is "like a man in a cataleptic state: he cannot speak, he cannot move, he suffers no pain, and yet he is perfectly conscious of everything that is going on around him." John Nance Garner, who served under Franklin Delano Roosevelt, once said to his fellow Texan, "I'll tell you, Lyndon, the Vice Presidency isn't worth a pitcher of warm spit." Harry Truman added, "Look at all the Vice Presidents in history. Where are they? They were about as useful as a cow's fifth teat."

So far Agnew has not contributed much to the published literature on the horrors of the Vice Presidency. The closest he came to sounding unhappy in public was in an interview with the Nixon Administration's semi-authorized biographer, Allen Drury. "I find up there [at the Senate], as I do in the Executive Branch, that I have no real power," said Agnew. "It's a damned peculiar position to be in, to have authority and a title and responsibility with no real power to do any-thing. . . . In the early days I used to say to myself, 'Now, tomorrow I'm going to do so and so' . . . and then I would stop and think, 'You aren't going to do anything, you don't have the power.' "

15

"My view is that one should not break up
a winning combination."

President Agnew?

The bruises from the 1970 election were just beginning to
fade when William F. Buckley invited Spiro Agnew over
to lunch at his Manhattan apartment. About fifteen other
guests, mostly Buckley's friends or potential advertisers for
his magazine *National Review,* were on hand to meet this
curious man who was their Vice President.

Anyone looking around the room could tell that these
were men who mattered, men who would be listened to not
only on Wall Street but at 1600 Pennsylvania Avenue. There
was Jeremiah Milbank, Jr., finance director of the Republican National Committee. There was Roger Milliken, the
former Republican National Committeeman from South
Carolina who helped lock up the 1964 nomination for Barry
Goldwater. There were the board chairmen of National
Distillers, General Electric, Allstate Insurance, Chemical
Bank, and General Motors. There was the past board chairman of the First National City Bank. And there were the
presidents of Prudential Insurance, Brown & Williamson

Tobacco Company, Eastern Airlines, Mutual of New York, American Airlines, and United States Steel.

It was at William Buckley's off-the-record luncheon that Spiro Agnew uttered one of the strangest statements a Vice President has ever made about a job he might inherit at any moment. "Let me disabuse you of one notion," said Agnew. "I can't think of anything more repulsive than to be President." That is the exact quotation of what he said on December 14, 1970, as tape-recorded by his Press Secretary, Vic Gold, and released to me nine months later.[1]

No matter how repulsed he says he is, one has to take very seriously the possibility that sometime in the next five years Agnew will become President. The chances of an Agnew Presidency will obviously diminish if he is dropped from the Republican ticket in 1972, but even then we may not have heard the end of him. It wouldn't be the first time he has been dumped from one office only to rebound higher.

As 1972 rushed toward him, Richard Nixon had not flatly decided the problem of whether to jettison his Vice President and pick a new one. It wasn't a pleasant decision for him, either personally or politically. He had gone through the tortures of nearly being dumped by President Eisenhower, both in 1952 and 1956. Beyond that, the Wally Hickel episode illustrated how little stomach he has for firing anyone.

It is a close question whether removing Agnew would help the Republican ticket, and late in 1971 Nixon commissioned a series of very sophisticated polls on Agnew through his political arm, Citizens to Reelect the President. Only Nixon, John Mitchell, and Bob Haldeman were expected to see the results. Meanwhile, at the offices of Citizens to Reelect the President they hung twenty-three glossy blowups. There was

Nixon sitting on the steps of the Rose Garden, Nixon with Secretary of State Rogers, Nixon walking on the beach, Nixon with John Ehrlichman, Nixon with a little boy in a red coat. To be on the safe side, they didn't hang any picture showing Spiro Agnew.

Nixon's dilemma was that Agnew is both very popular and very unpopular. Without access to Nixon's private surveys, the best evidence is the Harris Poll, which has tracked Agnew more frequently than any other published survey.[2] Judging from the Harris Poll, the trend line of Agnew's nationwide acceptability has zigzagged downward ever since Inauguration Day. In the second half of 1971, after nearly a year of what was supposed to be a low silhouette strategy for Agnew, his Harris ratings were worse than during the bitterest month of the 1970 campaign. These were the Harris Poll's disastrous numbers, compiled in response to the question: "How would you rate the job the Vice President is doing—excellent, pretty good, only fair, or poor?"

AGNEW RATING

	Excellent or Pretty Good	Only Fair or Poor
November 1969	40	42
February 1970	47	42
April 1970	45	44
September 1970	39	45
October 1970	40	50
February 1971	42	47
August 1971	35	52

And yet, it isn't all that obvious that Agnew's core of intensely loyal followers would forgive Nixon for replacing him, even if the replacement was another conservative. The more it seemed that Nixon would dump Agnew, the louder was the anguish on the right. First the 60,000-member American Conservative Union endorsed Agnew for renomination "in the strongest possible terms," calling him "the most impressive moral leader American politics has seen in more than a generation." Then, a year before the Republican Convention in San Diego, the 70,000-member Young Americans for Freedom held a mock nominating convention in Houston and chose Agnew for President over Richard Nixon. Meanwhile, Lee Edwards, a conservative Republican public relations man, began working the conservative mailing lists to establish a "nationwide grassroots organization which will do everything in its power in the next twelve months to insure that Agnew will be on the ticket again in 1972."

Late in September 1971 the White House felt compelled to drape a quasi-endorsement around Agnew's shoulders. In a letter to a New York Conservative Party leader, White House Special Counsel Harry Dent declared, "Despite what you read in the press, there is no plan to drop Mr. Agnew from the ticket in 1972. President Nixon has great respect for his Vice President and values the job he has been doing." Nixon's problems with the Republican right continued to grow, however. And after the decision by Congressman John Ashbrook of Ohio to run against Nixon in the New Hampshire primary, a more passionate embrace seemed called for. Thus, Nixon said on nationwide television early in 1972, "My view is that one should not break up a winning combination. I believe that the Vice President has handled his difficult assignments with dignity, with courage. He has at times been a man of controversy, but when a man has done a good job in a position, when he has been part of a winning team, I believe that he should stay on the team. That is my thinking at this time." Clearly, Nixon was trying to convey the impression that he had made up his mind to keep Agnew. In fact, all he had decided was to keep him through the California primary and then take up the Agnew question afresh before the Republican Convention.

There have been crosscurrents even among the aides working on Nixon's reelection. One school of thought held that Agnew was just one of those unfortunate people who seemed to attract criticism—and even though much of it was unfair, he would hurt the ticket. The countervailing theory was that Agnew would help carry the border states and the South, particularly if George Wallace was running.

In that pool of uncertainties, quite a few people around Nixon expect Agnew to decide his own future—by dumping himself. They recite Agnew's loyal statements that Nixon "must find the strongest running mate he can." They whisper that Agnew really didn't like his job anyway. Or that he isn't a man with a strong ambition. Or that he is anxious to go back to Maryland and make money.

Indeed, at least half of Agnew would just as soon go back to practicing law. He's also toyed with the idea of writing a column on the side or starting his own TV program, something like "The David Frost Show." "I've never been a person who wanted to be rich," he told one interviewer. "But I would like to—in my later years—at least be comfortable. . . . And of course I recognize that I could probably be a fairly easily employable person in a lot of places that would be stimulating to me and much more monetarily rewarding than the Vice Presidency." Incidentally, one indication of Agnew's earning power is that Robert P. Walker, head of a Boston lecture agency, has offered in all seriousness to guarantee Agnew half a million dollars for one year of lecturing.

Still, one has to wonder whether a man who once had so much political ambition in his blood could suddenly lose it within sight of the mountaintop. This, after all, is the same Agnew who wrote to his money-raiser Al Shuger six years ago, ". . . It would seem to me that it is much more important to you and me that I amass the utmost political strength so that I can continue to be successful. . . . Out of office, I am completely ineffectual." So accustomed is this man to the rhythm of politics that every two years since 1956 he has either thrown himself into an election campaign or tried to move to a higher political office. For most of that time, it looked to the outside world as though he had no further ambitions. Repulsed by being President? Methinks he doth protest too much.

Even if Agnew doesn't become President, he could eventually turn up in the Senate someday. In his interview with Allen Drury, Agnew said enough to make the two incumbent Republican Senators from Maryland tremble slightly about their job security. "I find the Senate very exclusive and withdrawn into itself . . . almost an arrogance in the club feeling up there," Agnew said. "It makes it difficult to deal with them, even in the rather remote fashion that I now do. And yet, you know, the Senate might not be such a bad place to be, someday. . . ." There are even people who foresee Agnew getting appointed to the Supreme Court or replacing J. Edgar Hoover as Director of the FBI.

Before laughing off these visions, one must always remember the luck of Spiro Agnew. The man would very likely never have become Vice President:

1. *If* the Republicans hadn't pulled an upset in the 1956 local elections in Baltimore County, thus winning a patronage job for an obscure lawyer named Spiro Agnew; or—

2. *If* he had succeeded in his desire to become a judge or a Workmen's Compensation Commissioner; or—

3. *If* the Democrats hadn't decided to drop him from the zoning board in 1961; or—

4. *If* the Democrats hadn't split and picked their worst candidate in the 1962 race for County Executive; or—

5. *If* Agnew had given in to his temptation to disavow Barry Goldwater in 1964; or—

6. *If* the Baltimore papers had decided in 1965 to assign a team of investigative reporters to check into his conflicts of interest; or—

7. *If* some other Republican had wanted to run for Governor in 1966; or—

8. *If* the Democrats had nominated anyone besides George Mahoney to be their gubernatorial candidate in 1966; or—

9. *If* William Scranton hadn't changed his mind about accepting the chairmanship of the Draft Rockefeller movement in 1968, and if Al Abrahams hadn't thought of Agnew as Scranton's replacement; or—

10. *If* Nelson Rockefeller had telephoned him before 2:00 P.M. on March 21, 1968; or—

11. *If* Nixon had needed Jim Rhodes' Ohio delegation to win on the first ballot; or—

12. *If* NBC had gotten film of Agnew stuck on top of the golf course fence in Miami Beach; or—

13. *If* Robert Finch had accepted the Vice Presidency when Nixon offered it to him; or—

14. *If* the *New York Times* had been able to document

all its charges in October 1968 about Agnew's financial dealings, or—

15. *If* the South Vietnamese government had not ruined Hubert Humphrey's chances by announcing three days before the election that it would not go along with President Johnson's bombing halt and peace initiative.

Agnew's luck has not totally abandoned him in Washington. In his first three years in office, five men have been built up in the press as Vice Presidential replacements in 1972. One by one, four of them have been harmed or destroyed by unforeseen events. First, Robert Finch made a poor showing as Secretary of Health, Education and Welfare and had to be whisked off in a state of nervous exhaustion to the White House staff. Soon the telegenic George Bush of Texas lost his campaign for the Senate and then lost his conservative spurs during the United Nations debate over China. Then Ronald Reagan dropped in the polls when word got around that he hadn't been paying any state income taxes. Finally Nelson Rockefeller had to preside over the bloodletting at Attica State.

Only John Connally, a Democrat, has survived the first three years of speculation, and he will need the luck of an Agnew to keep his luster through the coming months, in which political futures will trade up and down like pork bellies. In the end, Agnew's competition is likely to come from some little-known quantity, perhaps Senator Howard Baker of Tennessee or Senator Robert Dole of Kansas.

When a man moves from vice-president of the Kiwanis club to Vice President of the United States in nine years, it is clearly time to start thinking about what sort of a President he would make. In Spiro Agnew's case, there are enough clues strewn throughout his life to warrant some predictions, at least about the superficial aspects of his Presidency.

One thing for sure: he will always look like a President. *Playboy*'s fashion editor, Robert Green, was right when he described Agnew as "violently neat" and "the best-dressed man in government." Neat he has always been, to the point that he reportedly doesn't like toothpaste tubes squeezed in the middle. His law associate Joe Pokorny remembers that on a business trip about 1960, he once made a point of arising at dawn to see if Agnew slept with his hair combed. During 1966, aides marveled at the candidate's ability to campaign all day without getting sweaty and rumpled. "It's just a matter of control," he would tell them. It wasn't long before *Men's Hairstylist and Barber's Journal* named him as one of the ten Americans who had done the most to provide "good grooming leadership to the rest of his fellow citizens."

A second certainty is that we don't have to worry about the Agnews putting on the airs of a royal family. They are plain people with plain pleasures, like ping-pong, Patti Page, and pepperoni pizza. Judy Agnew, his wife of thirty years, has a charming, unaffected quality that lets her get away with saying things like "I majored in marriage" or "I have a wig." She could be your next-door neighbor. Or another Mamie Eisenhower.

The Agnew children seem unlikely subjects for the glamor treatment. If their father has anything to do with it, they will probably be neither seen nor heard. To quote Cynthia Rosenwald, "In his own family he's got problems, and he takes them very hard, and he keeps them very much to himself."

Agnew's only son, Randy, finished a stint in Vietnam three

years ago and has been working as a construction worker and part-time weight-lifting instructor since his separation from his wife, Ann. "Randy is so different from his father that it is hard to believe they are father and son," says Mrs. Alice Fringer, Agnew's longtime secretary. Lately Randy has been attending Towson State College in pursuit of a degree in physical education. One bit of publicity that has pained the Vice President was the Jack Anderson column in September 1970, reporting that Randy "has broken up with his wife and has been living for the past month with a male hairdresser in Baltimore."

The Vice President's eldest child, twenty-eight-year-old Pamela, is a very quiet girl who decided not to move to Annapolis with her father so people wouldn't say, "There goes the Governor's daughter." Agnew has said Pamela was "completely disinterested in school" until her senior year in high school, but was later able to elevate her grades and graduate from a teachers college. She now works for the Welfare Department in Baltimore County and is married to Robert DeHaven, an official of the Maryland mental retardation program.

Agnew's middle daughter, Susan, twenty-four, passed up college to become a salesgirl, then a fingerprint clerk, and more recently the coordinator of volunteers at a state hospital in Cambridge, Maryland. Her longtime romance with Colin Macindoe, a Maryland state trooper, ended in the fall of 1971 with a broken engagement.

Agnew's youngest child, sixteen-year-old Kim, is the only one living at home. "We have kept her out of the limelight as much as possible," says Judy Agnew of her tall, shy daughter, who has been getting nearly straight A's at Washington's

National Cathedral School. They haven't always succeeded in sheltering Kim. During the 1969 Vietnam Moratorium, Agnew had to prevent her from wearing a black armband to school, a fact he later put out to a columnist. Then *Time* reported that Kim "was known to have experimented with marijuana." Since then, the Agnews have made sure that Kim never sees the press.

Mrs. Judy Agnew provided an interesting glimpse at her husband in his role as father in an interview published in *Today's Health* in July 1971: "I always did the disciplining at home when the children were little, and I dealt with problems on the spot. When something happens involving a small child, you don't wait to tell Dad later on or discuss procedure with him, because the incident has passed. The child has forgotten it."

Following a few peripheral predictions, one runs out of certitudes. There is obviously no way of knowing how any man would perform in the most demanding job in the world. One can only look at his past and make guesstimates, which may be no more than hunches. Here, for what they are worth, are mine:

Would President Agnew be a conservative President? No. While he would still talk tough on social disorders, he would startle everyone, including Nixon, by his willingness to spend federal money to attack domestic problems. Both as County Executive and Governor he was a sort of Republican New Dealer, and in another chief executive's position he would line up on his former ideological hashmark.

What would be Agnew's style of governing? He would be a remote figure. Like Nixon, he would operate the Administration through a rigid staff system and deal at arm's length with Congress. Ceremonial appearances by the President would be less frequent, and he would seldom press the flesh in crowds. "I don't really like to be around strange people," Agnew told a Maryland newspaperman in early 1968. "They make me nervous, uncomfortable." Even so, on television he would be seen quite regularly and he would meet the press more often than Nixon has.

What would be his strengths? From hundreds of hours of briefings, he knows the job of President much more thoroughly than he knew his previous jobs before he took them—and in both he did tolerably well. He is an intelligent, tough-fibered executive who wouldn't back away from making a decision. He can absorb a new problem quickly.

What would be his weaknesses? As Joe Pokorny once said, "He's not a guy who can take defeats—he takes it personally, not politically." In his mind, political opponents become enemies, and differences become grudges. Thus when Senator Charles Goodell was defeated in the 1968 election, Wally Hickel heard Agnew saying, "We killed the sonofabitch! We killed the sonofabitch!"

In times of emotional stress or national crisis, Agnew would tend to be overdecisive and too quick with the inflammatory phrase. His pattern has been all too consistent: on the morning after the Cambridge riots, he announced he wanted to lock up Rap Brown and throw away the key; a week after the Baltimore riots, he lectured the black leaders before the TV cameras; four days after the Vietnam Moratorium, he produced his "effete corps of impudent snobs" speech; and the day after the shock of Nixon's China announcement, he bitterly assailed "most" American black leaders. It was unsettling that he made all these pronouncements without or against the advice of his responsible advisors. In a President, overdecisiveness is not the most comforting trait.

If Spiro Agnew goes no further than Vice President, his will still go down as perhaps the most stupefying Horatio Alger story in twentieth-century American politics. Very seldom has anyone so little grown so big so fast. Sometimes it appeared that he was simply floating on a geyser of good luck. But a man with less brains would have lost his buoyancy long before now. A man with less courage could never have risen above his first forty years of mediocrity.

The end of his political career has to come sometime, and Agnew is ready. He said it best on a Chicago TV show in 1970: "If in the process of rendering support, something happens to me politically through the hard partisan role I must play, through being the lightning rod for many of the things I'm saying, then that's the way the ball bounces. I think getting to be Vice President is pretty good for an immigrant's son."

Notes

CHAPTER 1

1. Although Agnew was on the Board of Appeals in 1957, he had nothing to do with the rezoning for the apartment building at 11 Slade Avenue. That rezoning was granted by the County Council, of which Agnew was not a member.

CHAPTER 2

1. Actually, there is some evidence that the elder Agnew worked as a barber before leaving Greece. When the Vice President's secretary, Mrs. Alice Fringer, visited Gargalianoi in 1971, she was shown a barber shop where the elder Agnew was supposed to have worked.

CHAPTER 3

1. After an interview with Agnew, author Jim Lucas wrote in his book *Agnew: Profile in Conflict:* "He [Agnew] vowed that if he became a father, none of his children would have Greek names. He kept that promise. The Agnew children are named Pam, Randy, Susan and Kim." Asked about this, Vice Presidential Press Secretary Vic Gold wrote me: "With regard to the naming of the Agnew children, there was no deliberate effort not to name them 'by Greek names.' In this regard, it might be noted that the children are, after all, of Greek descent on their father's side only."

CHAPTER 5

1. When Hubers' case came up in court, the indictment was dropped on the grounds that his alleged malfeasance, while it might have been morally reprehensible, was not a crime. However he resigned from his job on the Board of Appeals.

Two years later, A. Gordon Boone, then Speaker of the Maryland House of Delegates, was indicted by a federal grand jury for mail fraud in connection with a new company called the Security Financial Insurance Company. He was found guilty and sent for three years to the penitentiary. During his trial it was disclosed that Senator Pine served as an incorporator of Security Financial as a favor to Boone, and was subsequently given 500 shares of its stock. However no charges were brought against Pine.

CHAPTER 7

1. The February, 1965, issue of *American Opinion,* a John Birch Society publication, ran a 12-page article documenting how the residents of Baltimore County had risen up to defeat the urban renewal bond issue. Perhaps fortunately for Agnew's later political career, the article did not mention him or his role in pushing for the approval of the bond issue. In a note to the readers, Managing Editor Scott Stanley Jr. said the article "dissects, and thereby destroys, what has come to be euphemistically known as urban renewal."

CHAPTER 9

1. It just so happened that January 2, 1962 was a red letter day for both Spiro Agnew and the partners in Opfer-Dickinson, although for different reasons. For Agnew, it was the day he bought his new $35,900 white colonial house by the beltway, after living for 11 years in an $11,000 row house. For Jones and his two partners in Opfer-Dickinson, it was the day the $474,000 deal for the first 40 acres of rezoned land went through.

As it turned out, the builder which sold Agnew his house was the Shetland Construction Company, a firm closely affiliated with Opfer-Dickinson. In fact Jones' two partners in Opfer-Dickinson, Richard W. Opfer and Edward H. Dickinson, were the founders and owners of Shetland Construction Company. Agnew assured me the identity of his builder was a coincidence. "We looked at houses around there and we bought one and we paid the going rate for it," he said. When he sold it in June, 1967, he received $43,500, which was just about the average increase in value of houses in his neighborhood.

2. Agnew's justification for the Opfer-Dickinson rezoning: "It was an area which in our planning concept we thought would be a good place for light industrial uses, which were so vital for the tax base of the county."

3. When I got back to my office and played the tape, I found that Agnew had asked the bank for his balance on the wrong date—January 2, 1965, instead of July 2, 1965, when the loan was granted. The balance Ryan gave him for the earlier date was $7,694.13. I then telephoned Agnew's personal lawyer, George White, and he later telephoned the bank to obtain the July 2nd balance. The figure White gave me was $10,327.40

Actually, the $15,000 loan on July 2, 1965 wasn't the first unsecured loan granted to Agnew by Chesapeake. Exactly one year earlier, according to bank president Robert Baker, Agnew borrowed $1,500 with no recorded collateral. The first loan was paid off on July 2, 1965, on the day the second loan was granted. My efforts to determine what Agnew did in 1964 with the $1,500 loan failed.

4. George L. Rayburn, Maryland Assistant Commissioner of Small Loans, was asked in October, 1971, whether it was unusual in Maryland for anyone to get a $15,000 unsecured loan from a national bank. "Very unusual," he replied. "You must understand that banks rarely make unsecured loans over $500." Until 1967, the maximum interest on personal bank loans in Maryland was six percent. In 1967, a new law was passed permitting eight percent loans, provided that the bank and the borrower agreed in writing to the higher rate. Rayburn said a good many loans were cancelled in Maryland when the borrowers refused to agree to higher interest rates. There is no indication whether Agnew was asked by the bank for an increase in the interest rate on his loan.

5. White was referring to *Newsday*, of which I was then Washington Bureau Chief. White also warned me of the possibility of a libel suit, saying: "I am a trial lawyer. If you were on the witness stand, I'd tear you apart."

A few days later, *Newsday*'s editor David Laventhol decided against printing a series I was in the process of writing about Agnew's early career, one part of which included the information now disclosed in Chapter 9 about Agnew and Jones. Although Laventhol had been informed of White's threat, I am sure he decided against running the series for other reasons. As he explained his decision to me, he believed 1) that the fresh information about Agnew's business deals amounted to "infelicities" and not to crimes, and thus did not justify a long investigative article, and 2) that for space reasons it wasn't possible to present the new material in proper context.

CHAPTER *10*

1. At a Colts football game in November, 1966, Agnew explained what kind of a rooter he was. "I'm not a demonstrative rooter," he said. "I don't have to jump up and down and scream." But Agnew liked his football well enough to change the traditional once-a-year public visiting hours on New Year's Day at the Governor's Mansion so that he could watch the bowl games on television.

CHAPTER *11*

1. In an interview with columnist Nick Thimmesch published on September 3, 1971, Agnew prefaced an attack on some present-day black leaders with a revealing paragraph about his motivations three years earlier. "This takes me back," Agnew said, "to 1968 when I had to dress down the Negro leaders in Baltimore after they made no effort to stop the rioting we had then."

CHAPTER *12*

1. Agnew, in a jocular moment, said at a luncheon in Washington on September 28, 1967, sponsored by Republican Congressional aides: "Some of my constituents in Maryland are contemplating an Agnew for Vice President campaign. This drive began almost immediately after we raised taxes, making it rather obvious that they are putting what they consider the best interests of their state before the best interests of the country. My claim to be a noncandidate of course parallels the assertions of Richard Nixon, George Romney, Nelson Rockefeller, Ronald Reagan and Charles Percy. Therefore I should probably announce that I am an eligible candidate for this great office so you will be convinced beyond a doubt that I am not."

2. The details of what was said in their closely guarded conference room in the Sheraton-Blackstone Hotel stayed secret less than twenty-four hours. In a copyrighted story in the *Chicago Sun-Times,* Carleton Kent and I reported on July 29, 1960 that Nixon first listed eight potential candidates and then asking each man present to discuss their pos and cons, in terms of what they would add to the ticket. As Nixon explained the problem, "We have to win."

Lodge then picked up the predictable support of liberals at the meeting, like Governor Mark Hatfield of Oregon, Charles Percy of Illinois, Senator Hugh Scott of Pennsylvania and Thomas E. Dewey of New York. But he also unexpectedly won the praise of former Senator John W. Bricker of Ohio, a longtime isolationist leader, who cited Lodge's "remarkable war record not as a staff officer but as a fighting officer."

The opposition to Lodge was led by Governor William G. Stratton of Illinois, who said at one point, "You can say all you want about foreign affairs, but what is really important is the price of hogs in Chicago and St. Louis." Stratton and a few others at the meeting preferred Senator Thruston Morton of Kentucky. After everyone had spoken, Nixon summed up, beginning with this remark: "Frankly, it's a hell of a tough decision." At that point there were four remaining candidates: Lodge, Morton, Rep. Walter Judd of Minnesota and Treasury Secretary Robert Anderson.

Nixon praised Anderson, but observed that he would not add much to the ticket. He disclosed that Judd did not believe he had sufficient vigor for the tough campaigning ahead. As for Morton, Nixon said he would probably be the favorite of most sitting Republican Congressmen as well as new Republican Congressional candidates. But, Nixon said, both he and Morton appealed fundamentally to the same people.

The "only hope" against the Democrats, he added, was to keep the campaign concentrated on foreign policy. "If you ever let them campaign only on domestic issues, they'll beat us," he told the group. It was apparent before Nixon finished his summation that his choice was Lodge. He offered to put it to a vote of the meeting, but the conference said the decision was his. After two hours and five minutes in the room, Nixon went out before the microphones to announce his decision to run with Lodge.

CHAPTER 13

1. A reference to Agnew's remark to reporters that Hubert Humphrey was "squishy soft" on Communism. After Senate Minority Leader Everett Dirksen and House Republican Leader Gerald Ford held a press conference to rebuff the charge against Humphrey, Agnew retreated, saying: "If I'd known I'd be cast as the Joe McCarthy of 1968, I would have turned five somersaults. I said 'squishy soft' and I'm not proud of it."

2. The "fat Jap" remark came shortly after Agnew's first ethnic gaffe of the campaign: referring to Polish-Americans as "polacks" in an off-the-cuff remark in Chicago. Agnew later explained that he had heard his Polish friends refer to each other as "polacks," and he was unaware that the appellation could cause offense.

3. One Agnewism which came out sounding much worse than it might have was his 1968 comment when a reporter on a Tennessee TV panel asked him why he was not bringing his campaign to the ghettos. "When you've seen one slum, you've seen them all," said Agnew. What he meant was that a candidate could not learn by grandstanding in the

ghettos. In a cover story on Agnew in November, 1969, *Time* was right in observing: "The odd thing is that the line makes a certain cockeyed sense; there is a miserable monotony about urban slums. If Agnew had made the point with any sensitivity the effect would have been the opposite of the one he achieved."

While he was County Executive, Agnew made at least one well-publicized tour of the slums of Eastern Baltimore County. "I knew that things were bad down there but I can truthfully say I was shocked," he said in October, 1964, after seeing an area where septic tanks overflowed into open ditches. "The overall impression as you drive through the area is that this can't be part of the United States."

4. The *Washington Post* and *Time* magazine both reported that the Gridiron gags were written by Paul Keyes, producer of television's "Laugh-In." The *Post* said Keyes had been a friend of Nixon since Jack Paar introduced the two, suggesting to Nixon that Keyes was "an Irish Catholic from Boston who voted against JFK in 1960." The *Post* said its reporter reached Keyes in Agnew's office, but he wouldn't confirm or deny writing Agnew's jokes.

5. Mrs. Katherine Graham, president of the Washington Post Company, replied that each outlet was a separate enterprise with separate editorial policies. Arthur Ochs Sulzburger, president and publisher of *The New Yorw Times,* pointed out that the story about the Congressional endorsement of Nixon's policies was published in later editions even though it did not make the edition delivered to Washington.

6. By January, 1971, Agnew had slipped a notch and was the fourth most admired man in the world, according to the Gallup Poll. Edward Kennedy had moved up to third, with Nixon and the Reverend Graham still one and two, respectively. By January 1972 he had dropped to sixth.

Chapter *14*

1. The reason Agnew's vote wasn't needed was that the key roll call in the Senate came on an amendment aimed at deleting the funds for th ABM. Under parliamentary rules any amendment fails in case of a tie.

2. One source of Agnew's knowledge about the foster care problem is his daughter Pamela, whose job is placing children in foster homes for the Baltimore County Welfare Department.

3. According to statistics compiled in the Senate Press Gallery, Agnew presided over the Senate 60 of the 927 hours the Senate was in session in 1969, or six percent of the time. In 1970 Agnew was in the chair 16 hours and 15 minutes out of a total of 1,424 hours, 51 minutes the Senate was in session, or one percent of the time. In the first nine

months of 1971 Agnew presided 11 hours and 53 minutes out of a total of 861 hours, or one percent of the time.

By contrast, Vice President Humphrey presided over the Senate for 25 out of a total of 1,090 hours in 1967, or two percent of the time. In 1968, when he was campaigning for President, he was in the chair 12 hours, 44 minutes out of a total of 870 hours, or one percent of the time.

CHAPTER 15

1. The rest of the quotation, as provided by Gold: "I think we have a pretty good President at the present time. I undertook my responsibilities as Vice President in full belief that President Nixon was the kind of man who would project the ideas that he campaigned on, which were basically the ideas of his heritage and my heritage and your heritage." Gold said he went on to talk about the difficult burdens of the Presidency.

2. Another bit of evidence, which surfaced at the end of 1971, was the result of the respected California Poll, issued by pollster Mervin D. Field. The California Poll found that among Republican voters, Agnew was the most popular Vice Presidental candidate, with 31 percent of the sample, followed by New York Governor Nelson Rockefeller with 23 percent, and Treasury Secretary John Connally with 16 percent. However, the poll also found that Agnew "alienates a majority of Democrats and others who do not identify with either of the two major parties." When Democrats were asked which candidate they were most likely to vote for as Nixon's running mate, 29 percent of those polled said Governor Rockefeller, while 22 percent said Secretary Connally, and 20 percent named Agnew. Pollster Field concluded: "In a state where more than 60 percent of the voters are not Republicans, a Vice Presidential candidate who repels a large segment of voters could be a serious drag on the G.O.P. ticket."

A nationwide survey of 300 scientifically chosen voters conducted in late 1971 by the *Washington Post* produced somewhat similar results. The *Post* concluded: "Statistically, the reaction of those interviewed by the *Washington Post* (almost half of them 1968 Nixon-Agnew supporters) were strongly anti-Agnew. Twenty-three percent of those we talked to praised Agnew; 49 percent criticized him; 20 percent gave him mixed reviews; and only 8 percent said they did not know enough about him to comment."

Acknowledgments

Without knowing whether it would help them or hurt them, Spiro Agnew and most of his close associates were very generous in granting the interviews that made this biography worth writing. Even when they began to suspect that the book might contain some unpleasant disclosures, they made no effort to cut me off from further interviews. For their cooperation I am most grateful.

The main source for what I have written has been interviews with 124 men and women who figured in Agnew's life. Of these, two-thirds were on-the-record interviews, many of them tape-recorded. The remaining interviews were with government officials, Senators, and newspapermen who would not speak frankly if they had to be quoted by name. The next four paragraphs contain the names of those interviewed on-the-record.

I am particularly grateful to Vice-President Agnew himself, who saw me on February 8, 1971, and again eight days later. To Victor Gold, Herbert Thompson, Charles Bresler, Samuel Kimmel and J. Walter Jones Jr. go especial thanks for their willingness to grant me multiple interviews so that I could crosscheck facts supplied by others.

The following were extremely helpful for the chapters about Agnew's ancestry and his career in school, the Army, and the law: Miss Lucille Akers, his first cousin; C. J. Harkrader, James Ringold, Joseph L. Krieger, Andy Anderson, Dr. Emmett Queen, George Rowan, W. H. Callahan, H. Raymond Cluster, Alan Clarke, former First Sergeant John F. Bevilaqua, former Private Clarence F. Berry, former Major Warren

B. Haskell, former Colonel James O'Hara, Eugene Schreiber, Alvin Schreiber, Carl Gleitsmann, Thomas Kerrigan, Owen Hennegan, Judge Lester Barrett, Leon B. Schachter, E. Scott Moore, Ormsby S. "Dutch" Moore, Roy C. Manns, Edgar Fulton, Joseph Pokorny, Howard Medicus, J. Walter Jones Jr., and Samuel Kimmel.

For the chapters dealing with Agnew's political career before Richard Nixon discovered him, I am indebted to the following: Christine Nathan, Jeanette C. Harris, Edward Hardesty, George White, W. Lee Harrison, Mrs. Alice Fringer, Albert A. Shuger, Theodore McKeldin, Lester Barrett, Clarke Langrall, Dale Anderson, Vladimir Wahbe, William E. Fornoff, Arthur J. Sohmer, Robert J. Lally, James P. S. Devereaux, Edward Hanrahan, Brownlee Corrin, Michael Birmingham Jr., Michael Holofcener, Edgar Feingold, G. Mitchell Austin, Judge Kenneth C. Proctor, Everett T. Hay, George Arrowsmith, John K. Davis, Lou Cahn, Nat Molofsky, Ormsby Moore, Scott Moore, Charles Steinbock, Parren Mitchell, D. C. Lee, Marshall W. Jones Jr., Paul Sarbanes, Robert Goodman, Mrs. Cynthia Rosenwald, Robert T. Baker, John W. Steffee, Herbert Thompson, Charles Bresler, Samuel Kimmel, and J. Walter Jones Jr.

As for the chapters about Agnew in Washington, the custom of "background interviews" prevents me from identifying most of those who have helped me, but I do want to thank Walter Mote, C. D. Ward, Victor Gold, and Harry Dent.

In addition to my own interviews, I was able to draw on the excellent research files of Daniel St. Albin Greene of the *National Observer*, whose article "Agnew, Man and Boy—and the *Phenomenon*" (November 2, 1970) has been the best published account of Agnew's ancestry and early life. The transcripts of Greene's interviews with Agnew's stepbrother, W. Roy Pollard, and longtime friend, I. H. "Bud" Hammerman, as well as his father's friends Luke Carmen, Louis Lambros, George E. Phillies, and Anthony Raptis were important to me for chapters 2 and 3.

A good deal of new information on Agnew's life emerged from public documents. Among the sources in Towson, Maryland, which proved valuable: the minutes of the Baltimore County Council; the dockets and files of the Baltimore County Zoning Commissioner, the Board of Appeals, the Planning Board, the Department of Public Works, and the Budget Office; and the land transfer and election financing records filed with the Baltimore County Circuit Court. Other documentary sources included the Meat Cutters union financial reports, filed with the Labor Department's Bureau of Labor-Management Reports in Silver Spring, Md.; the 1860-1880 census records and the Confederate Army personnel records at the National Archives in Washington; the

World War II unit records at the Federal Records Center in Suitland, Maryland; the military personnel locator at the National Military Personnel Records Center in St. Louis, Missouri; the files on promotion policy at the National Archives and the Army Office of Military History in Washington; the Lester Grogg files at the Federal Courthouse in Balitmore; the land and zoning records of Anne Arundel County, Maryland, and St. Croix, Virgin Islands; the McCormick & Company registration statements and annual reports at the Securities and Exchange Commission in Washington; the State of Maryland's incorporation records in Baltimore and election financing records in Annapolis; the City of Baltimore's partnerships docket; the Register of Marriages kept by the City Clerk of Lynchburg, Virginia; the city directories for Bristol, Virginia; Schenectady, New York; Washington, and Baltimore at the Library of Congress in Washington. A word of thanks is due to all the keepers of these documents, who found them for me with efficiency and good grace.

Several troves of clippings proved helpful. I am indebted to Sam Kimmel and E. Scott Moore, who made it possible for me to use Moore's 13-volume scrapbook covering the period when Agnew was County Executive. Also valuable and much appreciated were the clip files of the Field Politics Center at Goucher College, the County Executive's Office, in Baltimore County, the *Towson Jeffersonian,* the *Baltimore Sun,* the *Baltimore News-American,* the *Washington Post,* the Washington Bureau of *Newsday,* and *National Geographic.*

For Agnew's years in Washington, it was important to assemble as many as possible of his published or broadcast interviews. The Republican and Democratic National Committees, the Vice-President's Press Office, and *U.S. News & World Report* were extremely helpful. Among the interviews I found most revealing were one by Jim Naughton in *The New York Times Magazine* on December 27, 1970, and one by Allen Drury which first appeared in *Look* on October 19, 1971, entitled "Inside the White House 1971."

I want to thank Andrew Mayer, Susan Soper and LaVerle Mitrovitch, who enthusiastically helped with the research; Rose Appel, who uncomplainingly typed the manuscript; Sterling Lord, my perceptive agent, and his helpful assistant, Townsend Blodgett; my deadeye editor, Tom Lipscomb, and his able assistant Margot Shields; and most important of all, my wife Madeleine K. Albright, and my mother, Josephine P. Albright, who evaluated, edited and encouraged from start to finish.

Naturally, any errors in fact or judgment are my own. If inaccuracies have found their way into print, I would be glad to hear about them for future reference.